Cambridge Opera Handbooks

Richard Wagner
Der fliegende Holländer

RENEWALS 458-4574

DATE DUE

MAY 01 2009			

| GAYLORD | | | PRINTED IN U.S.A. |

Richard Wagner
Der fliegende Holländer

Edited by
THOMAS GREY

Associate Professor of Music
Stanford University

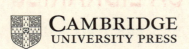

CAMBRIDGE
UNIVERSITY PRESS

PUBLISHED BY THE PRESS SYNDICATE OF THE UNIVERSITY OF CAMBRIDGE
The Pitt Building, Trumpington Street, Cambridge, United Kingdom

CAMBRIDGE UNIVERSITY PRESS
The Edinburgh Building, Cambridge CB2 2RU, UK   www.cup.cam.ac.uk
40 West 20th Street, New York, NY 10011-4211, USA   www.cup.org
10 Stamford Road, Oakleigh, Melbourne 3166, Australia
Ruiz de Alarcón 13, 28014 Madrid, Spain

© Thomas Grey 2000

This book is in copyright. Subject to statutory exception
and to the provisions of relevant collective licensing agreements,
no reproduction of any part may take place without
the written permission of Cambridge University Press.

First published 2000

Printed in the United Kingdom at the University Press, Cambridge

Typeface Times NR (MT) 10 on 12.25pt   *System* QuarkXPress™   [SE]

A catalogue record for this book is available from the British Library

Library of Congress Cataloguing in Publication data

Richard Wagner, Der fliegende Holländer / edited by Thomas Grey.
      p.   cm. – (Cambridge opera handbooks)
Includes bibliographical references and index.
ISBN 0 521 58285 7 (hardback). – ISBN 0 521 58763 8 (paperback)
1. Wagner, Richard, 1813–1883. Der Fliegende Holländer.   I. Title: Der Fliegende
Holländer.
II. Grey, Thomas S.   III. Series.

ML410.W132.R48   2000
782.1 – dc21   99-059951   CIP

ISBN 0 521 58285 7 (hardback)
ISBN 0 521 58763 8 (paperback)

WITHDRAWN
UTSA LIBRARIES

Library
University of Texas
at San Antonio

Contents

Illustrations

General preface

This is a series of studies of individual operas, written for the serious opera-goer or record-collector as well as the student or scholar. Each volume has three main concerns. The first is historical: to describe the genesis of the work, its sources or its relation to literary prototypes, the collaboration between librettist and composer, and the first performance and subsequent stage history. The history is itself a record of changing attitudes towards the work, and an index of general changes of taste. The second is analytical and it is grounded in a very full synopsis which considers the opera as a structure of musical and dramatic effects. In most volumes there is also a musical analysis of a section of the score, showing how the music serves or makes the drama. The analysis, like the history, naturally raises questions of interpretation, and the third concern of each volume is to show how critical writing about an opera, like production and performance, can direct or distort appreciation of its structural elements. Some conflict of interpretation is an inevitable part of this account; editors of the handbooks reflect this – by citing classic statements, by commissioning new essays, by taking up their own critical position. A final section gives a select bibliography and guides to other sources.

Acknowledgements

I would like to express my sincere thanks to the other contributors to this volume for their excellent work; to Stewart Spencer and Peter Bloom for their kind permission to reprint translations of texts included in Appendix A; to Victoria Cooper and Ann M. Lewis at Cambridge University Press for their assistance at various stages in the production of the text; and to Mary Cicora for her expert help with the proofs and the index.

1 *The return of the prodigal son: Wagner and* Der fliegende Holländer

THOMAS GREY

Lebensstürme (life's storms)

The figure of the "Flying Dutchman" is a mythical creation [*Gedicht*] of the people: it gives emotionally compelling expression to a timeless feature of human nature. This feature, in its most general sense, is the longing for peace from the storms of life.

> Wagner, *A Communication to my Friends* (*GSD*, vol. 4, 265)

The storm scene that opens Act I of *Der fliegende Holländer* rings with echoes of Wagner's own life-experiences: his "famous sea-voyage" (as he had already styled it in a letter to Ferdinand Heine in 1843) from the Baltic coast of East Prussia through the North Sea, down to the English Channel, and finally up the Thames to London.[1] By the summer of 1839 rising debts and the termination of his post as Kapellmeister in Riga had made it expedient for Wagner to put into action his characteristically over-ambitious project to conquer Paris – and from there, the rest of Europe – with the five-act grand opera he had recently begun, *Rienzi*. (Both the opera and the career move he hoped to found on it were modeled after the spectacular success of Giacomo Meyerbeer during the past decade.) After escaping by the skin of their teeth from the Russian-controlled Baltic provinces and across the Prussian frontier, without passport, Wagner and his wife Minna – along with their mammoth Newfoundland dog, Robber – boarded a trading vessel "of the smallest sort" called the *Thetis*, bound for London.[2] A series of violent storms more than doubled the expected length of the voyage, in addition to occasioning a good deal of physical and mental distress; but these storms also afforded Wagner a variety of experiences that would ultimately contribute to the novel and authentic coloring of *Der fliegende Holländer*.

At the center of this nexus of real-life impressions resonating through the opening scene of *Der fliegende Holländer* (and the overture, by extension) is, in fact, a literal echo effect. In the one passage from his autobiography, *Mein Leben* (*My Life*), in which Wagner specifically connects the impressions of his sea-voyage with the eventual composition of the opera, he describes how a short rhythmic cry emitted by the crew of the *Thetis*, preparing to moor the ship, echoed across the fjord along the southern coast of Norway where they had been driven for shelter during the last days of July 1839:

A feeling of indescribable well-being came over me as the granite walls of the cliff echoed the chantings of the crew as they cast anchor and furled the sails. The sharp rhythm [*kurze Rhythmus*] of their call stuck with me as an omen of good fortune and soon resolved itself into the theme of the Sailors' Chorus in my *Fliegende Holländer*, the idea for which I had already carried within me at the time and which now, under the impressions I had just gained, took on its characteristic musical-poetic coloring.[3]

The three-note descending idea Wagner alludes to here as the motivic basis of the Sailors' Chorus in Act III, "Steuermann! Laß die Wacht!" also figures in the re-creation of the very scene described in *My Life* at the opening of Act I: as they secure their boat in the shelter of a Norwegian fjord, in an attempt to escape the tumult of the storm raging about them, the crew of Daland's ship cries "Hallojo!" to a more emphatic, "sharper" version of that same rhythm, which is echoed in the orchestra alternately by valved horns, *fortissimo*, and natural horns, *forte* (see Chapter 3, Ex. 4a).[4]

In the scenario Wagner originally drafted, as well as in the original libretto, the setting of the action had been some unidentified point on the coast of Scotland, evidently following the example of several recent treatments of the Flying Dutchman legend, such as Heinrich Heine's (see Chapter 2). Prior to the eventual première of the opera in the first days of January 1843, however, Wagner transposed the action to the Norwegian coast, altering the names of the principal characters accordingly. It has been suggested that Wagner decided to distance his dramatization of the story from Heine's and from *Le Vaisseau fantôme* of Pierre-Louis Dietsch, recently mounted by the Paris Opéra and nominally based on Wagner's own scenario. Whatever the other reasons behind this last-minute transposition of setting, though, there can be little doubt that the change confirmed the close association between the composer's own experiences and his conception of the opera. Thus when the Norwegian captain Daland identifies the neighborhood of his ship's haven as "Sandwike," the name of the fishing-village where the *Thetis* had sought respite from the North Sea storms during Wagner's summer voyage of 1839, it is a kind of personal signature inscribed by the composer into the text of his work. The change of fictional setting was not so much an afterthought, then, as a decision to authenticate an aspect of the work that was truly Wagner's own intellectual (or imaginative) property (however widely familiar the underlying elements of the story may have been): the maritime local color that he had absorbed first hand in the course of his tempestuous North Sea crossing with its Norwegian coastal interlude.

Wagner would always be fond of identifying himself with the characters and situations of his dramas. In one way or another he could always fancy himself as the heroes of his works. In a few other cases, too, biographical anecdotes served as the foundation for particular scenes or episodes, such as the midnight brawl in Act II of *Die Meistersinger*, whose prototype Wagner claims to have participated in during a visit with his sister Klara and her husband in Nuremberg in 1835 (*ML*, 105–07). But, apart perhaps from the notorious case of *Tristan und Isolde* and the Mathilde Wesendonck affair, the strongest parallel between Wagner's life and his art is to be found in *Der fliegende Holländer*. And while the echoes of his own seafaring experiences are especially vivid and precise, an even more extensive parallel exists between the mythic-dramatic figure of the Dutchman and Wagner's inner, "artistic" biography, as he himself construed it in later life.

No one has ever questioned Wagner's assessment of *Der fliegende Holländer* as a crucial turning point in his career as composer and dramatist. "I am unable to cite in the life of any other artist," Wagner wrote in the introduction to the first volume of his collected writings, "such a striking transformation accomplished in so short a time" as occurred with him between the composition of *Rienzi* and *Holländer*, "the first of which was scarcely finished when the second one, too, was nearly complete" (*GSD*, vol. 1, 3). Despite the numerous traditional or even regressive details one could cite, Wagner's overall achievement in *Holländer* represents the first of two distinct quantum leaps in his artistic development, the second constituted by the much more protracted upheaval between the composition of *Lohengrin* and *Das Rheingold*, between 1848 and 1853. (The compact and revolutionary character of *Rheingold* makes it a counterpart of sorts to *Holländer* within Wagner's career.) Both of these phases of intellectual and psychological upheaval coincided with periods of exile. After his participation in the socialist uprisings in Dresden in May 1849

Wagner became an actual political exile from Germany, and the factors of political agitation and geographical exile were certainly catalysts to the inner, creative "revolution" that gave birth to the *Ring* project. The period spent in Paris between 1839 and 1842 was, on the other hand, a self-imposed exile. Yet its effect on Wagner's psyche was equally drastic.

Living the life of a struggling artist in 1840s Paris – that of Henri Murger's original Bohemians – may have had its colorful aspects, in retrospect; but it was scarcely the *vie de Bohème* that drew Wagner to the French capital. His failure to become a second Meyerbeer, indeed, his near-failure to make any kind of living at all during these years, is surely the root of many salient traits of his future character: his demonization of Meyerbeer himself, along with all Jews (and Frenchmen); his deep-seated sense of social and artistic persecution; his peculiarly egocentric brand of aesthetic nationalism; and his genuine socialistic convictions, even if colored (like his nationalism) by a self-centered aesthetic utopianism. Against all odds Wagner had staked everything on a brilliant popular success in Paris, and by 1841 it was becoming evident that he had lost this wager. By then it was clear that his grand-historical Meyerbeerian blockbuster, *Rienzi*, would not so much as receive an audition by the personnel of the Académie royale de musique, the official operatic institution of Paris (commonly known as the Opéra). His hopes of having a translation of his previous operatic effort, *Das Liebesverbot*, produced by the Théâtre de la Renaissance foundered with the bankruptcy of that institution. (This was the first of several pieces of bad luck which Wagner's suspicious imagination transmuted into evidence of Meyerbeer's insidious double-dealing with him; but even if plans for the production had moved ahead, it is more than likely that the French would have dismissed this overwrought *opéra comique* as an impossible freak.) Finally, Wagner's hopes of receiving a commission for a short opera in one or three acts on the subject of the Flying Dutchman and his "phantom ship" – perhaps with a notion of capitalizing on the successful Parisian revival of Weber's *Freischütz* in 1840 and recent French interest in spectral themes of the Gothic and "fantastic" – dissolved early in his negotiations with the new opera director, Léon Pillet (see Chapter 2). By the time *Rienzi* was accepted for production back home, in Dresden, and Wagner had managed to sell off the French rights to his "Dutchman" scenario (as *Le Vaisseau fantôme*) to the direction of the Paris Opéra, he was ready to turn his back on Paris entirely. Now he would direct all his energies toward re-establishing a career in Germany, on a more secure and respectable footing than when he had left in 1839. It was in this frame of mind that he set about the composition of the "Dutchman" material (as *Der fliegende Holländer*) in the early summer of 1841, about nine months before he and Minna finally returned to Germany.

There's no place like home

It was thus in the course of his two-and-half-year Parisian "exile" that Wagner first consciously began to construct his identity as a German artist. A variety of factors were involved in this process, which was more than mere *ressentiment* occasioned by his failure to attain a brilliant Parisian success. The performances of Beethoven's symphonies by the "Societé des Concerts" of the Paris Conservatoire under François Habeneck, which had achieved a kind of cult status among the musical cognoscenti by the time of Wagner's visit, reawakened his appreciation of Beethoven and the Viennese Classical tradition. In particular, Habeneck's rendition of the Ninth Symphony galvanized his musical imagination: "the scales fell from my eyes," Wagner recalled many years later in his essay "On Conducting."[5] Beethoven's still-enigmatic masterpiece had fascinated him as a youth (he had made his own piano arrangement of the symphony around 1830), but he had never as yet encountered a performance that made sense of it. Performances of Berlioz's *Roméo et Juliette*, *Symphonie fantastique*, *Harold en Italie*, and *Symphonie funèbre et triomphale* during his first year in Paris also made a deep, if partly disturbing effect on Wagner. This remarkable body of new music aroused the ambitious young composer to look beyond the horizons of *Rienzi* and grand opera. The initial result of this inspiration was the decidedly Romantic project of a *Faust* symphony, which, however, soon took the more pragmatic form of a concert overture (*Eine Faust-Ouvertüre*, WWV 59).

Thus as time wore on, an ever-increasing disaffection with the world of commercial music-making in the French metropolis set in, along with a bitter resentment over his own inability to make headway as a musician beyond the hack-work of piano arrangements of music by Donizetti, Halévy, and Auber, as well as assorted potpourris for strings, flute quartet, and the latest rage, the *cornet à pistons*. (The fact that this "degrading" work was carried out for Maurice Schlesinger, son of a German-Jewish publisher in Berlin, was probably another contributing factor in the early development of Wagner's anti-Semitic psychology.) In the essays and reviews Wagner provided for the younger Schlesinger's *Revue et gazette musicale*, and in the notices on Parisian musical life he provided to the Dresden *Abend-Zeitung*, Schumann's *Neue Zeitschrift für Musik*, and several other German papers, Wagner gave vent to a splenetic view of musical circumstances in the French capital and, by contrast, an idealized view of German music and its institutions. This new strain of musical patriotism was less an expression of nostalgia for what he had left behind than of the utopian desires that he would continue to cultivate throughout his career. In the 1840 essay "On German Music" (originally published as "De la musique Allemande"), Wagner "could not help, at that [particular] time, holding forth with enthusiastic exaggeration on the intimate and deep nature" of German musical culture, as he remarks in *My Life* (*ML*, 186). The short story, "An End in Paris" (originally "Un musicien étranger à Paris," 1841), transmutes the composer's own tribulations into a still more tragic tale of young idealism and genius victimized, brutalized, and ultimately extinguished by modern urban capitalism and the emergent "culture industry." This bit of thinly disguised social criticism followed the story "A Pilgrimage to Beethoven" (originally less reverentially titled "Une visite à Beethoven"), which fantasizes a sympathetic encounter between a similar idealistic young musical protagonist and the aging Beethoven. Where the Beethoven-fantasy had been well received, Maurice Schlesinger was rather taken aback by the gloomy and acerbic tone of the second novella (although it elicited sympathetic remarks from Heine, Berlioz, and a "poor clerk" in Schlesinger's office, according to Wagner). With this piece, as he later observed, he exacted vengeance for all the shame he had endured.[6]

These details of biographical and psychological context explain, to some extent, what might have seemed at the time to be an odd miscalculation on Wagner's part in deciding to compose *Der fliegende Holländer*, an apparent return to the outdated, provincial *Schauer-romantik* of the Weber-Marschner-Spohr variety at a time when new genres were ruling the European operatic stage: historical grand opera in Paris, Romantic-historical *melodramma* in Italy, and the lighter *Spieloper* with spoken dialogue in Germany (Lortzing, Flotow *et al.*). As Wagner actually composed it, of course, the *Holländer* was anything but a throwback. Even a number of early critics (cf. Chapter 4) noted how the popular German "dark Romanticism" of an earlier generation had been infused with elements of grand-operatic orchestration (even traces of Berlioz), as well as Meyerbeer's sense of stage spectacle. (The stage machinery and decorations of the Paris Opéra were another influential revelation for Wagner during this period.) And in retrospect, at least, one can already detect a distinctively Wagnerian leaning towards "psychological" drama and increased musical continuity. But if *Holländer* did benefit from the composer's experiences in Paris – whether or not he cared to admit it – it remained above all a gesture of musical and cultural solidarity with the "homeland" toward which he was now turning his sights. Just as he had composed *Rienzi* with his eye fixed on the conquest of Paris, so the *Holländer* was composed as an offering of sorts by the prodigal son preparing to return home and recommence his operatic career on a newly reformed track. (We should not forget, of course, that it was really *Rienzi*, his bid for a brilliant, worldly success abroad, that paved his way back to Germany and to a respectable Kapellmeistership in Dresden.)

The autobiographical construction of *Der fliegende Holländer* as an embodiment of Wager's own yearning for the maternal bosom of "German music" and as the redemptive agent (in spirit, if not in fact) of his own artistic repatriation following the misadventures of his Parisian campaign was variously elaborated up to the early years at Tribschen, when the initial portions of *My Life* were dictated to Cosima. Wagner's identification with the Dutchman as a symbol of the alienated, exiled artist seeking redemption from the consequences of an impetuous and foolhardy transgression (the Dutchman's oath to round the Cape of Good Hope at all costs, Wagner's ill-advised bid for a brilliant career à la Meyerbeer) was evidently as vital a motive in the composition of the opera as his experience of weathering the North Sea storms along the coast of Norway.[7]

During his last months in Paris and the first ones back in Germany (where Wagner returned in April 1842) he became increasingly contrite about his misguided attempts to establish himself in Paris, while expressing enthusiasm at the prospect of a new beginning back home. He had already given fictional expression to the dangers Paris posed for naive idealists like himself in the story "An End in Paris," mentioned above. And he repeated the warning in several of the essay-reports he submitted to German publications, such as the one headed "Parisian Fatalities for Germans" printed in August Lewald's cultural review, *Europa* (1841).[8] An open letter to Robert Schumann from the early weeks of 1842 containing the first signs of Wagner's antipathy toward Meyerbeer (slightly toned down in the text printed in the 22 February issue of the *Neue Zeitschrift für Musik*) offers Wagner's experiences as an object-lesson for his countrymen: "How happy we should be if we could break *completely* free from Paris! It has had its Grande Epoque, which, admittedly, had a good and salutary effect upon us. But that is now a thing of the past, and we must renounce our faith in Paris!"[9] (The letter ends with an apology for having gotten rather carried away.) Writing about a month after his return to Germany to Ernst Benedikt Kietz, a young art student and former companion of his Parisian *misère*, Wagner reflects on his mixed feelings about having abandoned the French metropolis and makes a pointed attempt to convince himself – as well as Kietz – that he has taken the proper course:

Paris for people like *us* is no more than a resplendent grave in which all our youthful energies ebb away, untapped. The devil take it! – This is something I would scarcely have admitted a week ago: the first impression you feel on returning from Paris to any of our larger cities is dreadful; it is almost impossible to say why this should be so . . . – Here – I feel – is my *homeland*, this is where I belong, & my only desire is to have my friends here with me, since all that has made them dear to me is similarly a part of this homeland. What do you have there? Hunger & – inducements, yes, but let it be in Germany that you accomplish all that you feel induced to do. Whenever I find myself growing too much enamored of Paris, all I need do is pick up the latest issue of the *Gazette musicale*: my love for the place vanishes in an instant – the devil take it!   (letter of 12 May 1842, *SL*, 92).

The brilliant success of *Rienzi* in Dresden later the next year heartened Wagner in his resolve to rebuild his career at home. Subsequently, he tried his best to read encouraging signs into the fitful progress of *Der fliegende Holländer* following its Dresden première in January 1843. But after only a handful of performances in Dresden, Berlin, Kassel, and Riga by the end of 1844 the opera sank all too quickly into the very oblivion its protagonist so fervently invokes. And in fact, *Holländer* never did achieve more than a marginal existence in the repertoire, at home or abroad, during the composer's lifetime. Within a few years Wagner himself lost interest in the opera, though he did revive it for a few performances in Zurich in 1852 (as the most practical of his mature works up to that time) and advised on the "model" production mounted under King Ludwig's patronage in Munich in 1864 (cf. Chapter 5, pp. 99–101).[10]

This increasing distance from the opera is not surprising, considering the nature of Wagner's development as a composer over the next two decades. But just as understandably, he continued to regard *Holländer* as the crucial step in his path toward genuine "musical drama" and continued to elaborate, from time to time, the parallel between his own situation in the years around 1840 and the mythic import of the Dutchman figure. Already the brief account of the opera's genesis that concludes the "Autobiographical Sketch" of 1843 juxtaposes that with the sentimental scene of Wagner's return to Germany, the implicit setting for the next, more glorious chapter in this life-in-progress: "For the first time I saw the Rhine – with hot tears in my eyes, I, poor artist, swore eternal fidelity to my German fatherland."[11] ("Eternal fidelity," *ewige Treue*: written around the time of the *Holländer* première in Dresden, these closing words of the "Autobiographical Sketch" must have contained for Wagner some echo of Senta's redemptive oath.)

The most extensive ruminations on the significance of the Dutchman figure and his legend occur in another autobiographical context, *Eine Mitteilung an meine Freunde* (*A Communication to my Friends*). This reflexive analysis of his artistic career up to 1851 and the first phase of the *Ring* project was written as a preface to the publication of the librettos of *Der fliegende Holländer*, *Tannhäuser*, and *Lohengrin*. An implicit premise of the undertaking is the status of these three operas, beginning with *Holländer*, as the foundation of Wagner's career as an original and distinctively German artist. Wagner's account of *Holländer* here has often been taken to task in recent times for its fairly transparent attempt to interpret the opera as an incipient "music drama," in terms of the later theories of *Opera and Drama* (in particular, to represent the score as organically unified by a network of motives in the manner of the *Ring* or other later music dramas). Equally tendentious is the construction of the drama, and even the music, as symbolic representations of the composer's own spiritual homesickness for "true German art" following an extended period of artistic waywardness coupled with empirical, geographical wandering and "exile." Whatever one makes of the retrospective reading of the opera as "music drama" (on this, see also Chapters 4 and 7), the parallels to Wagner's own life and career are less easy to refute. Allowing for an inevitable element of idealization and hyperbole, we probably must accept them, along with most aspects of his aesthetic self-analysis, as fundamentally valid.

The *Communication* is concerned primarily with "inner," artistic biography rather than external facts, dates, and events. Wagner's self-identification with the Dutchman there focuses on the theme of spiritual, psychological alienation as the lot of the Romantic artist, which condition becomes more poignant still for the artist who – like Wagner – has sacrificed his deeper artistic convictions along with his native roots in the vain pursuit of fame and fortune. In true Romantic fashion, Wagner yearns for a homeland he has never actually known, a utopian artistic "space" that is more a state of mind than any real place. (Of course, Wagner was writing here from the perspective of his second exile, following on his participation in the insurrection of 1849, and his faith in both the political and artistic conditions in Germany was at a low point.) He cites the "ardent, yearning patriotism" newly awoken in him at the time he composed *Holländer*, after receiving word that *Rienzi* would be produced in Dresden, news that strengthened his resolve to return to Germany. But he immediately qualifies this as a cultural, distinctly non-political patriotism – a rekindled faith in the potential of "German art" and, implicitly, in his own destined role within it:

It was the feeling of utter homelessness in Paris that awoke in me a longing for my German homeland. Yet this longing was not directed toward some old familiar thing that was to be regained; rather, its object was something new, as yet unknown, which I intuitively desired, but of which I only knew one thing for sure: that I would certainly never find it here in Paris. It was the longing of my Flying Dutchman for a woman . . . the redeeming woman whose features I beheld as yet only indistinctly, but which hovered before me only as the feminine element in general. And now this element expressed itself to me in terms of the *homeland* [*Heimat*], that is to say, the sensation of being embraced by some intimately familiar community [*Allgemeinen*], although a community I did not truly know, but only longed for, as the realization of the idea of a "homeland." Previously it had been the notion of something thoroughly foreign that, in the confining circumstances of my earlier existence [i.e., in Magdeburg and Riga] had beckoned to me with the promise of salvation, and which had driven me towards Paris in order to find it.   (*GSD*, vol. 4, 268)

For Wagner, writing ten years after the *Holländer*, this dreamt-of "homeland" was not the Germany of the 1830s or 1840s, but an undiscovered country: the Germany (or Europe) of the "future" as this had been imagined and theorized in the post-revolutionary writings he had recently completed.

The nexus of parallels between *Heimat*, woman, and an ideal artistic community maps onto the roles of Senta and the Dutchman within the *Holländer* interpreted as a *Künstlerdrama*, a dramatic representation of the artist's condition in symbolic terms.[12] This interpretation naturally reflects Wagner's conception of himself with respect to society at large, but also patterns in his personal life. As an individual, he was – from this time onward – forever in search of a woman who would demonstrate absolute, unconditional faith in him, ready to sacrifice everything for the sake of his mission and his person (Jessie Laussot, Mathilde Wesendonck, Cosima von Bülow). His ideal of the public audience for his work mirrored this personal dynamic: the public had only to surrender itself wholly and unconditionally to his vision and his works, and all would be mutually "redeemed" (the public spiritually and socially, and he, not least of all, fiscally). The selfless, self-sacrificing, unconditionally yielding woman was thus also a figure for the ideal audience, the public "of the future." Wagner's own "male" persona adopts a role partly conjugal and partly paternal with respect to this (implicitly) female construction of the public. Such a gendered allegorical embodiment of the relation between artist and public also helps to make some sense of Wagner's otherwise rather inscrutable identification, in this same context, of the object of Dutchman's desire as "the woman of the future" (*GSD*, vol. 4, 266).

Angels to the rescue

Reading backwards in the *Communication*, however, a more concrete application of the redemptive female to the circumstances of Wagner's own "inner" biography materializes – one that draws on the metaphorical constructions of music as "woman" in *Opera and Drama* and music's role as the redemptive (metaphorically female) agent within the aesthetic union of the *Gesamtkunstwerk*.[13] It is music, Wagner says a few pages earlier, that came to his spiritual rescue in the dark days of penury and degradation in Paris – specifically music in its "pure" and "German" guise (instrumental music, Beethoven), as might be aptly embodied in the pure and Nordic person of Senta. The frustrating and depressing circumstances of his life in Paris and his disaffection with the modern culture industry, he reflects, might easily have led to the continued dissipation of his creative energies in ineffectual gestures of literary and critical protest. But having discharged his accumulated ironic, bitter, and sardonic impulses in the assorted journalistic efforts of this period,

Wagner asserts, he was rescued from the career of a mere hack critic and arranger by the revitalization of his authentic creative impulses, and specifically, the impulse to composition.[14]

"I have more recently expressed myself at sufficient length on the nature of music," Wagner writes, alluding to the major series of "reform" treatises written immediately prior to the *Communication*. "Here I only want to call to mind how it [music] acted as my good angel, who preserved me as an artist, or indeed, only truly rendered me an artist in the first place now, at a time when my feelings were roused to an increasingly strong sense of indignation toward our entire artistic conditions" (*GSD*, vol. 4, 263). The widespread revolutionary sentiments of the age, he maintains (already with a eye toward his own post-revolutionary political rehabilitation), were in him transmuted into revolutionary *artistic* impulses, nurtured by a new musical consciousness and – to infer from the broader context – by the maternal bosom of the German art (music) he now consciously re-embraced:

Just now I identified [music] as my good angel. This angel was not sent down to me from heaven, though; rather, it came to me through the toil of human genius over the centuries. It did not simply touch my brow with an imperceptible, shining hand; rather it nourished itself in the dark, warm-blooded interior of my vehemently longing heart, strengthening a generative power [*gebärende Kraft*] directed to the daylight world without.

(*GSD*, vol. 4, 264)

The gender identity of this musical angel of salvation becomes somewhat complicated. Following the norms of German grammar, Wagner speaks of this angel in the masculine (*der Engel*), and he is clearly being figured here as an emissary of the pantheon of (male) German composers of the modern era, from Bach and Handel through Gluck, Haydn, Mozart, and Beethoven. But precisely at this point in the text Wagner takes a new metaphorical tack, identifying music with the abstract notion of "love" (*die Liebe*), figurally and grammatically feminine.[15] Where Wagner's "capacity for love" (thus also, for music) had been injured and repulsed by the cold, soulless "formalism" he had encountered in Parisian culture, this same experience kindled his "need for love" (for music) all the more (*GS* vol. 4, 264). Wagner figures his relationship to music in terms of desire, psychological as well as sexual (echoing the explicitly sexual, biological metaphors of music and drama developed in *Opera and Drama*). But there is also an element of Romantic, even courtly chivalric love in this figurative relationship. At the time of *Der fliegende Holländer* Wagner is suddenly activated by a desire to rescue the honor of true (German) music, threatened by the loveless forces of modern capitalism and urban culture, even while his own aesthetic salvation, in turn, is effected through the agency of the "good angel" of German Music.

All of this is finds a reflection in the role of Senta (that dreamy, ingenuous, yet fanatically resolute Nordic maiden) with respect to the Dutchman. He several times apostrophizes her as his "angel" – or potential angel – before addressing her directly as such. "Wird sie mein Engel sein?" ("Will she be my angel?"), he asks himself, aside, at the moment of closing his bargain with Daland toward the end of the first act. "Can I still indulge the wild hope," he ponders in the last part of his duet with Daland, "that an angel will take pity on me?" ("Darf ich in jenem Wahn noch schmachten, daß sich ein Engel mir erweicht?"). In the duet with Senta in Act II he wonders, yet again (still to himself), "will [my salvation] come to me through an angel such as this?" ("würd' es durch solchen Engel mir zutheil?"). Finally, as their duet nears its climax, he exclaims:

> Du bist ein Engel, – eines Engels Liebe
> Verworfne selbst zu trösten weiß . . . !
> Ach, wenn Erlösung mir zu hoffen bliebe, –
> Allewiger, durch diese sei's!
>
> [You are an angel, – an angel's love
> can console even a lost one [such as I] . . . !
> Ah, if salvation remains within my reach, –
> Almighty one, let it be through her!]

But there is, in fact, another angel inhabiting the text of *Der fliegende Holländer*, if not the visible stage drama. In Wagner's version of the legend it was an "angel of God" who instructed the Dutchman as to the one possible means of salvation open to him, a woman who will plight him eternal troth and remain good to her word.[16] (In Heine, appropriately, it is the Devil who fixes these terms – "not believing in woman's constancy, fool that he is.") Hence the various references within the internal narratives of the drama (the Dutchman's monologue, Senta's Ballad) to *Gottes Engel* and the promise that this angel would someday point the Dutchman to the chosen woman who will be true to him. The gender of this particular "angel of God" remains indeterminate (though again, grammatically male). Yet, as the passages of text just cited suggest, and as the end of the opera confirms, Senta herself assumes the role of redeeming angel over the course of the drama. In her final lines prior to her redemptive *salto mortale* into the sea, Senta proclaims that she now fulfills the angel's promise:

> Preis deinen Engel und sein Gebot!
> Hier steh' ich – treu dir bis zum Tod!
>
> [Praise your angel and his decree!
> Here I stand – true until the end!]

By fulfilling the terms of the angel's promise to the Dutchman, Senta herself is beatified. Wagner made the point in his stage directions: "Senta and the Dutchman rise from the sea in transfigured guise." This "phantasmagoria" of disembodied, sanctified forms floating heavenwards is scarcely something we expect to see realized in modern productions (though it forces certain questions that confront us throughout Wagner's oeuvre: what *are* we to make of all the talk about redemption, finally, and how *is* redemption to be staged?).

Senta's angelic transfiguration was evidently a serious point for the composer, at any rate, since it seems to have been the principal impulse behind his subsequent revisions to the ending (mainly those of 1860; see below and Chapter 3). The ten measures appended to the closing scene in 1860 – from the revised conclusion of the overture – sound the "redemption" theme from the refrain of Senta's Ballad in paired flutes and oboes to the celestial accompaniment of strumming harps, a sonic counterpart to the "brilliant gloriole" that is meant to surround the ascending images of Senta and the Dutchman at the final curtain. The "psalmodic" contour of $\hat{1}$–$\hat{2}$–$\hat{4}$–$\hat{3}$ (familiar from the Finale to Mozart's "Jupiter" Symphony) is harmonized as a minor plagal cadence to terminate the angelic transformation of Senta's theme, while reinforcing the gesture of angelic beatification. At key moments in the original score, as well, the music indicates Senta's provisionally angelic status: the hushed, a cappella refrain the women's chorus supplies to the third strophe of her Ballad (while she is momentarily sunk in a visionary trance), and the pulsating high woodwind chords that illuminate the musical texture of the Senta–Dutchman duet with a new "celestial" radiance strongly contrasting with the preceding, storm-tossed developmental material (Senta: "Wohl kenn' ich Weibes heil'ge Pflichten"). Senta's words – "Well I know a woman's sacred duty" – allude to the "eternal fidelity" set as the condition of the Dutchman's salvation. But they also remind us of the extent to which Senta's character is conceived as an apotheosis of the domestic "angel" of Biedermeier and Victorian social ideals, the virtuous helpmate whose entire being is dedicated to making the household a safe and tranquil haven for her husband when he returns home exhausted by "life's storms." (Wagner later construed his relation to Cosima in terms of the Dutchman and Senta: after singing the Act II Dutchman–Senta duet, apparently, with a certain Frau von Steinitz during a musical soirée at Tribschen, he remarked to Cosima how affected he was "to be singing this particular scene, in which he sees our whole situation, in front of my father" – *CWD*, 26 July 1873.)

If the music of *Holländer* assists in constructing Senta's redemptive angelic persona, what about its role as Wagner's own "good angel," leading the prodigal composer away from the false temptations of Paris and back toward his artistic homeland? In terms of outward pecuniary and domestic circumstances, as mentioned earlier, the composer was rescued by *Rienzi*, not by *Der fliegende Holländer*. There can be little question, though, that Wagner did really in some sense "discover himself" in the composition of *Holländer*. Modern scholarship has long been driven (and with good reason) by an impulse to deconstruct the personal mythography constructed by Wagner in the course of his lifetime. But the core of these personal myths often remains compelling and insightful, like those of his dramas. His sense for myth, after all, rivaled his sense for music.

After a decade of *Lehr-* and *Wanderjahre* (his artistic apprenticeship and journeyman years in Germany) Wagner underwent a rapid and remarkable sea-change – so to speak– toward the end of his stay in Paris. This creative sea-change seems indeed to have been triggered by a reaction against the conditions he faced in Paris and the false hopes that brought him there, as well as by a renewed orientation to German traditions, both operatic and instrumental. On the surface, *Der fliegende Holländer* still reflects much more of Weber and Marschner than of Beethoven, although the score does betray early signs of the supple motivic consciousness, as we might call it, that links Wagner's more mature works with Beethoven on a very broad level. At the same time, it should be admitted (as Wagner himself was loath to do) that much of what marks an advance over his German operatic forebears in the *Holländer* can be traced to the impact of Meyerbeer and Berlioz, and the spirit of French Romanticism as embodied by Victor Hugo, with its sense of theatrical panache, its grandly melodramatic gestures, and its new feeling for historical and local color.[17] On the whole, though, it is fair to regard *Der fliegende Holländer* as a new beginning for Wagner, drawing on a newly rediscovered enthusiasm for his German Romantic roots.

The fact that he so neatly closed the circuit of his early wanderings by returning to Dresden, where he had spent much of his youth, was to some extent a matter of chance, or at least of pragmatic concerns. Of the major operatic centers in Germany, this was the one to which Wagner had the most personal connections. *Holländer* was to have been created in Berlin, in fact, where it was first accepted, partly at Meyerbeer's recommendation. Only a series of administrative delays (which Wagner would soon blame on Meyerbeer) accounted for the eventual première in Dresden, at the beginning of 1843. And while the welcoming embrace extended by his native city to this "prodigal son" following his misadventures in the wide world was of course encouraging, it was also to some extent illusory. It was not so long before the terms and duties of his Kapellmeistership came to seem nearly as onerous as the privations of Paris. The conditions of German opera – both the repertoire and the institution – were disappointing. *Der fliegende Holländer*, which Wagner had proudly designated as his "offering to the German muse" in the first flush of his new-found cultural patriotism,[18] met with only a tepid success in Dresden, and the following year in Berlin. Attempts to get the work staged in Leipzig and Munich came to naught; the direction of those theatres, as mentioned above, viewed the piece as "unsuited to the German public" and to conditions of the German stage (cf. note 11).

Wagner's account (in the *Communication to my Friends*) of the "spiritual homecoming" represented by *Der fliegende Holländer* is suffused with nostalgic recollections of the homesickness he experienced during the latter part of his Paris sojourn. But at the time of the *Communication* (1851), Wagner had also come to realize that he was still far from finding the understanding that he had hoped for in Germany. The unconditional, unquestioning love that he required from his public in order to achieve artistic (or maybe just psychic) "redemption" was still a long way off. (The *Communication* is in large part a plea for that unconditional love.) Wagner was just then embarking on a whole new period of exile and wandering, as it turned out. And contrary to his original expectations, *Holländer* had failed to find a home on the German stage. Wagner did revive the opera for a few performances in Zurich, in 1852, and it was given a considerable boost by Liszt's production in Weimar the next year (and by the lengthy, appreciative essay he published in 1854). But it was not until after Wagner's death that the work really found a stable niche in the operatic repertoire and came to be generally appreciated as the first decisive step in his path toward the "music drama of the future."

Conception and composition: a brief chronicle

By way of epilogue to this account of *Holländer*'s role in the composer's personal and artistic biography, let us briefly review some basic facts pertaining to the original conception of the work and the various stages of its composition and subsequent revision.

When Wagner undertook his "famous sea-voyage" through the Baltic and North Sea in the summer of 1839 he was already familiar with Heinrich Heine's satirical version of the Flying Dutchman story, as he confessed to his Dresden friend and colleague Ferdinand Heine (see Appendix C, pp. 190–91). He could well have known several other versions of the legend from German popular literature of recent decades, such as von Zedlitz's "Das Geisterschiff" of 1832 or the "Geschichte vom Gespensterschiff" by the short-lived Wilhelm Hauff (1802–27).[19] Thus, whether or not he was actually regaled with stories of the Dutchman by the sailors aboard the *Thetis* (as the early "Autobiographical Sketch" would have it), there is no reason to doubt that he did have occasion to reflect on this legend in the course of his sometimes stormy and harrowing sea-voyage, and that – as he also maintains in the 1842 "Sketch" – the legend acquired for him "a distinctive coloring as only the experience of such an adventure at sea could provide" (*GSD*, vol. 1, 13–14). Upon arrival in Paris in the fall of 1839, the first order of business was to complete *Rienzi* while also beginning to lay the groundwork for its triumphant Parisian première – at least, as the still idealistic young composer imagined it. But knowing as we do Wagner's habit of storing up and working out in his mind promising dramatic themes, often over great lengths of time, there is every reason to believe that he did continue to meditate on the operatic possibilities of the Dutchman legend throughout his first months in the French capital.

The decision to pursue the Flying Dutchman project was probably influenced by a mixture of practical and aesthetic factors. Even before having completed *Rienzi* Wagner was forced to realize that the prospects of a production at the Paris Opéra were negligible, at best.

The influential conductor François Habeneck had given Wagner to understand, in the meantime, that he would have better luck with a small-scale opera in one or two acts that could sooner help meet the requisites of the Opéra's seasonal programming needs (a mixture of new grand opera, shorter works, older repertoire operas, and ballets).[20] The Flying Dutchman material, Wagner realized, was naturally suited to the proportions of a one-act "curtain-raiser." At the same time, the cold water cast on his original hopes for a Parisian *Rienzi* had the effect of warming him towards the thought of a return to an "authentically German" style and genre, as suggested earlier in this chapter.

The delusion of providing an immediately practical work, as would later attend the births of *Tristan* and *Die Meistersinger*, was perhaps less exaggerated in the case of *Der fliegende Holländer* (or *Le Hollandais volant*, as it was first sketched). But, while Wagner held on to hopes of a Parisian production of this new project for almost a year, these hopes would also have to be relinquished, even before serious work on the score had begun in the spring and summer of 1841. Wagner seems to have made the first steps toward realizing the *Holländer* project within six or seven months of his arrival in Paris. On 6 May 1840 he sent a sketch of his plan to the celebrated playwright and librettist Eugène Scribe in the hope of getting Scribe to produce a French text for it. (This was presumably the same as the still extant French prose draft reproduced, in translation, in Appendix A, pp. 169–73.) Would Scribe still be willing to consider versifying "un petit opéra en un acte" on the basis of the enclosed sketch, Wagner inquires, as he had intimated earlier? (*SB*, vol. 1, 390). Whatever polite promises he may or may not have extended, Scribe seems, unsurprisingly, to have ignored this request when it was formally proposed. By 26 July 1840 Wagner is writing to Meyerbeer again encouraging him to put in a good word "for me and my 'winged Dutchman' (1 act)" with the new director of the Opéra, Léon Pillet, who is on his way to meet with Meyerbeer at Bad Ems. Wagner adds that he now has "several numbers" ready for audition.[21] Evidently these pre-composed "audition numbers" for the project consisted of Senta's Ballad, the dance-chorus of Norwegian sailors that opens Act III, and some simplified, autonomous version of the "spectral chorus" (*Spukgesang*) later in Act III. In *My Life* Wagner mentions these as having been written before the rest of the score for this purpose, with texts translated into French by Emile Deschamps.[22]

Despite his best efforts to pull strings with the power elite of the Parisian operatic world, no audition of Wagner's *Holländer* excerpts was forthcoming. The project remained on hold through the spring of 1841, until he finally gave into pressure from Pillet to relinquish his prose sketch to the Opéra management for their own uses.[23] In May Wagner went ahead and drafted a complete libretto on the basis of his sketch for a "Dutchman" libretto, now evidently staking his hopes on a production of the work back home in Germany. (The libretto was completed by 28 May.) Sometime over the next month it was settled that Wagner would receive 500 francs for the rights to his scenario. This was probably an unnecessary act of generosity on the part of the Opéra administration, since the general subject was well known, and the opera eventually composed by Pierre-Louis Dietsch to a libretto by Révoil and Foucher owes less to Wagner's sketch than to other existing versions of the story (see Chapter 2).

At any rate, these 500 francs along with the news that *Rienzi* was accepted for production in Dresden (both bits of good luck arrived in the first week of July) greatly heartened the composer after his long tribulations in Paris. He settled himself and Minna comfortably out in the country, at Meudon, to devote the summer to the composition of his new opera, now as *Der fliegende Holländer*. According to *My Life*, a complete draft of the opera (minus the overture) was finished within seven weeks, between the second week of July and 22 August 1841. An interesting detail in this account is Wagner's uncertainty as to whether he had already composed the Helmsman's song (from Act I) along with the other "advance" numbers mentioned above: the implication is that he had imagined the music (or *some* music) distinctly enough when writing out the text that he could later be unsure whether or not he had actually "composed" it. The orchestration of the opera was carried out through the fall of 1841, and this, along with the composition of the overture (which, in fact, Wagner did claim to have "carried around complete in his head" for some time), was completed by early or middle November.

Having placed *Rienzi* with the Dresden theatre, Wagner was now working on a Berlin première for *Der fliegende Holländer*. Partly thanks to Meyerbeer's recommendation, *Holländer* was indeed accepted early in 1842 for production at the royal theatre in Berlin. (For a time, Wagner even expected that Meyerbeer himself would rehearse and conduct the première.) But Count Redern, who had accepted the work, turned out to be a lame-duck Intendant and, as luck would have it, his replacement (Theodor von Küstner) was less enthusiastic. Küstner, in fact, had just turned down the work in his previous capacity as director of the Munich court opera. While negotiations with Berlin came to a standstill, Wagner had in the meantime moved back to Germany and enjoyed a tremendous success with *Rienzi* in Dresden, where the theatre administration declared itself eager to take on the composer's latest opera. And so at the beginning of January 1843 (a little more than two months after *Rienzi*, and just a month before Wagner came to be appointed Royal Saxon Kapellmeister) *Der fliegende Holländer* reached the boards of the Dresden court opera.

Wagner was understandably eager to see his newest and most original work produced. His letters from the time (see Appendix B, pp. 185–90) reflect his excitement over the event, which seems to have led him to exaggerate a good deal the warmth of the public's response. Recalling the première in *My Life*, on the other hand, he takes a much more sober view of it. He was genuinely inspired by Schröder-Devrient's performance of Senta. (While coaching her in the role he had became particularly intimate with the singer, for whom he had entertained a strong natural sympathy since first meeting and working with her in 1835.) But the rest of the cast, the stage sets, and very likely the orchestral playing were either merely adequate or worse, and the evidence suggests that the composer enjoyed at best a *succès d'estime* as the "composer of *Rienzi*" and a newly discovered, promising local talent more than for the merits of the new work itself. After only four performances the opera was put aside, and was never revived in Dresden during Wagner's tenure as Kapellmeister, nor for many years afterwards (not until 1865).

Almost exactly one year later the long-delayed Berlin production came to fruition. This took place in Karl Friedrich Schinkel's Schauspielhaus, as the old opera house on Unter den Linden had recently been burned out. Wagner was unexpectedly pleased with the staging and design, under the circumstances, and later cited it in his 1852 production notes (see Appendix C) as a "model" production. Yet, like the first production, it lasted only four performances. The first two were given on 7 and 8 January, conducted by Wagner, who was not at all pleased with the musical state of things when he arrived to take over the last dress rehearsal. The plan had been to invite Schröder-Devrient to reprise the role of Senta. For some reason, however, she did not participate in the performances conducted by

Wagner, but only in the second two (23 and 25 February), after he had returned to Dresden.

As soon as Wagner had decided to divide the opera into three acts, rather than risk his original plan of playing it without a break, he seems to have worried about the lack of a strong "curtain" for the first act. The musical-dramaturgical effect of the first- and second-act conclusions, in the customary three-act division, are indeed rather perfunctory – by Wagner's own standards, as well as those of contemporary grand opera. Thus his letters from Berlin express considerable relief and elation at the growing responsiveness of the audience in the course of the second act: "their interest grew," as he describes it to Minna, "tension turned into excitement, heightened involvement – finally to enthusiasm, and even before the curtain had fallen on the second act I was celebrating a triumph such as few, I am sure, have ever been granted" (8 January 1844, *SB*, vol. 2, 352; see also Appendix B, p. 190).

Nonetheless, the intense desire for public approbation of his newest opera, as expressed in Wagner's correspondence, was destined to meet with frustration. In between the Dresden and Berlin performances *Holländer* had been also produced at Riga (where local interest in the work of the former music-director was no doubt sparked by reports on the success of *Rienzi*), and in Kassel (where the composer and Kapellmeister Louis Spohr looked with a sympathetic eye on what others seem to have regarded as an untimely bid to revive the creaky, provincial genre of German Romantic *Schaueroper*). Plans for a Leipzig production in 1846 never materialized. After resettling in Zurich following his exile from Germany Wagner was persuaded to oversee a revival of his now nearly forgotten opera in the spring of 1852 (with performances on 25, 28, 30 April and 2 May), its modest dimensions being better suited to local forces than *Tannhäuser* or *Lohengrin*. Liszt produced the opera in Weimar the following year (February 1853), and a few other theatres picked it up over the next decade (Breslau and Schwerin in 1853, Prague in 1856, and Vienna in 1860). Yet *Holländer* was destined to remain a poor relation to Wagner's other "Romantic operas" of the Dresden years throughout his life and into the twentieth century, when its dramatic economy and its significance in Wagner's oeuvre came to be better appreciated.

Although Wagner himself had little contact with *Holländer* in performance after its relatively inauspicious première, he did have occasion to implement some second and third thoughts about the score. He evidently still entertained hopes of making a mark with the opera when the plans for a Leipzig production were floated in 1846. A year earlier, the Dresden publisher C. F. Meser had overseen the production of thirty lithograph copies of the full score.[24] On the basis of his interim experience with *Tannhäuser*, Wagner now wanted to rework the orchestration throughout, principally by reducing the role of the brass and thinning out the strings in places. (Berlioz had criticized an over-reliance on string-tremolo accompaniments after hearing the first performances in Dresden, and Wagner himself came to regard the tendency to reinforce melody and harmonic accompaniment alike with penetrating brass instruments as a bad habit acquired from modern French and Italian opera, with its striving for "effect.") He touched up a copy of the printed score accordingly, and sent it to Leipzig. Several years later, when he directed the Zurich revival (April 1852) and corresponded with Liszt about the Weimar production of 1853, Wagner attempted to recuperate his 1846 revisions, further refining the instrumentation of the overture's coda (and the analogous passage at the close of the opera), as well as adding an extra measure of unison tremolo (on A, m. 328) to highlight the entrance of the triumphantly transformed Senta/redemption theme.[25]

The most significant alterations were undertaken at the beginning of 1860 in conjunction with the concert programs Wagner organized to introduce himself to the Paris public prior to the ill-fated French première of *Tannhäuser* (which he had hoped would be a triumphant conquest of the site of his earlier struggles). Now it was the experience of *Tristan* that guided the tone of the revisions, just as it did – on a larger scale – the revisions to the *Tannhäuser* score at this time. "Only now that I have written Isolde's final transfiguration," the composer remarked in a well-known passage from his correspondence with Mathilde Wesendonck, "have I been able to find the right ending for the Flying Dutchman Overture, as well as – the horrors of the Venusberg" (letter of 10 April 1860, *SL*, 489).

The relevance of Isolde's "transfiguration" is immediately clear in the case of the *Holländer* finale, for this likewise involves the self-sacrificial death and mystical assumption of the opera's heroine, as anticipated at the conclusion of the overture. (Wagner made a point to see that the end of the opera and the overture corresponded at each stage of his revisions.) Musically, there are two points of contact. In place of the somewhat limited attempt at harmonic-developmental intensification in the overture's original coda (measures 346–69) Wagner inserted a much bolder series of chromatic sequences, based on the coda to Senta's Ballad, pressing from V^7 of E-flat through E major (measures 355–57) to V of F and beyond. These sequences are now set to the "ethereal" orchestration of harps and woodwinds, backed by a more energetic figuration in the strings. (This much recalls, if on a modest scale, the central intensifications of Isolde's great final scene.) Then, following a triumphant D-major statement of the Dutchman motive with an elaborate new swirling string accompaniment (measures 377–88), woodwinds and harp arpeggios return with the Senta/redemption theme, rounded off with a drawn-out minor/major plagal cadence (measure 389 to the end) that similarly recalls the cathartic, "transfigured" conclusion of *Tristan und Isolde*. The scoring, the cadential harmony, and the melodic rise to a sustained third degree in the upper voice are all comparable features of both endings.

As with his next opera, *Tannhäuser*, Wagner continued to think in later life about establishing a definitive musical text for *Der fliegende Holländer*. In particular, he contemplated a wholesale recomposition of Senta's Ballad (though this could not have included the Ballad's refrain-theme without seriously upsetting the conception of the overture and the other passages in the opera that quote or transform the theme). The idea of revising the Ballad may have originated at the time of the Munich revival of the opera in 1864, under the patronage of Ludwig II of Bavaria. A brief sketch of the opening phrase of the Ballad, with the text slightly altered and the melody completely recast (modulating from A-flat/C minor to A minor, though still in $\frac{6}{8}$) exists with the date "9 September," most likely 1864. From the primitive state of the sketch it is difficult to gauge the potential effectiveness of the new idea.[26] There is no evidence that this sketch was ever further elaborated, and on 17 October 1878 Cosima noted that he was still "thinking of revising Senta's Ballad, the beginning of which he finds quite like a folk-song, but not characteristic of *Der fliegende Holländer*." Intriguingly, Wagner mentioned to Cosima several years later a "new version he made of the Ballad in *Der Fl. Holländer*, which he has unfortunately lost" (*CWD*, 20 January 1880). Whether he really had made such a new version or whether he was referring to the brief sketch is not possible to say for sure, though it seems unlikely that a fully composed new version would have gone astray. Other comments from between these years (1865–80) suggest that Wagner contemplated a more radical reworking of the whole score, to bring it closer into the orbit of his mature ideal of the "musical drama."[27] Beyond linking the three acts into one, as Cosima did with the so-called "Bayreuth" version in 1901, it is difficult to see how the fundamental dramaturgical and musical structure or the motivic-thematic content of the work could easily be thus overhauled. But Wagner's plans, at least, confirm his own sense of the work's importance in his oeuvre, as the vessel that returned him to his native soil, in aesthetic terms, securely oriented on his route toward "the future."

2 *The sources and genesis of the text*

BARRY MILLINGTON

Sources

Of all Wagner's mature operas, with their mythic or legendary subject matter, it is that of *Der fliegende Holländer* that has the shortest pre-history. Indeed, it was as late as the very end of the eighteenth century that the legend of the wandering seafarer achieved literary form, in various English and German versions. Probably the best known of all the versions is also one of the earliest: Samuel Taylor Coleridge's ballad "The Rime of the Ancient Mariner" (first published in 1798). A poem of Thomas Moore (1779–1852) alludes to a superstition among sailors about a ghost ship called the "Flying Dutchman." Sir Walter Scott's pirate poem "Rokeby" (1813), according to its author, relates to "a well-known nautical superstition concerning a fantastic vessel, called by sailors the 'Flying Dutchman', and supposed to be seen about the latitude of the Cape of Good Hope. She is distinguished from earthly vessels by bearing a press of sail when all others are unable, from stress of weather, to show an inch of canvas." The legend crops up too in contemporary German sources, including *Der ewige Segler* (*The Eternal Seafarer*) of 1812 by H. Schmidt; the *Bruchstücken aus Karl Berthold's Tagebuch* (*Fragments from the Diary of Karl Berthold*) of 1826, by "Oswald" (pseudonym of Martin Hieronymus Hudtwalcker), *Das Geisterschiff* (*The Ghost Ship*) of 1832, by Joseph Christian Freiherr von Zedlitz; and a number of popular tales by Wilhelm Hauff, which were almost certainly familiar to Wagner.

Wagner's chief source, however, was Heinrich Heine's treatment of the tale. Heine published his first, brief account of the story – where it is outlined in a single sentence – in 1827, in volume 2 of his *Reisebilder* (*Travel Pictures*). A few years later he developed it in Chapter 7 of his pseudo-autobiographical *Aus den Memoiren des Herren von*

Schnabelewopski, published in volume 1 of *Der Salon* (with 1834 as the publication date, though it actually appeared in December 1833). It was also published in a French version in 1834, under the macaronic title *Reisebilder: Œuvres III*.

The French and German versions differ only in minor details (the latter is reproduced in translation in Appendix A, pp. 166–69) and Heine's ironic, anti-Romantic stance is evident in both. They tell how the accursed sea-captain is forced to roam the oceans until Judgment Day unless he be saved by a woman's devotion. Once every seven years he is permitted to go ashore to seek such a woman, but the constraints of bourgeois marriage are such that he returns to his ship with relief. At the end, endeavoring to save her soul, he releases her from her commitment, but "Mrs. Flying Dutchman," in a dramatic demonstration of her loyalty, leaps from the cliff into the sea. Heine's cynicism is encapsulated in the final moral: that women should beware of marrying a Flying Dutchman, while men should take care that they are not ruined by women.

Notable, too, is the structure of Heine's account, for he sets up a framing narrative that serves as an ironic commentary on the legend. Positing an imaginary production of a Flying Dutchman drama in an Amsterdam theatre, Heine breaks off in the middle of a flight of Romantic rhetoric to describe how "a girl of breathtaking beauty" ("Eve herself" in the French version) leant seductively over the balcony above his head. The biblical apple becomes an orange, whose peel is dropped nonchalantly on his head. Closer inspection of the female responsible in the upper gallery reveals at the same time "a picture of domestic propriety" and a pair of tender, ruby lips marked by a curious, serpentine feature. The ensuing seduction is titillatingly omitted by Heine's narrator, who returns to the theatre in time to witness "Mrs. Flying Dutchman's" redemptive leap into the sea.

The structural disjunction of Heine's narrative serves not only to titillate (the author's "revenge," as he puts it, on those hypocritical prudes who enjoy a good sex scene yet decry it as immoral), but also to put an ironic distance between a potentially sentimental tale and the worldly-wise author. In doing so, Heine incorporates the age-old dualistic trope of woman as angel/whore, the seductress who draws helpless man to perdition. What a modern reader might deem to be a reactionary element in the story, though, was, at the time, indicative of the progressive ideals of the Young Germans (for whom Heine was an inspirational figure), since the latter were as opposed to sentimentally conceived Romanticism as they were to conventional morality based on Catholic values.

Heine's own possible sources are to some extent a matter of speculation. The legend seems to have grown up during the period of Britain's naval supremacy in the eighteenth century: England had waged a series of three inconclusive naval and colonial wars against the Dutch republic between 1652 and 1674, and the skirmishes – arising out of trading disputes, which continued to occur in the following century – would have given rise to such sailors' tales, passed down from one generation to another.

Of the literary manifestations of the legend mentioned above, we know that at least the Hudtwalcker Bruchstücke were read by Heine (in July 1826)[1] and it is almost certain that he would have been familiar also with the tales of Hauff. Another important source that Heine may or may not have known is a tale that appeared in the May 1821 issue of Blackwood's *Edinburgh Magazine*, entitled "Vanderdecken's Message Home: Or, the Tenacity of Natural Affection". The story, published anonymously but believed to have been written by one John Howison, tells of the appearance of the ghost ship "scudding furiously before the wind, under a press of canvass [*sic*]" and of the vain attempt by a member of its crew to palm off some letters for delivery to long-dead relatives on land. (This mail-delivery motive, though looming large in many versions of the legend, including Heine's original *Reisebilder* summary, is relegated to a trifling detail by Wagner. There is no reason to suppose that the latter, who, incidentally, never gave his Dutchman a name, had first-hand knowledge of Howison's version.)

Another contemporary British, and rather more curious, manifestation of the legend is Edward Fitzball's play *The Flying Dutchman; or The Phantom Ship*. Fitzball was a versatile writer who specialized in adapting and arranging historical and other classic stories for the stage. The subjects of his many historical dramas included Joan of Arc, Peter the Great and Robin Hood, but he enjoyed his greatest successes with nautical stories such as Fenimore Cooper's *The Pilot* and *The Red Rover*, and, in 1826, *The Flying Dutchman*. The latter, described by Fitzball as "a piece of diablerie,"[2] was carefully calculated to catch the mood of the moment. In his autobiography, published in 1859, he places his *Flying Dutchman* in the tradition of Mary Shelley's novel *Frankenstein* (1818) and Weber's opera *Der Freischütz* (first performed 1821). The public appetite for horror and the supernatural, exploited in such works, was apparently insatiable. As the printer's preface to the published edition of the play put it, Fitzball's "wits, fits, and fancies, in dramatic diablerie, have contributed to make night hideous, to the infinite delight of an intellectual public, who think the day's meal incomplete until they have supped full with horrors."

Fitzball's *The Flying Dutchman* (subtitled "A Nautical Drama") was published in London between 1827 and 1829 by John Cumberland (who also, incidentally, published Mary Mitford's play *Rienzi* in 1828).[3] As in Howison's version, the captain of the cursed vessel is called Vanderdecken (the Blackwood narrative is acknowledged in the preface to Fitzball's play) but this time he proves to be the villain of a farcical theatrical trifle. Some idea of the tone can be gleaned from the printer's preface, which congratulates the author on a piece in which "mirth and moonshine – murder and merriment – fire and fun, are so happily blended!"

The *dramatis personae* include, beside Vanderdecken himself (who, as in Howison's narrative, attempts to have letters delivered to people who have been long dead), the venal Captain Peppercoal and his niece Lestelle Vanhelm (who is in love with Lieutenant Mowdrey, a young sea-officer, but who nonetheless does sing a ballad about the Flying Dutchman). Lestelle is abducted by Vanderdecken but rescued initially by Mowdrey; hero and heroine are finally saved from the water by the captain and others in a sloop. They hoist sail with a British flag and to shouts of "Huzza!" the curtain falls.[4]

The question of whether or not Heine was familiar with Fitzball's play cannot easily be answered. William Ashton Ellis, scornful of the notion that "Heine, or any one else, should ever have got any idea from such a jumble of burlesque and rant other than that of assaulting its author," argued that "there was but the remotest chance" of Heine having attended the play while he was in London.[5] However, Ellis's own research into the matter – impressively meticulous and highly entertaining to read – establishes quite the reverse of what he would wish: that Heine could have attended the play on the last night of its first run, 7 April 1827. Contrary to the generally reliable chronology of Fritz Mende,[6] according to which Heine arrived in London on 14 April (an asterisk indicating an element of uncertainty), Ellis shows that Heine had arrived as early as the 5th or 6th, presenting on the latter, to Rothschilds (whose records Ellis examined), two bank drafts drawn in his favor by his uncle Solomon Heine.

In any case, if Fitzball's play was indeed published that year, it is quite possible that Heine may have become acquainted with it in that form, or may have been told about it by an English acquaintance. Even 1829 publication does not rule out the possibility of a copy falling into his hands subsequently. As for the difference in tone between Fitzball and Heine, inspiration works in mysterious ways and it is by no means inconceivable that such a preposterous farcical treatment, deployed knowingly to commercial advantage, might have appealed to Heine's developed sense of cynical irony.

Genesis of the text

To what extent Wagner himself owed anything to sources of the Flying Dutchman legend beyond the versions of Heine must also remain undetermined. Suffice to say that Heine is the only source mentioned in Wagner's autobiographical accounts, albeit with varying degrees of emphasis, both between accounts and between different editions of the same accounts.

Whatever his inspiration, Wagner initially sketched, in French, an outline of a one-act opera based on the legend and sent a copy to Eugène Scribe, the celebrated dramatist and librettist, on 6 May 1840. The way for this approach had already been cleared by Giacomo Meyerbeer, as is evident from Wagner's deferential letter to the composer dated 3 May. Wagner's intention was to make his mark on the Parisian musical world, and the best way to win a hearing seemed to be via the reigning monarchs of that world.

Since at the Opéra, projects were decided on the strength of the libretto, Wagner's scheme was for Scribe to versify the text so that he, Wagner, could then be engaged to set it to music. Scribe had already attended an audition of excerpts from Wagner's *Das Liebesverbot* held in the foyer of the Salle Péletier (the Opéra) and pronounced the music *charmant*, but he seems not to have been persuaded by the virtues of the new text.

This first prose sketch (reproduced in translation in Appendix A, pp. 169–73) is notable for several things. In the first place, it is a remarkably detailed outline of the story as we know it from the opera, with many of the salient features in place: the Dutchman is allowed to go ashore every seven years; the merchant's daughter sits daily in front of a portrait of a "pale and handsome man," singing a ballad about his sad fate; she pledges fidelity to him even unto death; the singing of the merchant's sailors is obliterated by that of the Dutch crew; the young man who loves the girl recalls the happy times they spent together, thus precipitating the final catastrophe (the Dutchman releases her from her vow and sets sail, but her leap from a rocky promontory into the sea brings him redemption).

Also notable are the facts that the story is set on the Scottish, rather than the Norwegian, coast and that none of the characters has a name: they are referred to as "the Dutchman," "the Scotsman," "the young girl" and "the young man."

The sketch refers to three musical numbers – the Ballad, and the songs of the Scottish and Dutch crews – which may or may not suggest that Wagner already had a conception of these numbers (their texts, at least, if not their music). The editors of the authoritative *Wagner Werk-Verzeichnis* assume that the music of these three numbers was composed between May and July 1840.[7]

Making no headway with Scribe, Wagner sent a copy of the sketch a month later (4 June) to Meyerbeer in Berlin, in the hope that he would bring it to the attention of the Opéra management and use his influence to further the project. Later that summer Meyerbeer returned unexpectedly to Paris and Wagner took the opportunity to secure an introduction to the director of the Opéra, Léon Pillet. Meyerbeer took Wagner to meet Pillet, but all that came out of it was the suggestion – unacceptable to Wagner – that he collaborate with another composer on some music for a ballet. He did, however, succeed in leaving behind with Pillet his brief outline of the story. Hearing nothing from Pillet for quite a long time, he occupied himself with the composition of *Rienzi* and with hack-work for the publisher Schlesinger.

Wagner's account in *Mein Leben* goes on to describe how he eventually caught up with Pillet. The latter suggested that Wagner relinquish the sketch as he, Pillet, needed to furnish several composers with subjects for small-scale operas. The terms of Pillet's contract in fact obliged him to produce at least four new works a year, including "a grand opera in three, four, or five acts, of approximately three hours' duration," and "a second opera in two acts, or two operas of one act each, of which one may be a translation, with music by a foreign national."[8] Unsurprisingly, Wagner was unwilling to surrender his sketch for composition by another hand – this, after all, was the point of the exercise – whereupon Pillet told him that there was no chance of his receiving a commission to compose an opera for at least seven years, and he advised him to accept a small amount in compensation for the story which Pillet would give to another to have made into an opera.

Wagner then appealed to the influential Edouard Monnais, a member of the Commission Spéciale des Théâtres Royaux, which oversaw the activities of the Opéra, in an undated letter (?June 1841) which was published for the first time in 1984.[9] It is clear from this letter that, contrary to the indignation expressed in *Mein Leben*, Wagner was actually resigned, at this stage, to the prospect of relinquishing his scenario to another – and interestingly he declares a willingness "to communicate to whoever is given the task of versifying the libretto all my ideas relating to the *execution* of both the scenic and musical situations."[10] He even goes on (again *pace* the autobiography) to suggest that if he be required to surrender the scenario, he should be compensated by being invited to compose a one-act ballet.

Monnais replied frankly that Wagner should accept anything he could get for the Flying Dutchman story, as it had already been given to Paul Foucher to elaborate as a libretto, adding insult to injury by commenting that "he found nothing new in the plot, since the subject of *Le Vaisseau fantôme* was already quite familiar in France as well" (*ML*, 199). Realizing that he had been outmaneuvred, Wagner declared his willingness to fall in with Pillet's wishes. "I participated in a conference with M. Foucher," he continues in *Mein Leben*, "at which, as a result of M. Pillet's advocacy, the value of my scenario was fixed at 500 francs, a sum paid to me by the theatre cashier as an advance on any author's royalties" (*ML*, 199).

At one time it was unclear whether Wagner really had sold his sketch, as he claimed, for 500 francs. Doubt was cast on Wagner's account for a number of reasons. In the first place, by the date of the supposed sale (2 July 1841) Wagner had already made his own versification of *Der fliegende Holländer* (between 18 and 28 May 1841). In the second place, a search of the Opéra's correspondence files and accounts for the years 1840 to 1842 had revealed – as it seemed – no trace of Wagner's name, and no record of 500 francs being disbursed by the cashier. And in the third place, Paul Foucher's collaborator, Henri Révoil, gave a researcher some four decades later a quite different account: that Wagner had protested that he had been robbed, and Pillet, in order to get rid of the importunate composer, had taken out of his pocket five napoleons (worth about only 100 francs) and given them to Wagner.[11]

The mystery was solved, however, when Isolde Vetter rediscovered an entry in the accounts ledger of the Opéra (originally published in the French journal *L'Illustration* in 1936).[12] Evidently, previous research had been insufficiently meticulous. A transaction had taken place, more or less as recounted in *Mein Leben*, and the indigent Wagner had left the offices of the Opéra three days later (5 July) better off by 500 francs. The sale of the scenario, however, did not preclude the possibility of Wagner making his own version for performance elsewhere. And as mentioned above, by the beginning of July he had already made his own versification, preceded by a second, elaborated prose draft in German.

The latter (reproduced in English translation in Appendix A, p. 173), was dated spring 1840 by Otto Strobel, who first published it in 1933.[13] However, the editors of the *Wagner Werk-Verzeichnis* consider that a date of spring 1841 is more plausible, on the grounds that the document is closer in style and conception to the versified libretto of May 1841 than to the first prose sketch (in French) of a year earlier. The sketch in question survives only in fragmentary form, but its relatively advanced state is immediately obvious. The central scene for the Dutchman and the "young girl," for example, is dealt with in the French sketch in a short, prosaic paragraph, while the German sketch fleshes it out with poetic flights of fantasy, introducing vestigial dialogue that often pre-echoes the locution of the final libretto. The action is still set on the Scottish coast – as it was to be until shortly before the première itself – and the characters of Senta, Erik and Daland are named, respectively, Anna, Georg and the Scotsman.

It is also, perhaps, worth tracing the evolution of *Der fliegende Holländer* from its original single-act conception to the opera in three acts, which was its final, published form. Whereas the first (French) prose sketch of May 1840 shows no scene divisions at all, the second (German) sketch of spring 1841 divides the scenario into three scenes (*Aufzügen*), but within a single act. The final versified text (May 1841) was designated by Wagner as a "Romantische Oper," and laid out (still) in three "Aufzügen." In subsequent, slightly amended versions made over the next month or so, the designation was changed first to "Romantische Oper in einem Act u. 3 Aufzügen" and finally to "Romantische Oper in drei Aufzügen."

In spite of the division into scenes, however, the intention at this stage was still for continuous music. Only when, at the end of October 1842, Wagner retrieved his score from the Berlin Opera, where there had been hopes of a performance, did he divide the work into three separate acts (i.e. with a full-scale close at the end of each one, and intervals before the second and third acts). At this time the action was also relocated to the coast of Norway. It is possible that the elevation of the work into a three-act opera was instigated by advice from Berlin, though it is equally plausible that the recent success of the five-act *Rienzi* in Dresden encouraged Wagner's expansionist tendencies.

Whereas Wagner's original conception, then, had been a curtain-raiser in a single act, the score itself was initially cast in three large "scenes," essentially three acts but without any pause. The opera was, however, first performed and published in three discrete acts, an arrangement consistent with Wagner's ambitions at the time. Cosima Wagner's decision, when she introduced the work at Bayreuth in 1901, to give it in a single act was grounded in an ideological preference – instigated by Wagner himself in later years – for regarding the work as an incipient music drama (see Chapter 7). Both continuous and separate-act versions therefore have some claim to authenticity. In dramatic terms, it can be argued that the continuous version is tauter and more concentrated. On the other hand, the work in its final form is an evening-long entertainment, not a mere curtain-raiser, and when intervals are interposed, the overlapping musical material (evident on recordings) no longer poses a problem.

In conclusion, the story of what happened to Wagner's scenario after he sold it to the Opéra may briefly be told. Whether or not Foucher and Révoil, the librettists employed by Pillet, actually began work on *Le Vaisseau fantôme* before the sale of Wagner's scenario (2 July 1841) is unclear. The letter from Monnais (?June 1841), quoted above, suggests that the scenario *had* already been handed to Foucher, but Peter Bloom, on the basis of a little-known letter from Foucher to Révoil dated 1 August 1841, believes that even if the subject had been previously mooted, the formal commission to Foucher and Révoil probably came during July 1841.[14] A good deal of the libretto was evidently written in the early part of 1842[15] and finally printed in that year, with Foucher named as sole author.

The extent to which *Le Vaisseau fantôme* is based on Wagner's scenario, however, has been greatly exaggerated. Wagner was the first to assume that Foucher and Révoil had used his scenario,[16] and the claim was for a long time repeated by subsequent commentators. In fact, the French story bears very little resemblance to Wagner's scenario at all. The *dramatis personae* are as follows: Troïl (captain of the "phantom ship"), Magnus (a young Shetlander), Barlow (a rich merchant of the Shetland Islands), Eric (a young sailor and servant of Barlow), Scriften (steersman of Troïl's ship), Minna (Barlow's daughter), Shetlands citizens, sailors, and peasants.

Troïl once defied God by swearing an oath that he would round the cape (or "un cap" – unspecified). For his blasphemy he is condemned to sail the seas for eternity; only a woman faithful to death might save him. For one day every seven years he is allowed on land. Troïl's steersman had once rebelled against his evil works and been thrown into the sea, Troïl sustaining a wound which has remained open and bloody to this day. The steersman is revealed to have been the father of Magnus, now in love with Minna. Barlow returns home, having been saved from shipwreck by a brave Swedish captain called Waldemar (actually Troïl incognito, as it turns out), whom he proposes to give in marriage to his daughter. The Swedish and Shetlander crews engage in rival bouts of drinking and singing. Waldemar/Troïl enters and Magnus reluctantly relinquishes Minna.

In Act II, Magnus, who has taken holy orders, reveals his identity to Minna; he will officiate at the marriage of Minna and Waldemar. Troïl, alone with Minna, tells her that he must leave her, eventually revealing himself as Troïl, the ill-fated, wandering sea-captain. Minna pledges her fidelity even unto death and the wedding goes ahead. During the ceremony Troïl exposes his hand for the exchanging of rings. Magnus sees the bloody mark and denounces him as the murderer Troïl. He leaves and is followed by Minna, who leaps from a rock into the sea. The ghost ship is swallowed up with a terrible noise, followed by a brilliant apotheosis. Minna is seen leading the accursed one to the feet of God.

It is clear that while there *are* several points of contact with Wagner's *Fliegender Holländer*, there are also important divergencies. There is no wedding ceremony in Wagner, for example; nor does the Dutchman disguise himself or have to conceal a bloody wound. The characters' names are different too, with the exception of Eric (though in *Le Vaisseau fantôme* he is not Minna's lover). The presence of a character called Minna once led to much confusion. It had sometimes been assumed that in his original sketch Wagner named his heroine Minna, as a token of his wife's devotion, and that Foucher/Révoil took over the name while Wagner changed it first to Anna and then to Senta.[17] However, Wagner's original name for his heroine was undoubtedly Anna, as in his second prose draft (see

Appendix A), and Foucher and Révoil took the name not from Wagner but, as we shall shortly see, from a different source altogether.

The chief similarities of the two plots may be summarized as follows: the relation in song of the legend of a cursed seafarer; the daughter given in marriage to a demonic stranger by a father who lusts after riches; local sailors routed by the singing of the crew of a strange vessel; the heroine leaping from a rock into the sea; apotheosis with redeemed and redeemer in the sky.

The possible sources drawn on by Foucher and Révoil include Heine's telling of the legend, Hauff's tales, Fenimore Cooper's novel *The Red Rover*, and several poetic treatments of the legend. But the most suggestive sources are two other novels: Captain Marryat's *The Phantom Ship*, which features a steersman called Schriften, and Walter Scott's *The Pirate*, from which the French librettists took the names of Magnus, Troïl, and Minna.[18]

The original title proposed by Foucher and Révoil for their opera was, in fact, *Troïl ou le Vaisseau fantôme*. Their libretto was duly set to music by a mediocre composer called Pierre-Louis Dietsch. *Le Vaisseau fantôme* was performed on eleven occasions, each time as a curtain-raiser to a ballet (as had been Wagner's original intention). It was not, however, a success, and the all-powerful Commission Spéciale des Théâtres Royaux reported that it disappointed expectations on more than one count: neither the scenery nor the costumes achieved "the grandeur and magnificence" required in the capital's principal lyric theatre. Moreover, the report continued, the audience waited in vain for the appearance of the phantom vessel itself, and the apotheosis was feeble.[19] Wagner was less than pleased to find Dietsch's opera on the Paris stage just as his own was entering production. By January of the new year (1843), however, the French ghost ship was on the verge of sinking without trace, while Wagner's was just embarking on a perennial voyage worthy of its subject.

3   *Text, action, and music*
THOMAS GREY

While Wagner himself regarded *Der fliegende Holländer* as the first crucial step on his path toward the true "musical drama," he made no attempt to disguise its foundation in traditional musical-dramaturgical units or numbers. As with some of the more "advanced" operas of the time (particularly the recent French grand operas of Meyerbeer and Halévy), the individual numbers within an act are almost always elided, at least nominally, and some become quite extended in scope and complexity (the Senta–Holländer duet in Act II, for instance, which forms in turn just one section of a larger finale-complex, or the still more ambitious choral-ensemble scene that opens Act III). All the same, Wagner – already an experienced librettist and opera composer – conceived the action of the opera from the outset largely in terms of the traditional formal types of aria, ensemble, and scene, as the German prose-sketch demonstrates (Appendix A, pp. 173–78). (The success of Wagner's "naturalistically" through-composed music dramas, it could be argued, owes much to his earlier experience with traditional number-based opera and its time-tested principles of musical dramaturgy, which continued to inform the "music drama" in matters of pacing, contrast, and the strategic deployment of gestural vs. lyrical music.) The following synopsis and commentary therefore takes the formal divisions with in each act as a point of departure, explaining the action within the framework of the musical-dramatic units that delineate it.

Overture

As Wagner's own "programmatic commentary" indicates, the overture is intended as a kind of instrumental encapsulation of the drama (see Appendix C, pp. 192–93). His models for this were most likely Weber's *Freischütz* overture and Beethoven's Second and Third

Ex. 3.1

Leonore overtures. It was especially Weber's practice of deploying central thematic ideas from the opera as symbolic musical agents within the sonata-based musical "narrative" of the overture that became paradigmatic for subsequent Romantic composers up to around 1850. Wagner goes much further than either Beethoven or Weber in his modifications of the standard sonata form: his overture is really more an orchestral fantasy on themes from the opera, though he attempts to invest it with some structural integrity by limiting the amount of thematic material used, developing it at some length (especially the "Dutchman" motive and the "Senta" theme), and even revealing certain motivic interconnections among the different ideas.[1]

In what amounts to a double-function introduction-cum-exposition Wagner introduces the principal thematic ideas of the overture, corresponding to the principal agents of the drama: the Flying Dutchman as protagonist and Senta as redeeming heroine. The source of both musical ideas (and their dramatic associations) is Senta's Ballad of Act II, one of the numbers Wagner had drafted over a year before the composition of the opera as a whole (cf. Chapter 1). In fact, this Ballad, along with the theme of the Sailors' Chorus of Act III (likewise drafted before the rest of the opera), contains nearly all the raw material of the overture. Of these three main thematic elements – the Dutchman theme, the Senta theme, and the Sailors' Chorus – the first one comes the closest to prefiguring the leitmotif technique of Wagner's later operas. Like some of the fundamental leitmotifs of the *Ring* cycle (the Rhinegold motive, the motive of Freia's Golden Apples, the Sword motive, Siegfried's horn-call), it is an open-ended call or fanfare figure, composed of the most fundamental, "elemental" intervallic materials, in this case a perfect fourth and fifth (Ex. 3.1, accompanied by a sustained open-fifth sonority in woodwinds and string tremolo).

More than any other musical idea in the score, this one will recur at various crucial junctures of the opera with unequivocal symbolic intent. The motive clearly embodies the Dutchman himself, as the

Ex. 3.2

central dramatic figure. The Senta theme, pointedly introduced in the woodwinds (measures 65ff, see Ex. 3.2) as an expressive counterpart to the opening material, fulfills the same role in the Act II Ballad, where it serves as refrain, but there its dramatic-textual association is the promise of redemption held out to the accursed Dutchman. Its association with Senta as a character is only realized by virtue of her emphatic decision to become the agent of this redemption; the theme does not otherwise function as an identifying "tag" for her character as such in the course of the opera (hence the common alternative designation of this idea as the "redemption theme").

The Dutchman motive is juxtaposed with two other, faster-moving figures in the introduction/exposition of the overture, both of them likewise drawn from the source material of the Ballad. One is nothing more than a chromatic surge, obviously intended to convey the vertiginous ocean swells and the listing of the ship (Ex. 3.3a); the other is similarly surging but more tonally stable, outlining the tonic key of D minor, and could be said to constitute the actual main theme of the overture (Ex. 3.3b) on account of its structural placement both here and later in the movement. If the fourth-plus-fifth horn-call signifies the figure of the Dutchman himself, Example 3.3b appears to signify his fate: his endless and aimless navigation of the world's oceans, which appear in a state of perpetual agitation wherever he is present.

The "development" section of the overture begins with an evocation of these turbulent journeys (as Wagner also suggests in his "programmatic commentary"), implementing both Examples 3a and 3b – the latter now given a cadential consequent which Wagner presses into the service of a restless series of modulations. The striking novelty of Wagner's formal conception – one that would exert a significant influence on Liszt's symphonic poems – begins to unfold at this point: for the rest of the overture up to the coda (really the whole body of the piece, apart from the introductory "exposition") consists in the developmental working-up of the Dutchman material, into which the Senta theme and the Sailors' Chorus theme are interwoven

Ex. 3.3a

Ex. 3.3b

with overt dramatic intent. The storm-tossed Dutchman material undergoes various sequential and chromatic developments between measures 97 and 163, although the D tonic is never left very far behind. (The musical content of this section corresponds fairly closely to the central "Allegro molto agitato" of the Dutchman's Act I monologue, "Wie oft in Meeres tiefsten Schlund," where he describes for the audience the nature of his endless voyaging.) Then an oscillating figure on fifth and sixth scale-degrees and a descending three-note "call" (both of which will figure in the sailors' music at the end of Act I and the opening of Act III) are heard over an extended dominant preparation for F major. These motivic fragments contend with the chromatic agitations in the strings, until a robust cadence on the dominant (measures 195–99) ushers in a statement of the Act III Sailors' Chorus theme in *banda*-style scoring for winds and brass. The musical-dramatic image informing this next phase of the "development" is that of the uncanny "song-contest" between the hearty Norwegian and spectral Dutch crews in Act III; perhaps for the sake of thematic economy, Wagner does not actually bring the ghostly song of the Dutch crew ("Schwarzer Hauptmann, geh' ans Land") into the overture, but contents himself with the Dutchman material from the exposition. As later in Act III, though, the stormy-demonic, Dutchman-related music can be heard to chase desperate snatches of the Norwegians' song up the chromatic ladder. The process subsides for a while, as the Dutchman music gains the upper hand, and then resumes at a still higher pitch level in measure 267.

The final phase of this central, extended development comes with the arrival of the Senta or redemption theme in F major at measure

285 (where Wagner also draws attention to the $\hat{5}$–$\hat{6}$ oscillation of its motivic tail, which it shares with the sailors' music). Like the Sailors' Chorus, the Senta theme undergoes several upward transpositions. But the import of this upward sequencing seems to be different here: rather than being chased and harried by the storm, this music fulfills an ostensive function, pointing the way towards the promised goal that will be revealed in the coda as the Dutchman's eventual salvation. While it may seem problematic to maintain that this theme "pulls" where the other one was "pushed," one could point to the combined effect of the Senta theme's noble and dignified character, the *fortissimo* dynamics and full *tutti* texture, as well as the *poco ritenuto* Wagner indicates at each appearance of the idea. Furthermore, the Senta/redemption theme *does* prove to be the ultimate goal: the Dutchman motive (in B minor) is left poised melodramatically on a diminished-seventh brink, over the gaping abyss of a measure's rest (fermata), at which point a flurry of violins lead the G♯ diminished chord up to a triumphant D major $\frac{6}{4}$ and the heroic *alla breve* transformation of the Senta theme in that key.

As in the case of its prototypes (the Beethoven and Weber overtures cited above), Wagner's coda anticipates the spiritual triumph or breakthrough that is the goal of the drama. (Wagner goes beyond them in fashioning a precise correlation between the conclusion of the overture and of the whole opera, as he would do again in *Tannhäuser* – a correlation he was careful to preserve at each stage of his revisions.) The coda derives, more specifically, from the ecstatic transformation of the Ballad-refrain ("Senta theme") in Act II, where Senta is suddenly seized with the inspiration that she is the one who must fulfill the promise of the Dutchman's salvation ("Ich sei's, die dich durch ihre Treu' erlöse!"). In the overture this material is transposed to D major, reorganized, and expanded. The triumphantly assertive transformation of the $\hat{3}$–$\hat{2}$–$\hat{1}$ contour of the Senta theme is stated twice, enclosing a dozen measures or so of sequential harmonic intensification that recalls for a moment the storms of the development, and followed by a final, broad statement of the Dutchman motive, harmonized as D major and engulfed by swirling scales and tremolos in the rest of the orchestra.

This original version of the coda (1841) was twice revised.[2] In 1852, Wagner refined the orchestration in a number of small but significant ways, and added one extra measure of high string tremolo (a^2–a^3) to highlight the first entrance of the transformed Senta theme.[3] Then at the beginning of 1860, in preparing for the series of orchestral concerts he had scheduled for Paris (prior to the ill-fated *Tannhäuser* revival), Wagner rewrote and expanded by sixteen measures the central harmonic intensification of the coda, adding a final, "transfigured" recollection of the Senta theme at the end in the form of an extended plagal cadence (IV_4^6–iv_4^6–V^{4-3}–I). The new conclusion was certainly intended as a more suitable musical reflection of the lovers' visual apotheosis indicated by the stage directions for the close of the opera.

As with the much more extensive revisions to *Tannhäuser* from this time, those to the *Holländer* overture reflect, in a modest way, the recent experience of *Tristan*. "Only now that I have written Isolde's final transfiguration," he wrote to Mathilde Wesendonck in April of 1860, "have I been able to find the right ending for the Flying Dutchman overture, as well as – the horrors of the Venusberg" (*SL*, 489). The revised central portion of the coda (measures 347–71 of the 1860 version) shows how much more Wagner could now provide along the lines of chromatic sequential intensification than he was able to do in 1841. The passage begins with harp and woodwinds (a decidedly "French" touch, and a welcome textural relief at this point in the score); the same combination is featured in the opera's new "apotheosis," as well. The string figuration that carries the Dutchman motive into the safe haven of the transfigured Senta theme (measures 377–88) is the swirling principal thematic gesture of the overture (Ex. 3.3b), now in D major. The Dutchman's endless wanderings are thus symbolically brought to rest in this instrumental précis of the drama to follow.

Act I

No. 1 Introduction (Chorus of Norwegian sailors, Daland, Helmsman): "Hojohe, Hallojo!"

The first act opens in the manner of contemporary Italian and French operas with a choral-ensemble *introduzione*, an animated tableau presenting a number of secondary characters and enfolding a cavatina-like solo for one of these – here, the Helmsman of Daland's ship. (In keeping with the compact dimensions of this work, however, the *Holländer* "introduction" is more streamlined than those of grand opera, and ends "in the middle," in a sense, with the Helmsman's drowsy song interrupted by the appearance of the Dutchman's ship, rather than with the conventional return of the full chorus and ensemble.[4])

The scene is a narrow bay or fjord on the Norwegian coast, bounded by steep rocky cliffs. A storm is raging out at sea (in the background), although the force of the gale only penetrates the bay (in the foreground) from time to time.[5] The ship of the Norwegian merchant-captain Daland has just taken refuge in this bay and the crew is busy taking down the sails. An agitated prelude establishes the key of B-flat minor, and between chromatic swells and diminished-seventh gusts in the orchestra the chorus of sailors emit a variety of robust working-cries. The second of these is the rhythmically accented $\hat{3}$–$\hat{2}$–$\hat{1}$ motive of the Act III Sailors' Chorus, already antici-pated in the overture, and now uttered as an isolated call that echoes off the cliffs (first and second horns: see Ex. 3.4a). Wagner claimed to have experienced this effect first-hand in a similar locale during his 1839 North Sea voyage (cf. Chapter 1). The third call is a repeated neighbor-note oscillation on the dominant, likewise previewed in the overture in conjunction with the Sailors' Chorus theme (Ex. 3.4b). Daland appears on shore, where he has been taking his bearings. To a variable wave-like accompaniment he reports his findings – they have been driven some seven miles off-course by the storm – and exchanges words with the Helmsman on board. The key has shifted to the major mode (B-flat), and the accompanimental wave figure is relaxed, confirming Daland's hopeful claim that the storm is subsiding.

The Helmsman remains alone on deck to keep watch. A snatch of a theme that will be picked up at the end of the act (and in the festivities that open Act III) is given out by horns and bassoons, in between some more distant chromatic-diminished gusts. The introduction concludes with the Helmsman's song, Wagner's rendition of a folk-like sea shanty. The "naturalness" of the song is signaled by its unac-companied beginning, simple line, and strophic form. The song's text invokes the co-operation of the favorable southerly winds to speed the sailor home to his *Mädel*. Its refrain picks of the "Ho-ho-jo's" and "Hallo-ho's" of the opening chorus, which, in the mouth of the drowsy Helmsman, trail off into yawns. As he dozes in between verses the ship is struck by a large wave – quite out of proportion (to judge by its musical realization) with the abating storm. This anticipates a yet more violent incursion, following the second verse: the great crash of the Dutchman's ship casting its anchor.

An F♯ tremolo in the violins spreads out to an F♯–B open fifth,

Ex. 3.4a

Ex. 3.4b

heralding portentous statements of the Dutchman motive on these notes in the horns and bassoons, then trumpets and trombones. (B minor not only stands in marked contrast to the preceding B-flat tonality, but carries conventional associations with the supernatural and demonic.) The Dutchman's phantom ship has appeared, trailing storm-winds with it, and with a "terrible crash" in the orchestra its anchor is cast out. The Helmsman awakens for a moment, back in B-flat, but falls asleep again without noticing anything untoward. To a gloomy B-minor version of Example 3.4b and low echoes of the Dutchman motive the spectral crew silently lowers the sails while the Dutchman steps slowly ashore.

No. 2 Recitative and Aria (Dutchman): "Die Frist ist um"

Alone on shore, the Dutchman delivers the opera's one large-scale solo number. In four main sections, the piece follows another general model of contemporary French and Italian opera, the *gran scena e cavatina*, comprising an opening dramatic accompanied recitative (*scena*), a central aria (here in fast tempo), a free transitional section in *scena* or *arioso* idiom, and an intensified, faster concluding aria-section with coda. While the relative formality of the plan may seem to belie the popular designation of this number as the Dutchman's "monologue," the rhetorical intensity of the piece makes it a legitimate forerunner of the great baritone and bass monologues of the later music dramas, above all Wotan's in *Die Walküre*.

The opening recitative – through "und euer letztes Naß versiegt" – provides an interesting early case-study of Wagner's preoccupation with fixing stage gesture and action in orchestral accompaniment, as detailed in the composer's 1852 "Remarks on the Performance of the Opera *Der fliegende Holländer*" (see Appendix C, pp. 193–200). Later on such orchestral gesture would often resolve itself into associative "leitmotifs." This scene, however, still trades on the repeating, isolated figures of accompanied recitative or *scena* in the Franco-Italian tradition, related to the musically underscored histrionics of contemporary melodrama. Each step of the Dutchman's glacial and pessimistic progress on shore is marked, at first, by accented downbeats in double basses, tuba, and bassoon. His unsteady gait after seven years at sea is conveyed by sinuous chromatic sextuplets in cellos and violas. (Wagner had been able to study the effect first hand when he disembarked in London after his own adventurous three-weeks' voyage from East Prussia in 1839.) The Dutchman expresses with increasing vehemence his glum view of the prospects of salvation, until the wobbling string figures subside. One can perhaps hear them as being transformed here into the undulating theme of the Dutchman's wanderings familiar from the overture (Ex. 3.3b), now outlining the dominant of C minor.

This undulating figure, together with its surging chromatic counterpart (Ex. 3.3a from the overture), accompanies the first "aria" portion of the scene, in which the Dutchman paints a picture of his endless wanderings, his vain attempts to wreck his own cursed ship, and the fear he and his crew inspire even in the godless and hardened hearts of pirates. Some of this text is repeated as the material undergoes harmonic development (similar to that in the overture). Though such aria-like repetition of text for the sake of musical expansion is a point Wagner later criticized in his own opera, one might seek to justify it in this particular case as an apt representation of the "cyclic," repetitious nature of the protagonist's fate. A vocal climax on "Tod!" ("Death," measure 104, °vii⁷/C) signals the cadence of this central portion of the aria, which sinks down to the despairing silence that, in fact, articulates each major section of the monologue.

The transitional third section is set almost entirely to low, quiet string tremolo. The Dutchman addresses, rhetorically, the "angel of God" that once disclosed to him the conditions of his salvation: the discovery of a faithful woman. In an intensified version of the opening recitative ("Vergeb'ne Hoffnung! Furchtbar eitler Wahn!") he rejects this seemingly impossible condition, and in the final portion of the aria (Molto passionato, C minor) he sets his sights on his only remaining hope for surcease: the apocalypse and Last Judgment. The musical material is new, but recalls the central aria in its surging, wave-like chromatic-diminished string accompaniment. The Dutchman's apocalyptic invocations turn this powerful concluding section into a kind of operatic *Dies irae*. Massive G octaves in the brass greet his supplication of the world's end, followed by yet more massive *tutti* C-major chords as part of an extended minor-plagal cadence, in which the Dutchman motive is resolved upwards in a paroxysm of desperate hope (measures 276–85). In striking contrast to this seemingly final event of the aria, the ship's invisible crew echo the Dutchman's C-minor/major conclusion ("Ew'ge Vernichtung nimm' mich auf!"), *piano* in E minor/major. As the Dutchman lowers his head in despair, the music also contracts back to C minor, where the Dutchman motive resounds faintly in the first horn (natural horn in C).

No. 3 Scene, Duet (Daland, Dutchman) and Finale (chorus)

The remainder of the first act is comprised of this scene-complex, centered on the meeting of the Dutchman and Daland and the "bargain" they strike to exchange the former's store of priceless jewels for the hand of latter's daughter in marriage. The duet/dialogue that forms the core of the scene divides into four sections or phases: (1) a solo in which the Dutchman introduces himself and his plight, (2) an intermediate *scena* in which Daland learns of the Dutchman's precious cargo and his willingness to trade it for the prospect of a good marriage, (3) a lyrical duo in which the two men reflect on their respective interests in this bargain, and (4) an energetic coda in which the bargain is sealed.

Preceding this extended dialogue is a short introductory *scena*

Ex. 3.5

between Daland, the Helmsman, and subsequently the Dutchman. The captain arrives on deck and discovers (to a fragmentary statement of the Dutchman motive) a strange ship unexpectedly moored alongside his own. He rouses the sleeping Helmsman, who stirs with the refrain of his song still on his lips. (Neither the tremendous crash of the Dutchman's anchor nor the apocalyptic din of the Dutchman's monologue seems to have disturbed his slumbers.) He calls to the neighboring ship, but meets with no response. Daland spies the Dutchman on shore, and addresses him. His lugubrious answer is prefaced by a short orchestral phrase that assumes a quasi-leitmotivic status within the scene, suggesting the Dutchman's fatigue and pessimism (Ex. 3.5). Daland and the stranger identify themselves in a brief recitative – Daland more loquaciously, the Dutchman hollow and laconic.

The motive cited above (Ex. 3.5) introduces the first phase of the formal duet, a G-minor cantabile solo for the Dutchman in which he characterizes his unhappy state ("Durch Sturm und bösen Wind verschlagen / irr' auf den Wassern ich umher"). Where his monologue depicted the outer and inner storms he has endured for so long, this solo presents a more subdued image of aimless wandering, enacted by a steadily crawling line of legato eighth-notes in first violins and cellos, rising up from and sinking back down to the low G tonic. The intermediate *scena* that follows develops a fuller texture than the opening of the scene and moves at a faster pace, reflecting Daland's eager amazement at the stranger's wealth and apparent munificence. This is punctuated at last by a loud exclamation in woodwinds and brass (measure 217) that seems to express at once the Dutchman's suddenly excited hopes on hearing of Daland's "faithful child" and the latter's astonishment at the sudden proposition: "Sie sei mein Weib" ("she'll be my wife!").

This exclamation introduces the formal cantabile *a due* where the two characters, in classic operatic style, simultaneously reflect on the diverse feelings engendered in them by a surprising revelation. The

Ex. 3.6

Dutchman carries the melody throughout (G major, $\frac{6}{8}$). In between the phrases of this somewhat sentimental Biedermeier expression of the Dutchman's hopes and sorrows, Daland interjects more rapidly paced *pertichini* that reveal his affinity with the basso buffo character type. The episodic concluding phase of the duet is dominated by march-like rhythms expressive of the characters' mutual satisfaction with the bargain being struck. Daland makes a formal offer of Senta's hand in a bluff and easy-going tune in E flat ("Wohl, Fremdling, hab' ich eine schöne Tochter"), and the Dutchman responds eagerly but in some agitation. With the next favorable wind they will be home and the Dutchman may see for himself what a fine catch Daland's daughter is. A brief aside ("Wenn aus der Qualen Schreckgewalten"), recalling the Dutchman's anguished address to the "Angel of God" in his monologue, introduces an energetic coda in G major (Daland: "Gepriesen sei des Sturmesgewalten"). Both characters pursue their personal reflections, as before. Even within the conventional operatic language of this coda Wagner is able to differentiate somewhat the blustery good humor of Daland from the more troubled accents of the Dutchman, until they come together in a series of generically emphatic repeated cadences.

The Helmsman announces the arrival of a propitious southerly wind (flute and clarinet arpeggios) invoked by his earlier song, and the sailors' calls heard at the outset of the act resolve themselves (again in B flat) into the merry dance-tune which anticipated that song (Ex. 3.6). As Daland and the Dutchman take leave of each other the characteristic music of these propitious winds is heard again (measures 529–34) in woodwind arpeggios and high *divisi* string tremolos, strongly reminiscent of the same descriptive effect in Mendelssohn's overture *Meeresstille und Glückliche Fahrt*. The anchor is raised and the whole chorus picks up the Helmsman's song to the south wind, punctuated by boisterous string figuration. The chromatic surges of the opening scene are heard once more as Daland's ship prepares to set sail, but are now resolved into the cheerful cadence of the sailors' music.

Act II

Introduction (Entr'acte)

Wagner's original intention to cast the opera in a single act – dictated both by the functional requisites of his original Parisian plan to have the work accepted as a one-act "curtain-raiser" to ballet performances, and by the compact nature of the material itself — left practicable traces in the overlapping structure of the respective orchestral postludes and preludes to each act. Thus the brief orchestral introduction to Act II picks up the sailors' music from the end of Act I, and it is possible to elide the first two acts, without a pause, by proceeding directly from the last measure of chorus in Act I (No. 3, measure 582) to measure 19 of the Act II introduction (as done in the so-called "Bayreuth" performing version of the opera).[6] In an early example of his celebrated "art of transition" Wagner reworks the oscillating, double-dotted "Ho! He!" figure of the sailors' call over a stepwise bass motion and against a new whirring string accompaniment, so as to suggest the organic generation of the ensuing Spinning Chorus (No. 4) out of the preceding music (compare Exx. 3.7a–c). The men's working-music is thus "domesticated" as the scene moves indoors, and their voices are replaced by those of women at their spinning-wheels.

No. 4 Lied, Scene, Ballad, and Chorus (Spinning Chorus, Senta's Ballad, Chorus – Chorus of Girls, Mary, Senta, Erik)

Spinning Chorus. The text of the spinning song sung by the young Norwegian women is, in fact, directly complementary to the Helmsman's song, as reprised by the Norwegian crew at the close of the first act. The men sang to the south wind to speed them home, the sooner to regale their girlfriends with gifts from foreign climes. The women sing of their sweethearts (or "treasure," *Schatz*) out at sea, bringing home gold and other precious commodities "from the South." They fancy their spinning-wheels as windmills to breathe

Ex. 3.7a

Ex. 3.7b

Ex. 3.7c

wind into the ship's sails. The *Schatz* they anticipate is indeed twofold: golden trinkets and a prospective husband. Frau Mary (Senta's nurse) and the girls themselves remind each other that their industrious domestic productivity is the means toward securing these ends. The music Wagner provides for their singing (one of the numbers independently composed back in 1840) is a folk-like three-part strophic ditty of calculated popular appeal. The inevitably descriptive accompaniment suggests both the rapid turning of the wheels (violin 2, viola) and the rhythmic actions of the girls' feet on the treadles of their spinning-wheels (cello, bass). A naturalistic dramaturgical touch is the interruption of the song first by Mary, inadvertently, and then by Senta, on purpose. Like the Ballad that follows (No. 5), this chorus is thus highlighted as a natural or "phenomenal" song within the operatic context: the girls scold Mary for interrupting between the first and second verses, and then Senta forcibly vetoes the third verse ("Oh! Macht dem dummen Lied ein Ende!").

Senta refuses to participate in the conventional social economy celebrated in this song, just as her social status (as the sea-captain's daughter) and her non-seagoing boyfriend (Erik, a hunter) already mark her as an outsider to this collective. The other girls mock her difference and her infatuation with the "pale man" in the portrait. She reproaches them for their frivolity, but they drown her out by returning to their singing and spinning with exaggerated energy. Interrupting this third verse, then, Senta calls for the Ballad of the Flying Dutchman. Mary demurs, so Senta says she will sing it herself. The girls put their work aside to listen, and only Mary spins on (to a quiet trill in the violas).

Ballad. A ten-measure orchestral prelude to the Ballad is based on the already familiar music of the Dutchman: open fifths (violins, upper woodwinds) and the fourth-plus-fifth "call" motive (bass instruments, in an aggressive *fortissimo*), followed by a chromatic falling sequence and the "wandering" figure (Example 3.3b) as heard in the overture and the Dutchman's aria (No. 2). The jarring contrast between the A-major conclusion of the spinning scene (with its faint humming of the violas on A–G♯) and the G–D open fifths of the Dutchman motive would at first appear to have been introduced when Wagner transposed the Ballad down a step from A minor to G minor to better suit the range of the original Senta, Wilhelmine Schröder-Devrient. But in fact Wagner had begun this transposition twenty-eight measures earlier (at Senta's words "Laßt mich's euch recht zu Herzen führen"), preserving a whole-step tonal disjunction that had been there from the beginning (originally B to A).[7] The transposition does result in a greater large-scale tonal contrast between the Ballad (now in G minor) and the Spinning Chorus as a whole (still in A major), and this must have suited Wagner himself well enough, since he left the Ballad in the lower key. In any case, the tonal disjunction is apt to Senta's purpose in wrenching her audience away from their domestic complacency and into her own passionate sympathy for the tormented Byronic hero of the Ballad.

Also apt is the traditional designation of this number as "Senta's Ballad." It is "hers" in the sense of a solo number within the opera – in fact, her only solo number, and a modestly scaled one at that, offering

Ex. 3.8

nothing much in the way of virtuoso vocal display (as Wagner would have been quick to point out). But it also becomes hers in a more pointed way within the dramatic context. She claims it for her own in appropriating it from Mary ("How many times I have heard it from you," says Senta). She fixates on it (as we know from hearing her hum a snatch of it during the preceding Spinning Chorus), just as she fixates on the Dutchman's portrait. And finally, it becomes hers in a still more drastic way when, after the third verse, she actually steps into the narrative frame of the song with her impromptu response to its questioning refrain ("Where is she, whom God's angel pointed out to you? / Where is she, who will remain true unto death?"), and declares: "*I* am the one who will redeem you through her fidelity!"

As Senta sings it, the Ballad consists of three verses. The first recalls to the audience the figure of the "pale man" who is doomed to sail the seas forever on his ship with its "blood-red" sails and black mast. The second verse tells of his ill-advised hubris in swearing that he would round a stormy cape at all costs. The third explains the as yet futile "sabbatical" arrangement, whereby he may go ashore once every seven years to search for a faithful wife. Each verse is punctuated by a simple statement of the Dutchman motive. The first phrase of the Ballad melody (which is not used elsewhere in the opera) is characterized by a repeated falling fourth, inverting the Dutchman motive (see Ex. 3.8), while its heavy-set $\frac{6}{8}$ rhythms reinforce the plodding iambics of the Ballad text. The second phrase of each verse implements the "storm" material of the overture (chromatic surges, diminished-seventh tremolo, and the "wandering" motive of Ex. 3.3b), evoked by the refrain-like iterations of "Hui!" and "Johohe!" in the text. The refrain proper speaks each time of the promise of salvation, set to the second (Senta) theme of the overture, in B-flat major (originally C). The second time through the rapt audience of Norwegian girls joins in the refrain, in sympathetic harmony. With the third verse Senta has sunk back into her chair, overwhelmed by her passionate engagement with the Ballad. This time the girls sing the refrain entirely by themselves, completing the pattern of their own increasing engagement and providing a foil for Senta's startling intervention a moment later, which becomes a musical coda to the Ballad, in B flat ("Ich sei's, die dich durch ihre Treu' erlöse! / Mög Gottes Engel mich dir zeigen! / Durch mich sollst du das Heil erreichen!"). The conclusion of this brief, ecstatic coda is undercut by a deceptive cadence to a diminished chord (as will become the standard ploy of musical continuity in Wagner's later works). Mary and the girls leap up in astonishment and implore Senta to come to her senses. Erik, who has overheard Senta's improvised conclusion to the Ballad, is standing dumbstruck at the door. He tells the company that he has sighted Daland's ship approaching. This brief A-minor *scena* leads back to A major for a "chattering" chorus in which the girls express their excitement at this news while Mary admonishes them to prepare food and drink for the returning crew. The lively musical setting of this ensemble suggests that the example of Auber's *opéras comiques* had not been entirely lost on Wagner during his Paris years.

No. 5 Duet (Erik, Senta): "Bleib, Senta! Bleib nur einen Augenblick!"

Erik, Senta's erstwhile childhood companion and nominal fiancé, is wracked with doubts and troubling premonitions. The time has come for her father to offer her in marriage, but Erik fears that she is not committed to him, and that he is too poor to meet with the father's approval. Above all, he is troubled by Senta's *Schwärmerei*, her dreamy fixation with the portrait of the mysterious Dutchman and the Ballad of his legendary curse. These fixations do not bode well, he seems to sense, for her attachment to a simple, prosaic huntsman like him. This much of the duet-scene is built around a conventionally phrased cavatina melody ("Mein Herz voll Treue bis zum Sterben"), alternating with agitated, free *scena* material. Erik sings this material in B flat, but Senta twice responds in G flat ("Ach, schweige, Erik, jetzt" and "Wie? Zweifelst du an meinem Herzen?"), as if to underline the psychological distance that separates her from him, even when she consciously tries to enter into his conventional emotional – and musical – world.[8] After the second of Senta's evasive cantabile responses, Erik upbraids her for her fanatical obsession with the Dutchman legend, while she mocks him, in turn, for his apparent jealousy of a mere picture and a song.

This dialogue *scena* leads up to two solo *ariosi* that conclude the scene: a compact, sixteen-measure declamatory phrase in G minor for Senta in which she empathizes with the sad expression of the Dutchman's portrait ("Fühlst du den Schmerz?"), and a more extended declamatory *arioso*, known as "Erik's Dream." Just as she "willed herself" into the Ballad she appropriated from Mary, Senta now enters into the dream Erik recounts to her: "at the beginning of Erik's narration," Wagner's stage directions read, "[Senta] sinks as if into a magnetic [i.e. hypnotic] sleep, so that she appears to be dreaming the very dream Erik is recounting." Erik reports a vision that intimates more or less the action that will follow. He saw a foreign ship arrive on their coastline; Daland and a pale man in a dark costume appeared on the shore; the stranger (as Senta guesses) was the man in the portrait above them; Senta fell to the stranger's feet in an access of impassioned sympathy; they kissed, and sped away across the sea.

The declamatory dream-*arioso* emphasizes the monotone repetitions often characteristic of oracular, visionary speech in opera. Once the music moves away from B-flat minor the Dutchman motive enters in the bass. Stepwise rising iterations of the motive (G-flat minor–A flat–A minor; F–G flat) scan the rest of the narration and underline the rising tension of both parties. Senta prompts Erik at each step of the way, until – as with the Ballad – she is inspired to improvise a coda of her own (actually, an abbreviated version of that to her Ballad, transposed to C).[9] Once again, she insists on entering into the narrative frame as an active agent: "He seeks me! I must find him, I must perish with him!" In fact, this dream turns out to mediate between the fiction of the Ballad and the real life of the immediate future.

No. 6 Finale: [Scene,] Aria, Duet, and Trio (Daland, Dutchman, Senta)

After Erik has run off stage in despair, it is the Dutchman himself who steps from the world of legendary ballad and prophetic dream into the dramatic present. Senta remains in rapt contemplation of the Dutchman's portrait, as the Dutchman motive sounds in clarinet and horn. (The motive has become an *idée fixe*, in precisely the sense of Berlioz's *Symphonie fantastique*: Senta broods ceaselessly on the image of her "unknown" beloved, which image corresponds to a talismanic musical idea, representing, as it were, the interiority of that image.) As she sings the Ballad refrain to herself, *sotto voce* against soft string tremolo, she is interrupted by the image of the real Dutchman, in the flesh, when he appears at the threshold with her father. The apparition moves toward Senta with deliberate steps. The gestural language of this unexpected encounter between daughter, father, and stranger is described in detail in Wagner's 1852 production notes (see Appendix C, pp. 198–99), following closely the gestural detail of the score. Senta barely acknowledges her father's return, except to inquire about the mysteriously compelling stranger at his side.

Aria (Daland): "Mögst du, mein Kind." Daland introduces Senta to the Dutchman in a formal aria in D major ("Mögst du, mein Kind, den fremden Mann willkommen heissen"), though the tone of it is rather jovial and *in*formal, emphasizing Daland's hearty, unconstrained manner. Wagner is able to put to advantage the normally awkward silence such an aria poses on the other characters present: Senta and the Dutchman are indeed speechless, and their silence in the face of Daland's ingratiating pleasantries underscores their psychological distance from him. After addressing the Dutchman in a breezy, confidential tone in the mid-section of the aria ("Sagt, hab' ich sie zu viel gepriesen?") – confirming the high quality of his "merchandise," as it were – he turns back to Senta. He thinks to convince her of the match by exhibiting samples of the Dutchman's treasures. Meeting with no response, Daland observes the taciturn pair more closely (the hesitant gestural music of the introductory scene returns for a moment), and decides to leave the couple alone. He tries to reassure both parties, and himself, in a concluding return to the main theme of the aria, then withdraws slowly, turning back once or twice with puzzled glances. The Dutchman motive and the Ballad refrain confront each other in the orchestra (as they did just prior to the Dutchman's entrance), while the two characters themselves remain mute, in rapt contemplation of one another.

Duet (Dutchman, Senta): "Wie aus der Ferne." The extended duet at the center of the finale-complex is the longest, most ambitious number of the opera, appropriate to the centrality of its subject matter. This kind of spiritual-psychological recognition scene between kindred souls, predestined to a passionate and doomed encounter, clearly appealed to Wagner; he would go on to develop it in different ways in *Die Walküre* (Siegmund and Sieglinde) and

Tristan und Isolde. In the present case, the formal ambition of the scene is somewhat at odds with its frequently four-square, banal musical material in a way that is perhaps symptomatic of a discrepancy between musical-dramatic means and ends (material and concept) in Wagner's works prior to the *Ring*. Even here, though, the integrity of the dramatic conception is able to invest the musical execution with a certain conviction in the end.

The overall trajectory moves from stasis and brooding self-absorption toward passionate animation and interpersonal "connection" in avowals of love and mutual identification. (The third scene of *Die Walküre*, Act I, follows a similar trajectory, and the basic musical-dramatic pacing can be found in several other scenes in that work, such as Wotan's monologue, the "Annunciation of Death" scene, and the scene between Brünnhilde and Wotan at the end of the opera.) The Dutchman sings softly to himself ("Wie aus der Ferne längst vergang'ner Zeiten"), unaccompanied except for an intermittent shivering in the upper strings. Shivering tremolos and monotone pulsations characterize the accompaniment to the whole first phase of the duet (to measure 141), during which both the Dutchman and Senta speak only to themselves, first singly, then both at once. He asks himself if it is love he feels, and decides that it is rather "the longing for salvation." She meditates on the confusion between waking and dreaming that has long characterized her inner life, and which the Dutchman's appearance has intensified. This introductory "monologue *à deux*" (as it were) is rounded out by a soft plagal cadence (A to E) outlined by the "redemption" theme in the woodwinds, complete with a *religioso* 4–3 suspension.

At last the Dutchman breaches the dramatic space that has separated the two up to this point, addressing Senta directly (E minor, *un poco meno sostenuto*). Is she really ready to give herself up to a stranger? She responds in E major, *un poco più animato*: she is ready to obey her father (though her words and her music suggest more than this, a genuine eagerness for self-sacrifice). He flings himself at her feet, "in a transport of joy," as tempo and rhythmic activity continue to increase. An agitated episode in B minor (measures 244–79) recalls the "wandering" motive of the overture and the Act I monologue, as the Dutchman gets up suddenly and warns Senta of the possible consequences of her sacrifice, should she fail to remain true. Now Senta is able at last to assume the role of redeeming angel for which she has been longing (like an aspiring film actress for a glamorous part, to take a somewhat cynical view – but also like the Dutchman for his salvation). The Dutchman sinks "annihilated" to the ground with his B-minor cadence ("nennst ew'ge Treue du nicht dein"), and Senta "stands over him like a sublime angel," according to Wagner's directorial notes (see Appendix C, p. 200). Quick repeated chords in the woodwinds, in B major, illuminate her like a musical halo, or spotlight. The "wandering" figure shoots through this woodwind corona like another beam of light, rapid and ethereal.

With this assurance from Senta that she understands "eternal fidelity" the last, ecstatic phase of the long duet commences (Allegro molto, E major, measure 322). This is ushered in by a broad, triadic fanfare (B major, *piano*) in the natural trumpet, looking forward to the "Sword" motive in the first two *Ring* operas and backward to a similar effect in Rezia's "Ocean" aria from Weber's *Oberon* ("Ozean, du Ungeheuer!"). Now the two sing once again to themselves in what is, in effect, the cabaletta to this large duet-scene. Instead of alternating strophes, however, soprano and baritone sing overlapping four-measure phrases, underpinned by simple block harmonies. (Wagner tries to keep the energy level up through quick harmonic figuration in the violins.) The Dutchman exults in his imminent salvation and his triumph over an evil fate. Senta marvels at the "powerful magic" that impels her to his rescue. Wagner comes close to undermining the grand sweep of his duet by introducing a see-sawing tonic–dominant series in the most banal manner of his early period (Senta, "Was ist's, daß mächtig in mir lebet?"; Dutchman, "Du, Stern des Unheils, sollst erblassen"), but he has at least the good sense not to keep this up too long.

Trio (Senta, Dutchman, Daland). In the nick of time, as it were, Daland arrives. An E-major march tune accompanies him, which he deflects to C major as he begins to sing (a kind of tonal cold shower that signals his uncomprehending distance from the transports of the two lovers). Can he announce a betrothal to cap the festivities at his ship's return? Back in E major, Senta extends her hand as a token of her pledge. The three of them celebrate the moment in a short, energetic trio that is really nothing more than a brief coda to the duet. A sudden V_2^4/IV provides a harmonic boost to the closing cadences in E, and the three principal characters exit the stage, rejoicing (from their different perspectives) in the vows that have been concluded here.

Act III

Entr'acte

The orchestral introduction to Act III picks up from the ninth measure of the postlude to Act II (or measure 84 of the concluding Trio), allowing for the same splicing technique that Wagner provided for between Acts I and II. The bustling string figure of that postlude continues here in alternation with the second phrase of the Ballad refrain. From this emerges (*pianissimo*, and growing louder) several familiar ideas from the first act associated with the Norwegian crew (Exx. 3.6 and 3.4b), as well as a preview of the upcoming dance-song of the crew, already heard in the development section of the overture.

No. 7. Chorus and Ensemble (Chorus of Norwegian sailors, Chorus of Girls, Helmsman, Chorus of the Dutchman's crew): "Steuermann, Laß die Wacht!"

As the later (German) prose sketch for the opera makes clear (see Appendix A, pp. 175–78), Wagner conceived the last act – originally the third "scene" of his planned one-acter – in two overall sections: (1) a choral-ensemble number culminating in the macabre singing duel between the Norwegian and Dutch crews, and (2) a fast-paced, melodramatic denouement beginning with the duet-confrontation of Senta and Erik (originally Anna and Georg), and culminating in the Dutchman's departure and Senta's redemptive *salto mortale* into the sea.

The setting is the harbor of Daland's village. The two ships from the first act are once again anchored side by side. It is night-time, and the Norwegian crew is making merry aboard their vessel, while the Dutchman's ship continues to brood in uncanny silence and darkness. The opening chorus of Norwegian sailors ("Steuermann, laß die Wacht") was one of the three "characteristic" numbers composed a year before the rest of the opera, along with early versions of the Ballad and the *Spukgesang* of the Dutch crew that comes later in this scene.[10] The theme is "hearty" to an almost excessive degree, with strong rhythmic accents on the downbeats of every other measure that seem to demand a slow swaying back-and-forth motion from the chorus (Ex. 3.9). For all its aggressive simplicity, the tune does include two motivic "seeds" sown throughout the opera, especially in the first

Ex. 3.9

act (see "x" and "y" in Ex. 3.9), so that Wagner might well have cited this number as constituting, along with the Ballad, the "kernel" from which the rest was to grow.[11] The text, addressing the Helmsman, signals a parallel to his song in Act I. Like that song, the present chorus is framed by Example 3.6b, to which the sailors execute a galumphing hornpipe.

The chorus of Norwegian girls hurries on stage, mocking the sailors who are dancing with one another. Wagner carries over the dance-tune (Ex. 3.6b) into this *scène d'action*, which follows the preceding chorus without a break. And indeed, from the stolidly folksy chorus composed in 1840 now grows the most original musical-dramatic unit of the completed opera, stretching across 637 measures. As the girls enter the music dips into E minor. They approach the Dutch ship intending to extend their hospitality to the foreigners, and call out to them, while the Norwegian crew chuckles over their gloomy neighbors. The scene develops first as a formalized dialogue between sailors and girls, as the latter try to rouse the Dutch crew. At first the girls sing a series of eight-measure phrases in a bumptious, *Juchhe* idiom in Ländler rhythm, alternating with mock-somber responses from the men in contrasting key and mode (Ex. 3.10). Together they shout to the neighboring ship, at progressively higher pitches: "Seeleut'! Seeleut'! Wacht doch auf!" ("Sailors! Sailors! Wake up!"). Then, trading musical parts, the Norwegian sailors pick up the Ländler-like *Juchhe* phrases, cajoling both the girls and the invisible neighboring crew, while the girls sing to the hushed, somber phrases – no longer in jest, but genuinely spooked. The sailors, however, try to maintain the jest, alluding to the legend of the Flying Dutchman and his phantom crew without wanting to believe in it: "How many hundred years have you been at sea? No storm or rock can harm your ship! Have you no letters for land, addressed to our great-grandfathers?"[12]

Ex. 3.10

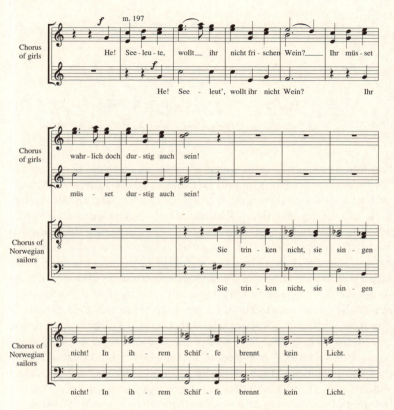

The *Ländler* theme subsides for a moment (back in C) as the girls go off stage, leaving the sailors to entertain themselves for a while longer. They begin a reprise of their earlier chorus ("Steuermann, Laß die Wacht"), which they preface with further loud provocations to the invisible crew of the Dutchman. But from the beginning of this reprise (measure 431), their hearty song is accompanied by faint, unsettling rumblings: first chromatic murmurs in the lower strings, then trombones begin to interject the Dutchman motive into the texture, as well as other familiar – but here chromatically altered – call-motives. The tension generated in this way is suddenly burst by the invisible chorus itself singing "Johohoe!" to the Dutchman motive, in B minor, against chromatic surging in the strings (likewise

Ex. 3.11

Schwarzer Haupt - mann, geh' ans Land,   sie - ben Jah - re   sind vor-bei!

Frei um blon - den   Mäd-chens Hand,   blon - des Mäd - chen sei   ihm treu!

familiar from Act I). This forms a prologue to their own macabre song, "Schwarzer Hauptmann, geh' ans Land" (B minor, Allegro $\frac{6}{8}$), with which they challenge the bravado of the Norwegian sailors (Ex. 3.11). Shrieking piccolos – Wagner asks for extra ones on stage, if possible – join with the chromatic-diminished surges in the strings to evoke the tempestuous "bridal music" (*Brautmusik*) of the Dutch crew's satanic shanty. (The score also calls for a wind machine.) The scene reaches its climax with the chaotic counterpoint of the two songs, the Norwegians making a vain effort to drown out the demonic music they have inadvertently stirred up from the bowels of the phantom ship.[13] The Norwegians start their song over several times, at progressively higher transpositions, as they try to out-sing their rivals. But at last they are silenced by the ghostly Dutch crew, whose own song reaches a pitch of Berlioz-like pandemonium before they suddenly break off with mocking, diabolical laughter, provoked by the sight of the Norwegians crossing themselves in terror. The strange "blue flame" that has illuminated the Dutchman's ship, according to the stage directions, is now extinguished. The Dutchman motive and Ballad refrain echo through the sudden silence, in B minor. The unison B of the cadence is held for several measures and yields to a hushed, harmonically alien C-minor chord (horns and bassoon, with tam-tam) in one last uncanny effect, serving also as transition to the F minor of the following scene.

No. 8 Finale

In the score Wagner divides the final scene into "Duet, Cavatina, and Finale." A more accurate representation of the structure would be "Scene [*a 2*], Cavatina, Scene [*a 3*], Trio, and Finale," where the formal

Ex. 3.12a

Ex. 3.12b

numbers (Erik's F-major Cavatina and the Senta–Erik–Dutchman trio in F minor) are sandwiched between freely composed action-scenes.

Duet (Erik, Senta). Senta and Erik rush out of Daland's house, where evidently Erik has returned to plead with Senta once more, witnessing the betrothal of Senta and the Dutchman ("Was mußt' ich hören, Gott! was mußt' ich seh'n?"). Their agitated encounter is organized around two ideas – one chromatic and frag-mentary, the other more tonally stable (Exx. 3.12a–b) – that will be further developed in the trio scene between Senta, Erik, and the Dutchman ("Fort auf das Meer"). The frenetic dialogue is brought to a halt by Erik's remark that Senta has sworn to be "eternally faithful" to him. Senta is horrified at this claim, which Erik proceeds to vali-date in a short, nostalgic "Cavatina."

Cavatina (Erik). Erik's solo ("Willst jenes Tag's du dich nicht mehr entsinnen?") is Wagner's attempt at Bellinian cantilena, a small vocal showcase for an otherwise dramatically and musically unrewarding role. There is more than a touch, too, of the Biedermeier or early Victorian sentimental parlor ballad to it, reinforced by the image of the young lover offering his lassie "the highland's flower" ("des Hochlands Blume") – a remnant, apparently, of the original Scottish setting. In the three quatrains of his Cavatina Erik recalls to Senta (1) how they once roamed the coastal highlands together; (2) how they watched her father sail away, leaving Senta in Erik's care; and (3) how, under these intimate circumstances, Senta promised always to be true to him. In the second quatrain an effective, though un-Bellinian, modulation through D flat to D accompanies the image of the father's ship sailing away. The third quatrain is similarly inflected with new, expressive modulations (to A flat) before returning to F and a modest ornamental cadenza.

Finale. As the song resolves, the Dutchman suddenly steps forward, having overheard Erik's reproachful reminiscences and been stung by the final line ("Tell me, was it not your promise to be true?"). To more agitated *scena* music (like that which began the scene-complex) the Dutchman resolves to board his ship immediately, and for the last time – abandoning all hope. Senta tries desperately to detain him.

A formal, "operatic" trio (F minor, Molto agitato: "Fort auf das Meer") serves as a musical and dramaturgical counterweight to the preceding F-major Cavatina. Though not indicated as a discrete number in the final score, it was already suggested as a set piece in the German prose draft (which designates this concluding scene-complex as "Duet, Trio & Finale" – see Appendix A, p. 176). The trio takes Example 3.12b as a main theme, and transforms the Tristanesque chromatic fragment of Example 3.12a into a somewhat more stable figure (Ex. 3.13a). A repeating dotted-rhythm motive (Ex. 3.13b) assumes a closing function in the trio, and is put through a sequential chromatic intensification that again forecasts the passionate gestures of the *Tristan* idiom. In the operatic fashion later abjured by Wagner, however, the three characters declaim their different texts at once, forfeiting any hope of intelligibility, aside from a few quick asides thrust between the principal phrases.

After repeated operatic cadences in F minor (in cabaletta style), Example 3.12a spills over into the final, climactic scene, where it serves to punctuate the Dutchman's self-revelations to Senta. Wagner seeks in this way to preserve some of the musical energy of the trio across the concluding, declamatory section of the Finale. Over quiet string tremolos the Dutchman begins to explain the conditions of his salvation from the curse he bears (the gesture anticipates Lohengrin's

Ex. 3.13a

Ex. 3.13b

"Grail" narration, though it breaks off after several measures). The tone intensifies as the Dutchman warns Senta to save herself from his fate. They have not yet been joined before God, and in view of what he overheard between Erik and Senta, he feels bound to release her. Senta tries once more to detain him (a flash of D_4^6 at "Ich bin's, durch deren Treu' dein Heil du finden sollst' foreshadows the musical conclusion). Alerted by Erik's cries for help, sailors and villagers gather on the shore. The Dutchman at last reveals his identity to the assembled crowd – somewhat anticlimactically, it must be said, since it would seem that no one except perhaps Daland is still deceived as to the identity of this pale sea-captain, so faithfully portrayed in the heirloom portrait hanging in Daland's own house.

At the revelation of his identity as the "Flying Dutchman," as if on cue, sustained open fifths on B are sounded in the orchestra along with the Dutchman motive itself, seconded by the invisible crew inside his ship. He leaps aboard and pushes off; Senta runs to the edge of a nearby cliff. (Both actions transpire with a rapidity that cannot help but call attention to the highly artificial topography of this stage-world.) To a condensed version of the overture's coda – corresponding either to the 1843, 1852, or 1860 score, depending on the performing edition – Senta leaps from the cliff, ensuring that she will indeed have remained "true unto death." The Dutchman's ship is seen to sink into the waves, and in an image that surely inspired Wagner to append the more ethereal conclusion in 1860, the embracing figures of Senta and the Dutchman "are seen rising from the sea, in transfigured guise." Senta's image gestures toward heaven with hands and eyes; a radiant halo-effect illumines the pair, while the cliff from which Senta has leaped "gradually takes in the appearance of a cloud" so as to assist in the heavenly assumption of the Dutchman and his redeemer.[14]

4   *Romantic opera as "dramatic ballad":* Der fliegende Holländer *and its generic contexts*

THOMAS GREY

I recall how, even before I set about writing the *Flying Dutchman* as a whole, I sketched Senta's Ballad in the second act, working out both the verses and music for it. In this piece I unconsciously set down the thematic seeds of the whole opera: it contained the condensed image of the entire drama, as this existed in my mind. And when it was time to give a title to the completed work I had a mind to designate it a "dramatic ballad."

A Communication to my Friends (*GSD*, vol. 4, 323)

Wagner has been taken to task repeatedly, in recent times, for his attempt to impute to *Der fliegende Holländer* something like the wide-ranging, "symphonic" leitmotif technique of his mature music dramas.[1] This attempt becomes even more pronounced (and transparent) in the passage that follows directly on those lines quoted above from the 1851 *Communication*:

When I eventually came to compose the rest of the opera, the thematic image [contained in the Ballad] spread itself quite naturally across the entire drama as a continuous network [*vollständiges Gewebe*]; all that remained to do, with no further conscious effort, was to develop further and more completely the various thematic seeds [*thematische Keime*] contained in the Ballad according to their own tendencies, and in this way I had all the principal moods of the poem before me, transformed into distinct thematic figures, quite of their own accord.

(*GSD*, vol. 4, 323)

The merits of these claims can be debated in either direction. Certainly there is more than a little exaggeration or wishful thinking involved here and, as Carl Dahlhaus and others have pointed out, an obvious attempt to read the earlier *Holländer* score in light not only of what had been done in *Tannhäuser* and *Lohengrin*, but especially what the composer was already now contemplating (in 1851) with respect to his ambitious new *Nibelungen* project. On the other hand, Senta's Ballad does have obvious and significant ramifications for "the entire drama," including the music: not only are the thematic materials of

65

the Ballad's introduction, refrain, and coda quoted in the overture and at various key points of the opera, but certain motivic "seeds" within these themes do indeed find their way into other, nominally independent themes (see, for example, the discussion of the ensemble-introduction and Act I finale in Chapter 3).

Apart from the retrospective, and debatable, attribution of a (proto-) leitmotivic coherence to the *Holländer* score (interesting as it is, from the perspective of the composer's artistic biography), what are we to make of the proposed genre designation, "dramatic ballad'? Whether the phrase "dramatic ballad" really did occur to Wagner in 1841, or only later (in the 1851 *Communication*), it seems to register something that he felt was significant about the work, and that set it apart from other operas. The centrality of Senta's Ballad to the conception of the opera reflects the pivotal position of the work as a whole in Wagner's oeuvre, with ties to the old world of German Romantic opera, as well as to the new, or future one of "music drama." The notion of *Der fliegende Holländer* as a "dramatic ballad" thus calls attention to both past and future contexts: the world of popular Romantic fiction, melodrama, and *Schaueroper*, on one hand (where such ballads were at home), and the musically continuous, motivically integrated music drama, on the other hand (with its sophisticated manipulations of dramatic and narrative temporal levels).

"A whole new genre"?

The Janus-faced character of *Der fliegende Holländer*, stylistically and generically, was a cause for some consternation among its first listeners. Wagner's recent accession to fame and good fortune was due to *Rienzi*, in which he had succeeded in translating the glamorous new genre of Parisian grand opera into an original German work. (The novelty of even this achievement is perhaps less often acknowledged than it deserves to be.) In the case of *Holländer*, unfortunate casting played some part in the cool reception of the first performances: in particular, the baritone Johann Michael Wächter, in the title role, lacked the vocal stamina and dramatic charisma necessary to bring the part to life. More than that, however, the opera was just not "the kind of thing" the audience expected from the composer of *Rienzi*. Even Wagner admitted this. "The public," as he later reflected in the *Communication to my Friends*, "was all the less inclined to demonstrations of approbation since it was put off by the genre of the work itself, having anticipated and hoped for something like *Rienzi*, rather than something so entirely *unlike* it" (*GSD*, vol. 4, 276; emphasis added). He felt compelled to defend himself (in the *Communication*) against charges of "regressing" in the direction of an outmoded type of "Romantic opera" with *Der fliegende Holländer* (even with *Tannhäuser* and *Lohengrin*) after Meyerbeer and Wagner himself had pointed in a new direction – beyond Gothic, chivalric, and legendary subjects – with their thrilling panoramas of early modern history in *Les Huguenots* and *Rienzi*, for example (allegories of social conflict and change that spoke more directly to the spirit of the times).[2]

The real difficulty of *Der fliegende Holländer*, however, lay in its peculiar, somewhat awkward conjunction of the old and the new, the *passé* and the avant-garde. (This could be said of the dramatic material and the music alike.) As Hans Sachs says in pondering the stylized innovations of a later Wagnerian hero: "es klang so alt, – und war doch so neu" ("it sounded so old – and yet was so new"). The Byronic-supernatural hero with his existential *Weltschmerz* may have seemed like a derivative compound of Faust, Manfred, and Lord Ruthven (or any number of vampires of recent popular fiction) – types that had been worn somewhat thin across the 1820s and 1830s. The numbers most calculated to please a general public (the Spinning Chorus, the Sailors' Chorus, Erik's Cavatina, and even Senta's Ballad, to some extent) succeeded in this, up to a point, but at the expense of highlighting the opera's affinity with Marschner, Spohr, Lortzing and lesser contemporaries, for whose works Wagner himself had little enthusiasm. Some aspects of both drama and music, on the other hand, were already "Wagnerian" in a way no one could yet fully appreciate: the extended, "psychological" colloquy of hero and heroine in Act II, for example, or the whole theme of "redemption through love." Likewise, the Senta–Dutchman duet, the overture, and the choral-orchestral duel between the two crews in Act III were distinctly "advanced" conceptions, likely to confuse and alienate a considerable portion of the operatic public of 1843.

At any rate, while the composer has been routinely – and perhaps somewhat unfairly – rebuked for his retrospective construction of *Der fliegende Holländer* as an anticipation of his later music dramas, he was profoundly aware of the opera's originality at the time of its composition. Writing to his sister Cäcilie Avenarius just after the

Dresden première he tells her how pleased and surprised he was with the work's warm reception (as he construed it), considering its uncompromising "difference":

After the brilliant, splendid, intoxicating operatic experience of *Rienzi* none of us held out great hopes for the effect of the *Dutchman*; I confess that I myself approached the matter with much trepidation, since it requires a good deal of imagination [*Fantasie*] to appreciate this opera, which offers little in the way of brilliant effects. It is something altogether different, a whole new genre (as many are saying), which will likely be slow to make headway . . .[3]   (*SB*, vol. 2, 203–04)

He still felt the same way a year later, at the time of the deferred Berlin production early in 1844, which he again took pains to construe as a popular success. "Imagine," he wrote to Minna back in Dresden, "I was appearing for the first time before a *completely unknown* audience with this fantastical opera of mine, a work totally remote from anything they had previously heard or grown to enjoy, and offering, on the face of it, so little that is appealing or rewarding!"[4]

Did *Der fliegende Holländer* really represent something "altogether different," "a whole new genre"? The opera's first critics were divided on this point, a few celebrating those qualities of novelty and difference they discerned, others dismissing them as forced and tasteless "effects," or failing to register them altogether. An anonymous reviewer of the Riga production later in 1843 took the side of novelty and innovation, even to the extent of wondering "whether *Der fliegende Holländer* is still an opera at all in the strict sense of the word?" – a rhetorical question that would surely have pleased the future author of *Opera and Drama*. The same critic (who must have been at least vaguely aware of Wagner's personal history since fleeing Riga in 1839) also reads the work, presciently, as a parable of the cultural mission Wagner was soon to be outlining for himself, a "hopeful signal that we will soon be redeemed from our aimless wanderings on the alien seas of foreign music [*von den wüsten Irrfahrten auf den fremden Meeren ausländischer Musik erlöst*] and find once again the blessed German homeland."[5]

If some of the earliest critics were impressed, favorably or otherwise, with the originality of the opera's style and conception (as Wagner's correspondence suggests), the kinship with a home-grown "German Romantic" genre was not overlooked. By the time Eduard Hanslick reviewed the Viennese première in 1860 the opera's dated aspects were even more pronounced. "In its musical treatment,"

Hanslick maintained, "*Holländer* reveals Wagner as an out-and-out epigone of the German 'Romantic' opera." To Hanslick, it looked like an effort to jump-start the somewhat tired idiom of Weber and Marschner by means of a few gaudy, electrifying orchestral effects, the "shrill orchestral innovations" of the neo-Romantics (*neu-Romantiker*) Berlioz and Meyerbeer. The opera's relative lack of success up to this time, Hanslick implies, reflects the extent to which it still inhabits the stylistic world of those "quickly forgotten dramatic compositions [*Tondichtungen*] of Lindpaintner, Reissiger, and Lachner," at least in terms of its melodic language.[6] Another critic of this Viennese production echoes Hanslick's views (perhaps directly): "*Der fliegende Holländer* [is] an interesting product of the post-Weber school . . . Spohr's *Faust* and Marschner's [*Hans*] *Heiling* are its godparents; Lindpaintner peeks through here and there, and Meyerbeer's incipient influence cannot be missed." Also echoed here is Hanslick's dissatisfaction with the character of melodic invention, though this other critic censures the "radical" elements along with the conventional ones: the dissolution of melodic phrases in *arioso*-recitative, sudden interruptions of the cantilena, lack of points of repose, an unfortunate striving for "bizarre descriptive effects," and "that exaggeratedly realistic tendency to characterize the demonic [*Unheilvolle*] by means of unpleasant progressions."[7] Here Wagner's attempt to reinvigorate the genre of earlier German Romantic opera is faulted as derivative and anarchistic at once, or by turns.

The earliest responses to the opera tended to emphasize, on the balance, elements of newness and difference, starting with the issue of genre. In pondering the question of what sort of piece this was, two early critiques strikingly voice the very notion Wagner later claimed (in the *Communication*) had occurred to him at the time: the idea of designating the opera a "dramatic ballad." A brief, enthusiastic report in the *Zeitung für die elegante Welt* (11 January 1843) confirmed that the new work had nothing in common with the "modern grand opera" (as represented by *Rienzi*), nor with the French *opéra comique*, nor the Italian "pathetic" opera [*pathetische Oper*]; "of all these genres there is no trace: the material, the structure [*Zuschnitt*], and the color are miles apart from everything that is now in fashion." The critic (who is conspicuously silent as to the "German Romantic" genre) goes on to assert that "this Dutchman is a *Ballad* from beginning to end, without elaborate ensemble-pieces or finales."[8] The panegyric tone and the close resemblance of certain points to some found in Wagner's own correspondence (for example, the suggestion that the work's success might be valued more highly than *Rienzi*'s, considering its serious, uncompromising character) raise the suspicion that the composer himself may have had some hand in it. In fact, the *Zeitung für die elegante Welt* was edited by a sympathetic acquaintance of Wagner, Heinrich Laube, who printed the composer's "Autobiographical Sketch" in the paper just about a month after this. But there is no direct evidence linking Wagner to the present review.

The role of Wagner's own hand is explicit, however, in the case of a slightly later piece in the Leipzig *Illustrirte Zeitung* (7 October 1843). This essay cites *in toto* a letter Wagner had sent to his friend and colleague from the Dresden court opera, Ferdinand Heine, during the summer of 1843, apparently for the purpose of generating some advance publicity for the upcoming Berlin production of the *Holländer* that winter. Strangely enough, though, the introductory remarks in the *Illustrirte Zeitung* article (which appeared unsigned) include the following passage on the new work's character and genre which does *not* figure in Wagner's letter to Ferdinand Heine, at least not as it has come down to us, but seems to originate with the critic himself – whether Heine or another writer:

Wagner calls [*Der fliegende Holländer*] a Romantic opera, yet in its overall nature and manner this work can hardly be assigned to any of the existing genres, and we would almost like to call it a *dramatic ballad*. Here is nothing of the usual stage effects, complicated intrigues, "interesting" episodes or any of the other typical means of enticement; Wagner offers us the Romantic idea in its own poetic atmosphere, prepared quite *au naturel*.[9]

If it was indeed Ferdinand Heine who supplied the framing remarks to Wagner's "open letter" in the *Illustrirte Zeitung* it seems more than likely that the composer may have fed him the "dramatic ballad" line in conversation or in some other piece of correspondence no longer extant.[10]

At all events, the notion found some wider resonance among early listeners and critics, including some who surely were not in direct communication with the composer. A correspondent for the paper *Unser Planet* (who assumes that he is dealing with an *earlier* work by the "talented and imaginative composer of *Rienzi* . . . possibly revised [*potenzirte*] here and there with respect to instrumentation") views the "ballad-like" character of the dramatic material in a more negative light, as a miscalculation with respect to the criterion of "effectiveness." "The choice of a subject more conducive *to a romance or a ballad* than to dramatic treatment," he submits, "has its drawbacks with regard to the scenic structuring of the text"; the librettist-composer has been moved to import extraneous musical-lyric material "to make up for the lack of external action on the stage."[11] The material is "by no means of grandiose nature," concurs another early Dresden critic; "it is rather meant as a kind of gothic folk-tale [*schauerliches Volksmärchen*], if you will," though the composer is charged with an inappropriate expenditure of grand-operatic means toward this simple, would-be *volkstümlich* end.[12] Finally, a feuilleton piece in the *Dresdener Abendzeitung* from later in 1843 varies the same theme of opera-as-ballad (perhaps under the influence of the earlier account in the *Illustrirte Zeitung*):

To us, the whole thing makes the impression of a *ballad* represented in dramatic form [*eine in dramatischer Handlung dargestellte Ballade*]; this explains and justifies much in the music that, by operatic criteria, would have to be considered a miscalculation. Even so, there remains a real question as to whether such an approach is actually suited to the stage [at all], and whether it does not inevitably result in a tiresome monotony, or whether the whole thing – in order to be effective as an aesthetic product – shouldn't have been much more condensed, and so on.[13]

This demand for greater "condensation" reminds us of Wagner's original plan to cast the opera in a single act. The decision taken just prior to the première to give the opera in three acts may well have been what dissuaded Wagner from calling it a "dramatic ballad" in the end (assuming he did originally contemplate it). For a ballad is by nature – even by definition – a single, continuous narration of events, a continuous "performance" that would resist parceling-out into separate acts. And while Wagner does not invoke the term "ballad" in the exegesis of his opera he supplied to Ferdinand Heine, he does contrast the "conventional arrangement into arias, duets, finales, etc." with the streamlined continuity of the *Holländer*, which "relate[s] the legend in a single breath, just as a good poem should [do]" (*SL*, 115). Those early critics who sensed and appreciated a "ballad-like" character in the opera seem to have appreciated the vestiges of this intended continuity and "condensation" even in the three-act version. Those who reacted negatively to the work's character and perceived genre (or "lack" of genre) responded to a dearth of dramatic features and to others that were more properly "balladic" than operatic or theatrical. For Wagner, however, the work's character as "dramatic ballad" turns precisely on the reflexive relation of the drama as a whole to its "condensed image" and origin in the ballad-number at its center.

"The condensed image of the whole drama"

When Wagner suggested, in the *Communication*, that Senta's Ballad contains within itself the "condensed image of the whole drama" ("das verdichtete Bild des ganzen Dramas"), he was actually making two different claims – one about the drama, and one about the music – which he characteristically confounds. The dramatic claim is relatively straightforward, even incontrovertible. It concerns the reflexive relationship of the background story, as told in the Ballad, to the dramatic action of the drama itself.[14] The legend of the "Flying Dutchman," presented as a piece of superstitious local lore handed down across generations, is indeed the "seed" from which opera's Romantic fiction develops, an open-ended myth of cyclic repetition to which the present drama provides redemption and closure. It is the musical claim, on the other hand, that has engendered critical resistance, the claim that the thematic-motivic "seeds" embedded within the Ballad provide the organic source material for the whole opera ("all that remained to do, with no further conscious effort, was to develop further and more completely the various thematic seeds [contained in the Ballad according to their own tendencies," as Wagner maintained in the *Communication* [*GSD*, vol. 4, 323]).

The musical setting of the Ballad, Wagner implies, provided the thematic or "leitmotivic" substance corresponding to the "principal moods" and situations of the drama. This musical substance, as noted, consists mainly of the Dutchman and Senta (or "redemption") themes, though it also extends to a small complex of chromatic-diminished storm gestures, the "main theme" of the overture (and the Dutchman's aria-monologue), and a few smaller separable motives that figure in the music of the Norwegian sailors in Acts I and III (cf. Chapter 3). Certainly any "network" of themes and motives here is much less extensive and less sophisticated than in the later music dramas. On the other hand, it is *more* extensive and, at least in some details, more sophisticated than in any other opera (by anyone) composed up to 1841. Furthermore, that Wagner should have recognized the potential for generating a motivic network on the basis of a musical narration of past events embedded within the "present" of the operatic action is in itself a point of critical and historical interest. It was precisely this layering of a dramatic present with its own pre-history, by means of affective-musical signs (or motives), that most intrigued Wagner when he tried to theorize a more advanced system of "motives of anticipation and recollection" in *Opera and Drama*. Reflecting on *Holländer* in 1851, Wagner seems to have sensed that the relation of the Ballad to the opera had something to tell him about the epic project he was then embarking upon, that is, about the need for a "prehistory" of musical and dramatic motives for *Siegfrieds Tod* (hence the expansion of that project into the *Ring* tetralogy as we know it).

The expository role of a ballad recounting some piece of prehistory crucial to the plot is typical of a whole spectrum of Romantic drama, operatic or otherwise. One parallel instance well known to Wagner is the *Romanze* sung by Emmy in Marschner's *Der Vampyr* (1828), "Sieh, Mutter, dort den bleichen Mann." Another is the ballad, "Jadis regnait en Normandie," performed by the *jongleur* Raimbaut in the first act of Meyerbeer and Scribe's *Robert le diable* (1830). Both the *Romanze* and the ballad have in common with Senta's Ballad, as often noted, the function of narrating the legend of a shady character, not quite human, who will intrude on the action of the drama itself by preying, in one way or another, upon an innocent female character.[15] The heroine of Fitzball's 1827 burlesque melodrama, *The Flying Dutchman, or the Phantom Ship*, sings a "ballad" she connects with the legendary sea captain, though it is merely a sentimental song to a distant lover: "Return to me, O my love." (The song returns in the play as a sonic "marker" of her character or presence, in the manner of other contemporary melodramas and earlier *opéras comiques*.) Two further instances that would have been well known to early audiences of Wagner's opera are Jenny's ballad of the "White Lady" ("D'ici voyez ce beau domaine") from Boieldieu's *La Dame blanche* and the Moorish *Romanze* "Wer klagt am Gitterfenster" from C. Kreutzer's *Nachtlager in Granada* (after a play by the *Freischütz* librettist Friedrich Kind). Both recount a piece of local lore involving restless spirits said to haunt the site on which the drama unfolds.

An effective parody of the expository ballad type and situation can be found in another Scribe collaboration from the same year as *Robert le diable*; the immensely popular *opéra comique* he created with D.-F.-E. Auber, *Fra Diavolo*. The dashing villain of the opera's title arrives at a country inn disguised as a "Neapolitan Marquis" and is (like Robert) promptly regaled with a ballad about himself – the notorious brigand Fra Diavolo who has lately been terrorizing the region. He shares with the Flying Dutchman, in fact, a reputation for looting gold and jewels from hapless travelers (on land rather than at sea), while relieving women of their honor and their peace of mind, as the innkeeper's plucky daughter, Zerline, narrates in her *couplets* "Voyez sur cette roche." As in *Robert le diable*, the undisclosed presence of the selfsame "diabolic" figure who is the subject of the song lends a certain farcical element. The balladesque, mock-Gothic character of Zerline's *couplets* is explicitly signaled by the "shuddering" cautionary refrain ("Tremblez au sein de la tempête, / Au loin l'écho répète: / Diavolo, Diavolo, Diavolo!"), which parallels Raimbaut's C-minor refrain, with its similarly shuddering triplets, "Funeste erreur, fatale délire! / Car ce guerrier était dit-on / Un habitant du sombre empire, / Foi de Normand, c'est un démon!" In *Robert le diable*, the assembled company echoes Raimbaut's refrain "with feigned terror," until the indignant Robert steps forward to reveal himself. Fra Diavolo's intervention is rather more gallant: still in the guise of the "Marquis," he steps in with a third *couplet* defending the reputation of this outlaw Don Juan, deflecting suspicion onto the exploits of local youths. The mock-ballad does conjure up an unexpected apparition: not the bandit himself (who remains incognito), but his bumbling sidekicks, Beppo and Giacomo, who suddenly stumble onto the scene disguised as "pilgrims."

Like its forebears in *Der Vampyr*, *Robert le diable*, and *Fra Diavolo*, Senta's Ballad performs an expository function, introducing the legendary reputation of an anti-heroic main character whose ontological status is, like his moral reputation, dubious. Does this shady character really exist, or is he just a popular fiction? It is in the nature of the ballad genre to equivocate on this point. The narration of any subject in the form of a ballad tends to overlay it with a patina of myth and fantasy. In some cases the ambivalent status of a figure's reality, within the fictional world of the ballad, is the central theme (Goethe's *Erlkönig*, for instance). The credulous peasant-folk who hear Emmy's ballad about the vampire are easily spooked by the story, though even they don't know for sure that such beings exist until Lord Ruthven's accursed identity is revealed at the end. The aristocratic Sicilian *chevaliers* who listen to Raimbaut's ballad are inclined to laugh at it, until Robert steps forward; and even then there's no evidence that he is the devil's brood the song reports him to be. Likewise, although the audience has seen the phantom ship in Act I and has overheard the Dutchman's own passionate testimony as to his spectral condition in his monologue, the Ballad is presented as a piece of popular superstition. It is only Senta herself who *believes* in the Dutchman. And she does so with an intensity that is able to summon his presence on the Norwegian coast, as if by telekinesis.

Senta's belief in the Dutchman and his tragic fate generates, of course, the crux of the Ballad – or rather of her particular rendition – and of the opera as a whole. After singing three verses of the Ballad she falls into a momentary trance (while the chorus of sympathetic listeners fills in the third refrain). Then suddenly she leaps to her feet, "carried away by a sudden inspiration," to improvise the B-flat-major coda (Allegro con fuoco), rending asunder the veil that separates fiction and reality, and opening up a window for the numinous Dutchman to penetrate the confines of her ordinary and unfulfilled existence. The chorus is aghast at this unseemly transgression of balladic myth ("God help us! Erik! She's lost her mind!"). But their surprise is perhaps not altogether justified. For one point in which Senta's Ballad differs markedly from its generic precedents is in the character of its refrain. Whether seriously or in jest, the refrains of the other ballads mentioned all serve to warn the auditors to beware the song's sinister, uncanny subject – devil, vampire, or bandit – and, for rhetorical effect, they each underline this admonition with an appropriate musical shudder. "Fatal error, fatal delirium, . . . flee, flee, you young shepherdesses," warns Raimbaut; "Tremble, amidst the tempest's gale," cries Zerline; "God save us, on earth, from ever becoming one of his kind," Emmy implores, echoed by the chorus.

Senta's refrain, on the contrary, embraces the plight of the accursed Dutchman: "Pray to heaven that he soon finds the woman who will be true to him!" The music of her refrain is appropriately beatific, consonant, and prayer-like. (The strings do indulge in a little discreet shuddering beneath the final phrase of the refrain, but the more direct analogue to the *Schauereffekt* of those other ballad-refrains, parodistic or otherwise, occurs in the chromatic-diminished storm-music that closes each verse of Senta's Ballad, *preceding* the refrain – e.g., "Hui, wie saust der Wind! Johohe! Johohe!" in the first verse – where Senta variously describes and sympathizes with the Dutchman's nautical wanderings.) We might even surmise that Senta has composed her own refrain to the Ballad, in keeping with the fluid nature of traditional oral transmission. It hardly seems likely that

Senta's crotchety nurse Mary – from whom she has supposedly learned the song – would bring such sentimental, girlish effusions to *her* telling of the tale. Senta's "recomposition" of the Ballad becomes explicit in the transformed "coda" she improvises on the spot. But anyone paying attention to Senta and her singing cannot be wholly surprised when she elects herself to redeem the wandering Dutchman (while the musical contrast of her sudden intervention can still elicit a jolt even from the listener familiar with the score).

"Let me be the one to redeem you through her faithfulness! Let God's angel direct you to me!," Senta trumpets in her brief but ecstatic transformation of the Ballad's refrain. She erases the conditional mood of the earlier refrains ("the pale man *might* find salvation if he *could* find a woman true to him on earth," "Ah! If only you, pale sailor, could find her," etc.) with bold, heroic, and aria-like assertions: "Let me be the one . . . ," "Through me you shall find salvation."[16] She "believes in" the Dutchman in two senses: she believes in his phenomenal existence, and she believes in his salvation as a cause, one which becomes her own, her mission and very *raison d'être* (whatever we choose to think of that).

Although Wagner does not specify it in his stage directions, it would make sense for Senta to address her peroration to the portrait on the wall, which has been the object of her trance-like meditations throughout the act. For now her text addresses the Dutchman directly in the second person, as a real, living being and not merely the subject of an old song. The Dutchman's portrait is the link between Senta's fantasy world (as embodied in the Ballad) and the "real" historical figure that is about to set foot in Senta's own house. The Ballad as such does not precisely contain the "condensed image of the whole drama," as Wagner claimed, but only the basic background of its central character, in the manner of other operatic ballads. Musically, it contains a central core of thematic ideas, although nothing like the "entire" motivic substance of the score. But watching over the performance of the Ballad, and over the action of the entire second act, is in fact the literal "image" of the Dutchman, in the form of his portrait (or "counterfeit," as Mary dubs it). As a stage prop the portrait suggests the visible legacy of popular melodrama and its conventions, a legacy whose remnants we can still recognize in the roving eyeballs of ancestral portraits in Gothic horror farces and cartoons of the twentieth century.[17] And yet, on a more elevated, symbolic (Wagnerian) level the portrait can be seen as a counterpart or complement to the Ballad: together they represent visual and oral artifacts, respectively, of a mythology which Senta (as a true Wagnerian) desires to "realize" in the present, as an edifying example for the future.

A song and a picture: Senta as creative artist

These complementary "artifacts" dominating the second act of the opera – the Ballad of the Dutchman and his portrait – are presented as family heirlooms of a sort. Senta senses herself as the one of her line destined to realize their potent significance; they absorb her thoughts (the Ballad) or hang over her (the portrait), almost like a family curse. Erik senses their fatal potency all too well, as registered in the following exchange from his duet with Senta in Act II:

> *Erik*. Was soll ich denken? Jenes Bild . . .
> *Senta*. Das Bild . . . ?
> *Erik*. Läßt du von deiner Schwärmerei wohl ab?
> *Senta*. Kann meinem Blick Teilnahme ich verwehren?
> *Erik*. Und die Ballade? . . . Heut' noch sangst du sie!
> *Senta*. Ich bin ein Kind, und weiß nicht, was ich singe!
>   O sag, wie? fürchtest du ein Lied – ein Bild?
> *Erik*. Du bist so bleich . . . sag! sollte ich's nicht fürchten?
>
> [*E*. What should I think? That picture . . .
> *S*. The picture . . . ?
> *E*. Will you not desist from your fantastic dreaming?
> *S*. Can I control the object of my gaze?
> *E*. And the Ballad? . . . You were singing it again today!
> *S*. I'm just a child, and know not what I sing.
>   Tell me, do you fear a song, a picture?
> *E*. You are so pale! . . . pray, should I then not be afraid?]

The accompaniment to Senta's patently disingenuous responses (a naively wandering line in the violins and flutes, alternately, over a static bass) seems almost to parody her efforts at dissimulation, and her response to Erik's subsequent dream-narration openly belies them, as does the "pallor" of her appearance here. Senta, for her part, surely appreciates the talismanic power of this song and this portrait. And the conjuring powers of her own vivid, "creative" imagination (like those of her dramatic cousin Elsa, in *Lohengrin*) will be demonstrated presently, when upon Erik's departure the Dutchman himself looms upon the threshold.

The Dutchman, together with the title heroes of *Tannhäuser* and

Lohengrin, has been interpreted as an allegorical embodiment of the Romantic artist – alienated from normal human society, misunderstood, torn by conflicting obligations to self and others, yearning for the unconditional love of an ideal woman (embodying the artist's public and patrons), but tragically compelled to forgo that love.[18] Here, as in the following operas, the allegory is plausible, if somewhat vaguely realized. In a rather more concrete sense, however, it is *Senta* who really assumes the role of the creative, imaginative "artist" in *Der fliegende Holländer* (in a way that also reflects, perhaps, the constraints imposed on that creativity by her sex). Although she did not paint the portrait – nor did she, strictly speaking, compose the Ballad – Senta's preoccupation with these objects is a matter of intense imaginative engagement. And the intended goal of this engagement is not only creative, but, in a properly Wagnerian way, redemptive. Indeed, it might not be stretching things too far to suggest that, in her passionate concern with poetry, melody, and picture in Act II, Senta acts as a symbolic impresario for the *Gesamtkunstwerk* of future Wagnerian theory. In any case, it is Senta's powers of imagination and visionary concentration (like Elsa's in *Lohengrin*) that mediate between the ordinary and the supernatural, the real and the ideal, thereby setting in motion the dramatic action.[19]

On the face of it, perhaps, Senta is just a passive consumer of "art works." She has learned the Ballad of the Flying Dutchman, we are given to understand, after having demanded time and again to hear it from Mary, the way a small child will demand repeated readings of a story to the point of learning it by heart.[20] The portrait is also a pre-existing work, of course, which Senta merely admires – if to an almost fetishistic degree (as brought out, for example, in Harry Kupfer's 1978 Bayreuth production, in which Senta carries it about with her throughout the whole opera, pressing it obsessively to her person). But her contact with these "works" takes on a creative, productive dimension both within the fictional world of the opera and on a broader symbolic or allegorical level. As suggested above (and in Chapter 3), Senta takes up a supposedly traditional ballad and makes it her own (thus, "Senta's Ballad"). The sympathetic strains of the refrain, in her rendition, are explicitly associated with Senta's character and her redemptive mission. Mary or others before her may have sung the basic "folk tune" of the verse or the stormy onomatopoeia evoking the Dutchman's wanderings on the high seas ("Hui, wie saust der Wind, Johohoe!"), but the refrain seems to be something new. (The captivated response of the other girls to Senta's singing would suggest this, too, though it could also be taken as a tribute to her impassioned performance.) And, as also mentioned before, her ecstatic "coda" ("Ich sei's, die dich durch ihre Treu' erlöset!") is explicitly improvised on the spot. (By interrupting the choral refrain in progress it also constitutes, if in a negative way, a "creative" intervention in the form.) This improvised peroration is the crux that unites the "fictional" world of the Ballad with the "real" world of the dramatic action.[21] Both the sense and the music of this crux will return at two key moments later on: first, at the end of Erik's dream-narration, and second, at the end of the opera. Those recurrences underscore the point that Senta's "revision" or recomposition of the Ballad is not fully completed until the end of the drama, the point at which ballad and drama ("fiction" and "reality") are conclusively merged.

Senta's successful impulse to merge art and life (the Ballad she sings and the drama she inhabits) is an eminently Romantic one. Berlioz, Liszt, and Wagner himself (his famous liaison with Mathilde Wesendonck during the inception of *Tristan*, for example) all provide familiar instances of the phenomenon. Her relation to the portrait embodies a similar allegory of the Romantic artist, though one with Classical roots. Like Pygmalion and his sculpted ideal, Senta "wills" the portrait of the Dutchman into life, at least symbolically, through the force of her sympathetic attachment to it. She rejects the real, everyday world of her companions, of Erik, and of her father – even while complying with his wishes – in favor of a fictional dream world, which she seeks to realize through the magnetic or telekinetic power of her imagination. The strength of her gaze fixed on the portrait, conjoined with her almost incantatory performance of the Ballad (recall that she begins with a gesture of pure, almost ritualistic vocalization: "Johohoe!"), draws the Dutchman out of his phantom existence and into her own sphere.[22] (The long duet they sing upon his arrival takes place in a half-waking, trance-like state on the border of dream and reality.) The beckoning of the Dutchman by means of Senta's fixation on the Ballad and the portrait becomes an allegory of the Romantic artist's "willing" the artwork into existence through the intensity of aesthetic inspiration and concentration.

"O, macht dem dummen Lied ein Ende!"

The Ballad is introduced into Act II of the opera as an alternative to another stage song, the "Spinning Chorus" of Senta's female companions. When Mary intervenes after the first strophe, the girls

scold her, "Frau Mary, be still! You know the song is not over yet."
When after the second strophe Mary, in turn, scolds Senta for not
spinning (or singing), the other girls join in a longer digression,
teasing Senta for her fixation with the portrait and its legend. The
third strophe is begun at an exaggerated dynamic as the girls resume
spinning "noisily" so as to drown out Senta's irritable remonstrances.
This time it is Senta who interrupts: "O, macht dem dummen Lied ein
Ende, es brummt und summt nur vor dem Ohr!" ("O, cease your
foolish song, its humming and buzzing grate so on one's ears"). If
Senta doesn't like it, they retort, why doesn't she sing something
instead? Senta asks Mary to sing "the Ballad" for them (Mary knows
which one is meant, without it being named). When Mary demurs,
Senta is moved to sing the Ballad herself. Her performance, as we have
seen, perpetuates the pattern of interrupted songs: her improvised,
ecstatic coda interrupts the girls' hushed choral refrain, only to be
interrupted in turn by the shocked response of Mary and the girls
("Hilf Himmel! Senta! Senta!") and by Erik's precipitous arrival
("Senta! Willst du mich verderben?").

There is good reason for this latter deferral of closure, even aside
from the simple dramaturgical one that motivates it.[23] Senta has been
suddenly inspired to conclude the tale by stepping into it herself; but
she can hardly effect a proper conclusion until she finds the
Dutchman, or he finds her. She must still wait, if only briefly, for the
circumstances that will allow her to take action. The subjunctive and
future tenses of Senta's text point to the conclusion of the opera:

> Ich sei's, die dich durch ihre Treu' erlöset!
> Mög' Gottes Engel mich dir zeigen!
> Durch mich sollst du das Heil erreichen!
>
> [Let me be the one to redeem you through my faithfulness!
> Let God's angel show you to me!
> Through me you shall be saved!]

But these tenses are not appropriate to the conclusion of a ballad,
which by nature sings of things long past and done. Senta breaks free
of the balladic narrative so that the ballad can "become" the opera;
or, vice versa, so that the opera can become a "dramatic ballad," a theatrical, live-action realization (and completion) of the unfinished
ballad.[24] Even apart from the nature of the subject matter and the
tone, or *tinta*, of its musical setting, Wagner might have been justified
in styling his opera as a "dramatic ballad" because of the way it stages

the stylized folk ballad at its center, transforming the narrative ballad into a dramatic action that will bring closure to the open-ended story. Senta heeds (as it were) her own injunction to her companions from a moment before: "Macht dem dummen Lied ein Ende!" ("make an end to your silly song!"). Her goal is to create a satisfying ending to the cyclic repetitions of Dutchman's story that has so long possessed her, to enact a definitive answer to the question posed in its refrain: "Where is the one who will remain true unto death?"

Senta's Ballad differs from both traditional folk ballads and literary ballads (though not so much from other operatic ballads) in the fragmentary, incomplete nature of its story. As an epic-narrative genre, the ballad normally builds towards a distinct climax or catastrophe, such as the death of its protagonist, followed perhaps by a reflective or moralizing epilogue. (Think, for example, of Bürger's "Lenore," Goethe's "Erlkönig," Schiller's "Die Bürgschaft," or Coleridge's "Rime of the Ancient Mariner.") Ballads within operas, or other dramas, may also recount a complete story, particularly if the story is meant to serve some didactic or exemplary function. But when, on the other hand, the function of the ballad is expository (as in *Holländer*, *Der Vampyr*, *Robert le diable* and *Fra Diavolo*, to some extent), its story will tend to be less clearly shaped, less conclusive. In each of these cases, for instance, the ballad simply serves to introduce the "legend" of the title character.[25]

In another respect, however, Senta's Ballad does embody one of the poetic genre's most common narrative tropes: recounting an act of transgression, blasphemy, or hubris, and the consequences of this act ("The Rime of the Ancient Mariner" would again be paradigmatic in this regard.) The simple structural formula of action and consequence, generally an act of defiance against the natural order followed by a moral reckoning (as James Parakilas sums it up), is fully represented within the three short stanzas of Senta's Ballad.[26] To this extent the story is "complete," as well as providing the necessary exposition for the operatic action (though, since Senta interrupts the song with her own impassioned outburst after the third strophe, we cannot know for sure whether we've heard the Ballad in its entirety or not.) The Ballad's refrain, in any case, explicitly invokes a closure that the story itself lacks. Senta longs to enter into the balladic "fiction" as an agent of closure, to deflect the endlessly repeating cycles of the Dutchman's fate. Alternatively, she longs to bring the "fictional" Dutchman into the active present of her own world, thereby transforming the fixed, static narrative of the Ballad into a dramatic action that presses toward a conclusion. To this end she will oppose the static "thesis" of the Ballad's refrain – the scarcity of faithful women – with a dynamic demonstration of her own fidelity, by way of antithesis.

The repetitive, stabilizing "ballast" of the refrain frequently serves to counterbalance the progressive, teleological dimension of balladic narrative, even where that is more pronounced than is the case with the Flying Dutchman's story. Carolyn Abbate speaks more generally of the "antagonistic tension between musical plot and textual plot that is characteristic of all strophic ballads" – that is, the conflict between the sameness of the repeating musical strophes (or the meter and rhyme scheme of the poetic stanza), on one hand, and the narration of progressive events, on the other.[27] The incantatory, ritualistic, repetitive quality of the Ballad is strongest in the refrain, where text and tune alike remain fixed. These repeating, cyclic qualities of the form are especially apposite to the case of the Dutchman, whose story itself resembles the ballad structure of stanza and refrain. After every seven years of new (yet dispiritingly similar) adventures on the high seas – encountering storms and shoals, affrighting pirates and innocent seafarers – the Dutchman is granted the opportunity to land and seek a faithful wife. The unvarying outcome of these intervals on land, ensured by the faithlessness and lack of poetic vision among ordinary women, becomes the tragic refrain of his cursed existence. These seven-year "stanzas" of his ceaseless voyaging are thus regularly punctuated by the "refrain" of his brief respites on shore – hopeful question marks answered every time in the negative. The text and music of the Ballad, as Senta performs it, underline this parallelism: the principal strophes evoke the stormy voyages, while the refrain holds out the repeated (but repeatedly unfulfilled) promise of salvation.

While the subjects of operatic ballads may, like the Dutchman, enter into the drama, Senta differs from the other operatic ballad-*singers* in her interventionist attempt to "recompose" the ending, as I have put it. Her "improvised" heroic transformation of the refrain ("Ich sei's, die dich durch ihre Treu' erlöse") is a sketch, so to speak, of the ultimate conclusion she has conceived for the story, likewise of the music that will accompany this closure. The conception itself is clear enough. In rescuing the Dutchman from his endless journeys through tide and time, she also seeks to establish a definitive close to the accretive, paratactic quality of his balladic existence. The accompanying musical strategy is similarly clear. The B-flat refrain to the Ballad, initially a tentative expression of hopeful promise, is transformed into an assertive closural (coda-like) gesture, Allegro con fuoco, its repeated cadential harmonies intensified by secondary-dominant progressions and neighboring diminished sevenths. Dramatically, of course, this moment can only be predictive, a decision to act rather than action as such, since the opportunity to carry out the decision has yet to arrive. Musically, as one might suppose, we will have to wait for the same transformation to occur in D major: the relative major of the Dutchman's characteristic key of B minor, and the parallel (tonic) major of the opera's overture, hence the framing "tonic" of the opera as a whole.

The second, very brief reference to this emphatic heroic transformation of the Ballad refrain following Erik's dream-narration occurs in C, up one step from the original B-flat major (Senta: "Er sucht mich auf! Ich muß ihn sehn! Mit ihm muß ich zu Grunde geh'n!"). It is still "one step away" from the final goal (D) in tonal terms (and figuratively, as well). There is also a broader logic to this brief recurrence. In content and in musical structure Erik's dream-narration is something like a ballad. It recounts a strange, marvelous, visionary event. The musical setting is repetitive and formulaic, like a ballad, but in loose, "dream-like" manner appropriate to the subject matter – a prophecy of things to come rather than a familiar and oft-repeated story. (Here the repetitions consist of sequential, tension-building restatements of the Dutchman "motive," while the vocal line remains freely declamatory.) In terms of the larger dramatic narrative, we are one step closer to the conclusion of the Ballad as Senta herself has dreamt it: an intermediate stage between the nominal "fiction" of the Ballad and the dramatic "reality" of the Dutchman's subsequent arrival and his eventual redemption through Senta.[28]

Only at the end of the opera, of course, will the dramatic transformation of the Ballad refrain be conclusively resolved. The relation of Senta's original stretta-transformation of the refrain – with its ecstatic cadence interrupted by the shocked response of the chorus – to the restatement and resolution of the material at the end anticipates the musical-dramaturgical conception of the Act II duet scene of *Tristan und Isolde* in relation to the conclusion of that work. In both cases an emphatic musical – and "dramatic" – cadence is interrupted at the center of the action (not unlike the mid-point interruption of a Schenkerian *Urlinie*) and completed only upon its reprise at the end of the opera. The apotheoses of the two heroines, Senta and Isolde, are similar mythical-dramatic gestures of redemptive "assumption" into the heavens. (The revised, so-called "Tristan" ending of *Holländer* underscores the parallel; see Chapter 3, pp. 41, 64.) Both heroines undergo a sacrificial self-annihilation in order to be reunited, on a transcendent plane, with their doomed or deceased lovers.

The redemption of the Dutchman likewise anticipates the Nirvana-like surcease of being that is the final goal of Tristan's and Isolde's physical and metaphysical raptures. In the later work it is of course Tristan's physical demise that precipitates this conclusion. In *Holländer* it is the Dutchman's own gesture of self-sacrifice (his intention to return to the sea rather than "ruin" the morally compromised Senta, as he perceives her) that precipitates the denouement. The Dutchman's moment of self-revelation also plays a part in bringing about the conclusion. Though presumably somewhat anti-climactic for the other characters (as well as for the audience), the Dutchman has to reveal formally his identity as the accursed seafarer – and the subject of Senta's Ballad – before the events can take their decisive turn:

> Befrag' die Meere aller Zonen; befrag'
> den Seemann, der den Ozean durchstrich!
> Er kennt dies Schiff, das Schrecken aller Frommen:
> den fliegenden Holländer nennt man mich!

> [Ask the seas of every clime,
> Ask the sailor who plies them!
> He knows this ship, dreaded by the pious:
> The Flying Dutchman, they call me.]

Anti-climactic or not, it is this act of self-revelation that makes an ending to the song (and the opera) possible. The Dutchman must confirm that myth has crossed into reality, that the Ballad has indeed entered the drama, or "become" the drama, before Senta can finally enact its end. And, befitting this shift from balladic epic to drama, Senta physically *enacts* the ending, rather than merely singing of it. Twice her vocal line gestures at an emphatic, conclusive cadence, poised upon a D^6_4 chord ("Ich bin's, durch deren Treu' dein Heil du finden sollst!" and "Preis deinen Engel und sein Gebot!"). But the transformed and transposed Ballad refrain (in D) only materializes, finally, in the orchestra, as Senta leaps to her death and ascends, "transfigured," with the Dutchman. The harmonically intensified cadences of the original stretta-like refrain transformation lead to a broad D-major resolution (or stabilization) of the open-fifth Dutchman motive and – in the revised ending – an extended plagal variant of Senta's refrain theme. The short but definitive orchestral coda that follows her last vocal cadence confirms, musically and symbolically, that the song is finally ended, the Ballad concluded, catharsis achieved. The Dutchman's self-revelation and Senta's self-sacrificial *salto mortale* are the climactic events necessarily absent from all earlier performances of the Ballad, now dramatically realized on stage. Through Senta's linking agency, fiction and (dramatic) reality, balladic narrative and operatic action are conclusively merged.

Romantic opera "redeemed"?

Looking back on the period of privation and moral-psychological degradation he experienced in Paris in the years around 1840, Wagner speculated with a shudder (in the *Communication to my Friends*) on the fate that might have overtaken him if he had continued to cultivate a literary-journalistic career at the expense of his higher musical calling. "Perhaps I might have followed in the path of our modern *literati* and playwrights who, under the petty influence of modern social conditions [*unserer formellen Lebensbeziehungen*], take up arms against the consequences of these conditions with each of their efforts in prose or rhyme" (*GSD*, vol. 4, 263). Wagner claims to have vented the irony and bitter sarcasm that motivate "all our journalist-poets" ("unseren schriftstellenderen Dichtern") in his contributions to various Parisian and German papers during his time in Paris, so that by the end of this period he was ready to devote himself to true artistic creation. Music, he writes, was the "good angel . . . that preserved me as an artist, or that truly first made of me an artist from that time, when my sensibilities became increasingly inflamed against the modern condition of the arts in general" (*GSD*, vol. 4, 263). Inspired by the spirit of music ("which I can conceive only in terms of love"), Wagner was able to become a genuine artist, rather than a mere writer and critic (*GSD*, vol. 4, 264). A renewed allegiance to the musical tradition of the German masters saved Wagner from a sterile, uncreative existence, the curse of the modern man of letters, rather as Senta saves the Dutchman from the curse of his weary and unproductive wanderings.

The opposition set up between the spiritually nourished musical artist and the sterile, modern journalist-critic-writer could be plausibly enough mapped (from Wagner's perspective) onto the opposition between Wagner himself and a figure like Heinrich Heine. The rhetorical invective wielded against the type of the modern writer in this passage from the *Communication* matches quite closely the language of Wagner's criticism of Heine scattered through his published writings and his correspondence. The attitude expressed here is also reflected in the nature of Wagner's adaptation of Heine's ironic-humorous literary vignette on the subject of the "Flying Dutchman" as a Romantic opera, quite purged of all modern irony, and drenched instead in an art-religious ethos of Romantic alienation, exaltation of poetic "feeling," sacrificial love, and redemption. Wagner invokes music as a means of "redeeming" the naive, traditional materials of myth, legend, folk tale, and broadside ballad from cultural obsolescence, rescuing them from the skeptical, ironizing, and sardonic gaze of the modern critical man of letters.

As Wagner must surely have sensed, Heine's "Fable of the Flying Dutchman" included in his *Memoirs of Herr Schnabelewopski* (see Appendix A, pp. 166–69) satirizes a subject that had, by the 1830s, become the material of melodramatic entertainment and popular fiction. Whether or not Heine had witnessed a performance of Edward Fitzball's "nautical drama" *The Flying Dutchman, or The Phantom Ship* (see Chapter 2) that played to great popular acclaim in London's Adelphi Theatre throughout 1827 (and continued to be reprinted through 1866), something like this semi-farcical melodrama was surely the model for the play his Schnabelewopski experiences at "a theatre in Amsterdam."[29] The novel of Captain Frederick Marryat, *The Phantom Ship* (1839) – which a number of the first critics of Wagner's opera assumed to be its source – forgoes the burlesque elements of Fitzball's stage piece, but has no aesthetic aspirations beyond the realm of ephemeral entertainment, no more so than the anonymous magazine piece, "Vanderdecken's Message Home,"[30] which seems to inaugurate the story's literary career. By way of explaining Wagner's elevation of this popular material to serious operatic status Carl Dahlhaus remarks: "It was by no means uncommon in the eighteenth and early nineteenth centuries, during the *Sturm und Drang* and Romantic eras, to ennoble old tales, which had

sunk to the level of broadsheet ballads, by writing new, poetic versions of them. Tragic subjects were sometimes parodied, but paro-
dies, vice versa, were also turned into tragedies."[31] (Goethe's *Faust*,
with its roots in fairground puppet-theatre, would be a classic case in
point.) In a certain sense, the ballad genre always tends to address
itself to the naive, childlike listener of a traditional oral, "unculti-
vated" culture – an idea Goethe himself expressed in his highly literary and self-conscious reflection on the genre, entitled simply
"Ballade," in which each stanza ends with the refrain, "The children,
they listen so gladly":

> O sing uns ein Märchen, o sing es uns oft,
> Daß ich und der Bruder es lerne;
> Wir haben schon längst einen Sänger gehofft,
> Die Kinder sie hören es gerne.
>
> [O sing us a story, and sing it again,
> That I and my brother might learn it;
> We've wanted so long for a singer to come,
> The children, they listen so gladly.]

While Wagner saw his heroine, Senta, as a naive child-of-nature,
performing her Ballad for an equally naive, pre-literate audience (cf.
his remarks on her character in the 1852 staging notes, Appendix C, p.
200), his own project in *Der fliegende Holländer* involved using the
naive folk ballad as a springboard for a newly sophisticated, aesthet-
ically ambitious cultivation of the genre of German Romantic opera.
The narrative ballad or romance was a typical marker of the genre, as
we have seen. A distinctive aspect of Wagner's achievement in
Höllander, noted by himself and some of his more sympathetic critics
(as cited earlier), was to turn the artificially naive "folk ballad" of
Senta not only into the fulcrum of the dramatic narrative, but also
into the source of a characteristic tone or color informing the work as
a whole. If modern audiences accustomed to the *Ring* and *Tristan* are
not so impressed by the musical-dramatic continuity of *Der fliegende
Holländer*, earlier critics registered surprise and even admiration at
the way in which the simpler requisites of the Romantic genre (such as
the folk ballad) were woven into the larger fabric of the opera, infus-
ing it with a balladic "color" or character even beyond the simple
recurrence of musical themes or the interdependence of ballad and
operatic plot.

A critic of the 1844 Berlin production, for instance, referred the
audience's reservations toward the piece – but also his own apparent

sympathy with it – to "the somber aspect of the Gothic subject [*des schauerlichen Sujets*] . . . , which the composer himself has dramatized after Capt. Marryat's interesting story [*sic*] and constructed in a quite novel form, without [spoken] dialogue or recitative, in continuous declamatory songs, ballads, duets, etc. and choruses, thoroughly appropriate to the Romantic character of the opera."[32] A critic of the Dresden première found that this increased continuity between numbers created a work "more epic than dramatic in nature," a response we might possibly construe as registering the expansion of balladic tone or character to encompass the overall opera (although this critic himself relates "epic" to "the symphony and its related forms").[33] Another reviewer of the 1844 Berlin production likened the piece to a "dramatic symphony with voices," anticipating a common reaction to Wagner's later works with regard to the perceived domination of the orchestra.[34]

Eduard Hanslick, as we have seen, heard the work as evidence of the composer's thoroughly epigonal relation to the earlier traditions of German Romantic opera at that earlier point of his career, while he also echoed other critics' views of its disproportionately "symphonic" character. Hanslick, however, relates this not merely to the density of the scoring, but to the very manner in which Wagner himself described the opera as evolving from the thematic kernel of the Ballad (citing the *Communication to my Friends*):

From this "condensed image [of the drama]" Wagner developed the whole opera rather in the way the composer of an instrumental composition derives the whole of it from the main theme. Such a conception, however, is not dramatic, but symphonic, whereas for the opera composer the image of the drama should unfold successively, as a process of "becoming" [*als ein Werdendes entrollen muß*]. But fortunately, the particular method of the present case harmonizes with the specific nature of the legend.[35]

The opposition between the symphonic development of a main theme and the "successive unfolding" of dramatic form is not entirely clear as Hanslick presents it here, though the imputation of a kind of higher "monothematicism" or thematic unity to the opera accords both with Wagner's claims for the centrality of the Ballad and with the complaints from other early critics about the unrelieved, somber "monotony" of the work's tone and color. (Even the composer's friend and advocate Heinrich Laube responded after the première, "I found the whole opera ghostly pale."[36])

Thus, from their opposing perspectives, the composer and his critics seem to agree about the dominating influence exerted by the Ballad on the opera as a whole. From Wagner's perspective, this concentration on a balladic "tone" at the expense of quotidian dramatic intrigue was an aspect of *Der fliegende Holländer* that made it a worthy predecessor to his later music dramas, where interior, psychological content is always privileged over the effective "situations" prized by conventional operatic dramaturgy. In *Music of the Future* he pointed to "the characteristic color of the legendary material" as an integral counterpart of the "inner motives of the action," to the extent that "this color itself became the action" (*GSD*, vol. 7, 122) – a paradox that might sound like a defensive apology.

Of course, what Wagner more controversially suggested about the relation of the Ballad to the opera was that the former contains the thematic germs or seeds of the latter, a proto-leitmotivic repertoire that "spread itself quite naturally across the entire drama as a continuous network," as he put it in the *Communication*. While modern critics have objected to the hindsight of this view, the position of the Ballad in the genealogy of Wagner's leitmotif technique is in some part validated by a remark in the early essay on the opera printed in the Leipzig *Illustrirte Zeitung* in 1843 (the one that reproduces the composer's "promotional" letter to Ferdinand Heine). The remarks on the Ballad's thematic importance allude to a figure (the "red thread") that plays a prominent role in the subsequent evolution of the leitmotif idea in the critical reception of Wagner's music up through the time of Wolzogen's motive guides of the 1870s and 1880s. (These remarks also appear to be unprompted; at least they do not derive from Wagner's own letter quoted earlier in the essay.)

We have thought it necessary to reproduce the entire Ballad here because it provides in a sense the kernel of the material [of the drama], just as the music [of the Ballad] constitutes the red thread running through the whole opera. The horn-tones that serve as a short ritornello introducing the Ballad also serve to announce each appearance of the phantom ship, or else that of the Dutchman; likewise do the other motives [of the Ballad] return, in accordance with the circumstances, whenever the Flying Dutchman is mentioned.[37]

The passage is not proof that the *Holländer* score is in fact rigorously leitmotivic. It does suggest, however, that the reflexive relationship of Ballad to opera was not without influence on the development of a leitmotif technique in later works.

It reminds us, moreover, of the broader genealogy of this technique that can be traced back precisely to the role of such ballads and romances in earlier Romantic and even pre-Romantic operas, from the works by Marschner, Meyerbeer, and Auber (or even Fitzball) cited earlier, to the *romances* "Un pauvre petit Savoyard" of Cherubini's *Les deux journées* and "Une fièvre brûlante" of Grétry's *Richard Cœur-de-Lion*. The narrative content of these *romances* may be immaterial to their dramaturgical function as the sign of a character's presence, but even this role of narrative song as sonic sign or marker points toward the exchange between epic past and dramatic present characteristic of the leitmotif. In *Der fliegende Holländer*, the incursions of the Dutchman's horn-call motto throughout Erik's dream-narration represent a transitional stage, of sorts, between this old-fashioned function of ballad-as-marker and the modern (or future) "psychological" leitmotif. Although he is nominally narrating a dream, the images (and sounds) of the dream have been suggested to Erik by the Ballad that so preoccupies Senta, and so unsettles himself.

In turning from *Rienzi* to *Der fliegende Holländer* Wagner was "saved by the good angel of German music," as he put it, from the threat of a career squandered in catering to the shallow tastes of a modern (Parisian-oriented) urban public. But in turning his attentions to the less glamorous, more homely genre of German Romantic opera he had grown up with, Wagner was hoping to rescue *it*, in turn (for by 1840 the home-grown genre was more than a little moribund). In his following works, *Tannhäuser* and *Lohengrin*, Wagner would seek to revive it through an infusion of grand-operatic *élan*. Yet he never quite overcame his own ambivalence toward the "Romantic" genre as he had first known it. Writing to Theodor Uhlig on 24 March 1852, shortly before the revival of *Holländer* in Zurich, he spoke with undisguised disdain of one of his work's direct generic forebears, Marschner's *Vampyr*, which was then playing at the Zurich Aktientheater. The public, he sneers, is not in the least put off by the "repulsiveness" of the subject.

The music, as a whole, disgusted me again, too: all this duet, trio, and quartet singing and drawling is so incredibly stupid and tasteless, since it remains quite void of sensual appeal and never really amounts to more than so many notes played and sung. The few exceptions I'm willing to accept as such. But now I really do see how infinitely far apart *my* operas stand from this so-called "German" genre; God knows, it's just Italian music re-soled in German leather, made learned and impotent – nothing more. – I was most amused, incidentally, by the poisoned flute in *Austin*.   (*SB*, vol. 4, 325)

The "poisoned flute" that serves as the instrument of an attempted regicide in Marschner's *Austin* (premièred in Hanover two months earlier, and evidently mentioned in Uhlig's previous letter) is an emblem of the genre's pedigree in popular melodrama, which composers like Marschner were either unable or unwilling to erase. In turning the melodramatic material of the Flying Dutchman and his "phantom ship" – with its mysterious portraits, invisible voices, *ersatz* folk ballads, and sentimental "romances" – into an allegory of Romantic alienation, love, and redemption, Wagner was aiming to rehabilitate this ailing branch of his artistic patrimony. Some of the ambivalence he felt towards this patrimony he eventually directed toward his own *Holländer*, after its failure to find a foothold in the German repertoire in the 1840s or 1850s. Wagner may have hoped that he could redeem the genre, as Senta redeems the Dutchman. But for all his heroic efforts, *Der fliegende Holländer* resembles the Ballad and its refrain more than it does the conclusion of the drama: a hopeful promise of future achievement, rather than the definitive act of "redemption."

5 Landfall on the stage: a brief production history

PATRICK CARNEGY

Dresden 1843 and the early performances

We can only reconstruct a relatively sketchy picture of the composer's earliest stagings of *Der fliegende Holländer*. What we do know is that despite Wagner's best efforts they were woefully out of tune with what he had imagined, and that this provoked him into lengthy descriptions of his intentions. Wagner's first idea had been for a compact one-act curtain-raiser to a full-length French ballet – a rather desperate bid to achieve his ambition of a performance at the Paris Opéra. But like so many of his projects it expanded far beyond the modest scope initially imagined, from "un petit opéra en un acte" into a "romantische Oper in einem Acte und drei Aufzügen" (a Romantic opera in one act and three scenes) lasting over two hours (see Chapter 1). Between the completion of the score in November 1841 and the Dresden première of 2 January 1843, Wagner made a substantial first round of revisions so that the work would be performed in the more usual form of three acts divided by intervals. This remained the way in which Wagner himself always performed the work (the emergence of a continuous performing version dates only from Cosima's Bayreuth production of 1901; see Chapter 7).

Wagner's first offer for the première had been from the Court Opera in Berlin. But the new Intendant (Theodor von Küstner, who, in his previous appointment at Munich, had turned the work down), although honoring his predecessor's commitment to the work, refused to give the work precedence over Franz Lachner's grand opera *Catarina Cornaro*. Wagner therefore demanded – and got – his score back so it could immediately be put into production in Dresden as a follow-up to the huge success he had had there with *Rienzi* in 1842.[1]

There was very little time to plan the staging of so technically demanding a work. Gottfried Semper's newly built court theatre (which opened in April 1841) was among the largest and best equipped in Germany but had been sufficiently taxed by the scenic demands of *Rienzi* that had included a conflagration anticipatory of the ending of *Götterdämmerung*. Within ten weeks the same stage had to contain the raging seas of *Der fliegende Holländer*, the arrival and departure of a huge ghostly ship, rapid transformations between seascapes and domesticity, and a concluding bodily resurrection from the waves for the hero and heroine.

In matters of staging Wagner demanded that everything depicted in the music should not only be shown on the stage but exactly coordinated with it. Equally important was that the singers should be totally inside their roles. In most of these respects Wagner was disappointed, though that did not prevent him writing to Schumann the day after the première to report a "triumph." After the second and third acts there had been tumultuous acclaim for the singers and himself. He was far prouder of this new success than he had been of *Rienzi*, the real reason being that, as he told his stepsister Cäcilie Avenarius, he had perhaps invented a new operatic genre.[2] In truth that was more important than whatever was, or was not, physically achieved on the Dresden stage that night. At any event, the "success" initially reported by Wagner was strictly limited, for after four performances the opera was pulled and replaced by the very much more popular *Rienzi*.

The staging appears to have been hastily cobbled together, most likely from existing stock. For a reasonably objective view of the première we can turn to Marie Schmole, daughter of Ferdinand Heine, close friend of Wagner's and costume designer at Dresden (though, strangely enough, not involved in this production). Marie had been a youthful member of the audience and, years later, she recalled that "The sea waves were produced in a quite primitive way and the ships made a pretty crude appearance and disappearance, but people then expected less of scenic equipment than they do now."[3] Marie recalled that the principals had done well enough, but that Johann Michael Wächter (the Dutchman), although a fine singer with a beautiful voice, had not projected the demonic nature of the character as Anton Mitterwurzer was to do later. Wagner had been in despair over the *Himmelfahrt* (bodily ascension from the waves) of Senta and the Dutchman, which had only been crudely managed. The only surviving visual records of the production are some costume drawings and

1ᵗᵉ Vorstellung im vierten Abonnement.

Königlich Sächsisches Hoftheater.

Montag, den 2. Januar 1843.

Zum ersten Male:

Der fliegende Holländer.

Romantische Oper in drei Akten, von Richard Wagner.

Personen:

Daland, norwegischer Seefahrer.	—	Herr Risse.
Senta, seine Tochter.	—	Mad. Schröder-Devrient.
Erik, ein Jäger.	—	Herr Reinhold
Mary, Haushälterin Dalands.	—	Mad. Wächter.
Der Steuermann Dalands.	—	Herr Bielezizky.
Der Holländer.	—	Herr Wächter.

Matrosen des Norwegers. Die Mannschaft des fliegenden Holländers. Mädchen.
Scene: Die norwegische Küste.

Textbücher sind an der Casse das Exemplar für 2½ Neugroschen zu haben.

Krank: Herr Dettmer.

Einlaß-Preise:

Ein Billet in die Logen des ersten Ranges und das Amphitheater		1 Thlr.	— Ngr.
„ „ „ Fremdenlogen des zweiten Ranges Nr. 1. 14. und 29.	1	—	„
„ „ „ übrigen Logen des zweiten Ranges		—	20 „
„ „ „ Sperr-Sitze der Mittel- u. Seiten-Gallerie des dritten Ranges	—	12½ „
„ „ „ Mittel- und Seiten-Logen des dritten Ranges		—	10 „
„ „ „ Sperr-Sitze der Gallerie des vierten Ranges		—	8 „
„ „ „ Mittel-Gallerie des vierten Ranges		—	7½ „
„ „ „ Seiten-Gallerie-Logen daselbst		—	5 „
„ „ „ Sperr-Sitze im Cercle.		—	20 „
„ „ „ Parterre-Logen		—	15 „
„ „ das Parterre		—	10 „

Die Billets sind nur am Tage der Vorstellung gültig, und zurückgebrachte Billets werden nur bis Mittag 12 Uhr an demselben Tage angenommen.

Der Verkauf der Billets gegen sofortige baare Bezahlung findet in der, in dem untern Theile des Rundbaues befindlichen Expedition, auf der rechten Seite, nach der Elbe zu, früh von 9 Uhr bis Mittags 12 Uhr, und Nachmittags von 3 bis 4 Uhr statt.

Alle zur heutigen Vorstellung bestellte und zugesagte Billets sind Vormittags von 9 Uhr bis längstens 11 Uhr abzuholen, außerdem darüber anders verfügt wird.

Der freie Einlaß beschränkt sich bei der heutigen Vorstellung blos auf die zum Hofstaate gehörigen Personen und die Mitglieder des Königl. Hoftheaters.

Einlaß um 5 Uhr.   Anfang um 6 Uhr.
Ende gegen 9 Uhr.

5.1 Playbill for the first performance, Hoftheater, Dresden, 2 January 1843 an artist's fanciful impression of Senta plunging down from the cliff while the Dutchman's ship sinks in the bay beyond.[4]

Marie's account squares well enough with Wagner's own later recollections. While performing the work in Zurich in 1852 (see below), the composer wrote to Wilhelm Fischer, the Dresden chorus master, that "now more than ever I have recognized how bad was the performance which Dresden gave of my work . . . When I recall what an extremely clumsy and wooden setting of the Flying Dutchman the imaginative Dresden machinist [Gustav Moritz] Hänel gave on his magnificent stage, I am seized even now with an after-attack of rage" (letter of 9 May 1852; *SB*, vol. 4, 360).

Some eighteen years later, in *Mein Leben*, he confirms his disappointment: "I had to learn from what was on the whole an unsuccessful performance how much care and forethought would be necessary to assure myself an adequate representation of my later works . . . The third act, in which the mightiest tempest in the orchestra was unable to disturb the quiet sea nor budge the ghost ship from its meticulous mooring, evoked amazement in the public as to how I could possibly offer, after a *Rienzi* during whose every act there was so much going on and in which Tichatschek shone in repeated changes of costumes, such an utterly unornamented, meager and somber piece of work."[5]

In the composer's view it was only the great singing-actress Wilhelmine Schröder-Devrient who had rescued the work from total disaster. Berlioz agreed with Wagner's high assessment of Schröder-Devrient ("in spite of one or two affected poses and the spoken phrases that she finds it necessary to interject throughout the role") but, not sharing Wagner's then unusual histrionic expectations of his performers, took a very different view of Wächter. He was excited by the "really remarkable and unspoiled talent [of] Wächter, who plays the doomed Dutchman. He has one of the finest baritone voices I have heard, and he uses it with complete mastery . . ." Berlioz professed himself greatly taken by "the sombre coloring of the music and by some remarkable effects of storm and wind which are an integral part of the dramatic character of the work."[6]

Der fliegende Holländer was quickly taken up by other theatres for whom the attractions of *Rienzi*, which had spread Wagner's name far and wide, were mitigated by its length and extravagant production requirements.

5.2 Costumes of the Dutchman, Erik and Senta in the first performance, as depicted in the *Illustrirte Zeitung*, Leipzig, 7 October 1843

Riga, Wagner's old theatre, produced the work on 22 May 1843 (Russian Old Style, or 3 June, New Style), and when Kassel did so on 5 June 1843 this was the first time any well-known German theatre outside Dresden had ventured a work by Wagner. The performance was prepared and conducted by Louis Spohr (known for his own earlier "Romantic operas" *Faust* and *Jessonda*). Spohr made a serious attempt to follow Wagner's scenic instructions: "Ships with full sails and rigging rocked about, dropped and weighed anchor, turned to port and starboard on the stage and departed seawards again – stormclouds, moonlight, radiant transfiguration, everything happened in front of our eyes as though by magic and with lightness of touch, perfection of illusion and artistic effect."[7]

In January 1844 Wagner himself conducted the work in Berlin, where it was originally to have been premièred in 1842. As the Royal Opera House had burnt down on 18 August 1843 the performances took place in a relatively small theatre, the Schauspielhaus on the Gendarmenmarkt, built in 1817–21 by Karl Friedrich Schinkel. Production plans for the aborted 1842 première offer vivid evidence of how theatres improvised scenery from stock. The designer Johann K. J. Gerst specified the following borrowings: the two ships (from a ballet *Der Seeräuber*), cyclorama and masts (Weber's *Oberon*), Daland's room (Gretchen's parlor in Goethe's *Faust* – a design by Schinkel) and the house in Act III (the Swiss chalet from Schiller's *Wilhelm Tell*).[8]

In the event Wagner may have been spared such a patchwork as the theatre's store was also destroyed in the fire. But whatever was invented in its stead was very likely still based on Gerst's sketches and impressed him so much that he commended it to other theatres: "I was most pleasantly surprised by the superb staging under the direction of the truly brilliant stage-director Blum, with the collaboration of his highly skilled and ingenious technicians" (*ML*, 263). The public seems to have given the production an enthusiastic reception, but the negative press response led to its withdrawal after four performances and the opera did not return to the Berlin stage until 1868.

For performances planned for Leipzig in 1846 (but aborted), Wagner lightened the brass (see Chapter 1). He made further adjustments when, now living in Switzerland with a price on his head, he was persuaded to produce and conduct performances in 1852 in Zurich with purpose-built sets by the Hamburg scenic artist Ludwig Caessmann. Despite the relatively primitive and cramped stage conditions Wagner rated the production far better than the Dresden one, commending it as a model for larger theatres to follow (letter to Wilhelm Fischer, *SB*, vol. 4, 361). The *Leipziger Allgemeine Theaterchronik* praised the fully functional ships, manned by crews of about a dozen each and maneuvering realistically: "In the final act we watched the Dutchman's ship sink *mit Mann und Maus* in the middle of the stage right before our eyes, and the Dutchman and Senta swept up to heaven in the same moment."[9]

Weimar 1853: Wagner's advice to Liszt

Liszt's request for guidance on how, in Wagner's absence, to produce the work in Weimar (February 1853) drew from the composer a detailed account of his intentions. His 1852 "Remarks on the Performance of the Opera *Der fliegende Holländer*" give a good idea of the persistent problems he had faced in previous attempts to stage the piece. (The full text of these "Remarks" is translated in Appendix C, pp. 193–200.) He is mostly concerned with characterization and with how he expected the singers to coordinate their movement and gestures with the music. That Wagner begins by asking the director to study the printed instructions in the score is evidence of the scant attention that was usually paid to them.

Wagner's principal scenic difficulty was that managements were interested only in decorative effects and had no conception of staging as an expression of the inner life of the drama. He therefore tries to get the conductor and singers to understand that his work has a dramatic rationale and is not merely a succession of numbers for vocal display. He explains that Daland is a doughty sailor, not a comedy figure; Erik a stormy romantic, not a sentimental whiner; Senta a tough Nordic girl, naive but not sentimental. Most of his "Remarks" concern the role of the Dutchman, the one that was hardest for his contemporaries to understand. If his measure-by-measure instructions seemed hardly likely to inspire singers to move as naturally and truthfully as he wished, one has to remember that he was out to eliminate the rhetorical posturing that appears to have been most directors' and performers' idea of acting.

Wagner's scenic requirements, totally impracticable at the time, were for an exact portrayal of sea and storm. He saw them as actors in the drama and therefore to be depicted with the same fidelity as the human characters. The sea had to be seen to rage and foam, Daland's ship to be naturalistic and to heave with the sea. Wagner cites the 1844 Berlin performances as a model for "the purely decorative aspects" of the production and suggests painted gauzes and subtle lighting to help achieve the sense of romantic illusion he wanted. He asks that "the stage directions given in the printed score be observed closely," while he leaves "the specific execution of these directions to the inventive power of stage designers and machinists." Quite how much of this Liszt was actually able to realize remains uncertain. His musical forces were certainly deficient but his production as a whole was regarded as so successful that it was taken as definitive by other theatres for years to come.[10]

Munich 1864: a royal command performance

It was with the new endings to the overture and third act (bearing the imprint of the recently completed *Tristan und Isolde*) that the opera was given at Ludwig II's court theatre in Munich in December 1864, shortly after the eighteen-year-old king had rescued Wagner from his creditors. It was the third staging given under his direction, and again he chose to perform the work in three separate acts. Wagner also added new stage directions, altered vocal lines and restored a chorus cut he had made in 1843.[11] The production was the first of the "model" performances promised by Ludwig to Wagner, the king's theatre specializing in the lush Romantic naturalism that the composer wanted. Ludwig's scenic artists were among the best of their kind, Heinrich Döll being responsible for Acts I and III, Angelo Quaglio for Act II. Wagner himself took charge of the staging, and also of the conducting, after the theatre's music director, Franz Lachner, had tried to make cuts and generally proved inadequate at rehearsals.

This was very much a theatre of illusionistic tricks. The arrival of the Dutchman's ship was effected by a small model ship passing in front of the seascape backcloth into the wings, then reappearing as a very much larger construction further downstage. The *Wellenballett* (dance of the waves) that Wagner wanted was enacted by the rapid movement of painted cloth-drops. Act II showed the living room of a prosperous seafarer with Dutchman's portrait, Senta's armchair and spinning wheels – everything as specified in Wagner's text. In Act III the ships had exchanged moorings, with the exterior of Daland's house on the audience's left and the rocky ledge from which Senta plunges on its right.

5.3 Model made in 1865 of Heinrich Döll's setting for Act I (steiles Felsenufer) in King Ludwig II's royal command production, Munich, 1864

The illusion of reality so painstakingly created was somewhat compromised in that the singers would have been out-of-scale with the ships, appearing far larger (or the ships far smaller) than they should have. There would also have been a serious limitation in that the settings were composed of "pictures" with inbuilt light-effects, illuminated by fixed gas lighting which could only be turned up and down. Wagner nevertheless took immense trouble to fine-tune the lighting effects.[12] The age of solid scenery and variable electric lighting still lay decades ahead.

Wagner was happy enough with the vocal and instrumental side of the performance, but frustrated by the staging's technical deficiencies. The gulf between the "model" intentions and what was actually achieved was still considerable, as the critics didn't fail to point out. The *Münchener Neueste Nachrichten* praised the painted scenery but was scornful of the small and ordinary ships, reporting that the *Wellenballet* often failed to function and that the supernatural effects in the third act were "more a cause for mirth than terror." The apotheosis of the hero and heroine was attempted with model effigies, but so clumsily that the *Bayerische Zeitung* (admittedly biased against

Ludwig's patronage of Wagner) remarked that nothing so tasteless and risible had ever been seen on the royal stage.[13] Wagner himself continued to feel that the work had still not found its definitive form. He contemplated further revisions (notably in 1866 and 1880) but died without attempting them.

In what follows I will attempt to describe how some of the more notable stagings of *Holländer* after Wagner's death have sought to interpret the work. These productions have tried to build bridges between the standpoint of the interpreter and the performance possibilities latent within the work itself. The composer would doubt-less have been happy that more has been found in the work than he was conscious of having put there himself (to perform is inevitably to interpret), but might perhaps have been surprised by some of these readings.

The *Holländer* weighs anchor

The *Holländer*'s conquest of foreign shores included first landfalls in Stockholm (1872, in Swedish), Budapest (1873, in Hungarian), Philadelphia (1876, in Italian; the US première), Copenhagen (1884, in Danish), Barcelona (1885, in Italian), Buenos Aires (1887, in Italian), Mexico (1891, in English), Lisbon (1893, in Italian) and Moscow (1894, in Italian).[14] The London production of 1870 was the very first Wagner opera to be produced in that city which, knowing opera as an essentially Italian phenomenon, gave the work as *L'Olandese dannato*.[15] George Bernard Shaw, reporting its 1891 revival (by this time in German, following a transitional English version), described Daland's ship as "a small copy of the *Victory* at the Naval Exhibition," rooted "so monumentally in the Shaftesbury stage that even I could ride out the storm without a qualm." Shaw was appalled by the chorus and impressed only by the Senta of Margaret Macintyre (*c.* 1865–1943), though he noted that "her notion of dra-matic singing at present hardly goes beyond intensely imagining herself to be the person in the drama, and then using the music to relieve her pent-up excitement." The props fooled no one: "there is one prima donna's spinning-wheel (practicable) out of *Faust* for Miss Damian [Grace Damian, as Mary], and three broken and incomplete ones (desperately impracticable) for the chorus." Shaw shows how so many attempts to follow Wagner's instructions have ended only in total disaster: "the curtain came down amid roars of laughter at the apotheosis of Senta, who had no sooner plunged into the deep in the person of Miss Macintyre than she rose resplendent from her dip in the person of a soft, plump, smiling, golden-haired lassie, whose extravagantly remote resemblance to Miss Macintyre took in nobody but the ghost of Vanderdecken, which hugged her with enthusiasm."[16] The *Holländer* did not arrive at the Paris Opéra until 1937 (disguised as *Le Vaisseau fantôme*) nearly a century after Wagner had hoped to have seen his work premièred there.[17]

Bayreuth 1901: the *Holländer* as music-drama

After Wagner's death it took Cosima a long time before she gave the work its first performance at Bayreuth – thus in 1901 completing what has ever since been its standard repertory of the ten operas from *Holländer* to *Parsifal*.

Cosima used the 1896 score edited by Felix Weingartner and in which she had had a hand (see Chapter 6, p. 142). It conflated the three separate acts into a single continuous span, Cosima's purpose in this, and in all other important editorial decisions, being to suggest that the opera was more of a music drama than the piece Wagner actually wrote. She took the 1864 Munich staging as her point of departure, using the Bayreuth veteran Max Brückner as designer; she knew he could be counted on not to rock the boat of nineteenth-century Romantic naturalism. Ever in search of historical exactitude (her solution whenever she was unsure of Wagner's intentions), Cosima researched meticulously into Norwegian coastal life in the seventeenth century and went all out for a Norwegian ambiance in the decor, props and costumes. As at Munich, wooden effigies of the Dutchman and Senta (now faithfully modeling the role's renowned interpreters, Anton van Rooy and Emmy Destinn) soared up into the flies at the end.[18] Siegfried's contribution lay in using electric lighting and mist-and-smoke machine effects to create atmosphere around the rather creaky handling of the tub-like ships and the action as a whole. In the 1914 revival of the production, cut short after two performances by the outbreak of the First World War, Siegfried's sea- and cloudscape effects gained greatly from his introduction of a large cyclorama.[19]

By the 1920s electric light projection and film were everywhere making a major contribution to meteorological and nautical realism,

5.4 Anton van Rooy as the Dutchman and Emmy Destinn as Senta, Bayreuth, 1901–2. A posed studio image, characteristic of the period, signed by van Rooy

5.5 Act III at Bayreuth, 1914. Only two performances were given before the curtailment of the Festival by the outbreak of the First World War. The settings were developed by Siegfried Wagner, using a large cyclorama, from those made by Max Brückner for Bayreuth's first production of the opera, 1901

as well as to the miraculous apotheosis at the end. But many had begun to feel that the triumphant wave of scenic naturalism was displacing the psychodrama at the core of the work. Among the few productions of this time to make an attempt to correct this was that at Königsberg in 1926 when "the set consisted simply of black rocky ledges and a blood-red cyclorama on which flashes of lightning were projected." The blood-red sky disappeared with the arrival of the Dutchman's ship, covering the whole width of the stage as it rose up out of the trap, sinister and ghostlike (while Daland's was consigned to the wings).[20]

Krolloper, Berlin 1929: Klemperer and the chill wind of change

Another tide in the Weimar Republic was running against every style of traditional operatic rhetoric, and especially that of the Bayreuth tradition. The decade of *Neue Sachlichkeit* was deeply suspicious of over-dressed productions, considering them servile to the supposed intentions of creators and in thrall to the taste of bourgeois society.

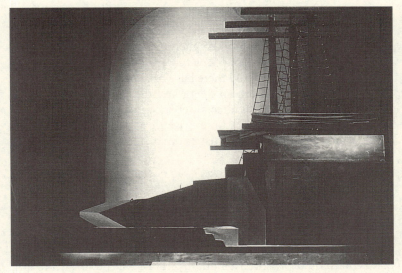

5.6 The Dutchman's ship in Act III of Otto Klemperer's 1929 production at
the Berlin Krolloper with designs of Bauhaus severity by Ewald Dülberg

Sobriety and truthfulness in theatrical performance were insisted on
by the radicals, none more so than by Otto Klemperer and his col-
leagues at Berlin's Krolloper which had been set up expressly as a
people's opera house in 1927. It was the Kroll's 1929 *Flying Dutchman*
which first crashed through "Senta-sentimentality" (as Nietzsche had
called it) into a tough new world of earthy realism and psychological
penetration.

Although the ascetic Klemperer had turned against Wagner's later
works, particularly in the lush performances conducted by
Furtwängler and Bruno Walter, he took up Richard Strauss's idea
that one should resurrect Wagner's original version of the opera.
Klemperer and his dramaturg Hans Curjel discovered in the
Prussian State Library the score used by Wagner himself for his 1844
Berlin performances (but see also Chapter 6, p. 140 n. 19). The raw
vigor of the opera in which the young composer discovered his voice
was, for Klemperer, a good way of settling his differences with
Wagner. Klemperer, his designer Ewald Dülberg, and his producer
Jürgen Fehling, were wholly antipathetic to Bayreuth's reverential
embalmings.

It was perhaps not surprising that the production premièred on 15 January 1929 (with police at the doors anticipating riots) should have been assailed as a mockery of Wagner and that Curjel should have been called before the Prussian *Landtag* (Parliament) to account for it. What other response could there have been to the first high-profile radical challenge in a German opera house to the accepted way of performing Wagner? Its architects were not the kind of men to seek scandal for its own sake but were driven by their mission to make audible and visible the "pure artistic core of the work," as Curjel put it.[21]

The collision between the *Sachlichkeit* of their approach and traditional Romantic production testified to the vigorous persistence of the latter (as a refuge from the rough winds of political and cultural change) in the new theatrical era of Piscator and Brecht, Meyerhold and Eisenstein, the cinema, the wireless, and the gramophone. Hence the outrage that the Dutchman should have been robbed of his beard, that Senta should have been a modern girl in a blue pullover, and that her plait-less companions should have been mending nets rather than toying with spinning wheels. It had not helped that the philosopher Ernst Bloch had written an introductory piece arguing that to treat the opera as a nautical adventure story by Captain Marryat, but with surrealistic overtones, was as good a way as any of liberating it from the *Traumkitsch* in which first Wagner himself and then his heirs had cocooned it.[22]

Klemperer gave the opera in the traditional three separate acts. Dülberg's sets (following his designs for *Fidelio*, with which the Krolloper had opened its doors) used only the most basic building blocks of ramps, platforms and steps, with the simplest of means to suggest the spars, masts and decks of the ships. "In the first and third acts," wrote the theatre-critic Bernhard Diebold, "the designs are still preoccupied with stylization. In the second act there is a complete translation of the sound world into colors: Senta's house is glazed like a lighthouse and stands as though surrounded by sea-mist. The tar-black spars of the ghost-ship tower over the roof. The Dutchman appears from the mist and materializes in the room in the dark form of a man. No beard, no hat. A gloomy man as though pictured by Th.[éodore] Rousseau: the most powerful atmosphere of the production was in the second act. Senta, as though possessed by the devil, springs up and sings the Ballad. Her ecstasy possesses the whole house."

Diebold considered that although she was somewhat overtaxed vocally, Moje Forbach's powerful acting as Senta conveyed an incomparable impression of heroic possession. In Forbach's fascinating account, " I wore a blue pullover, a grey skirt of coarse, stiff cloth and a startling red wig, smoothly combed back into a knot. This was of course extraordinary, because I'd previously always worn blouses and little bodices, skirts and petticoats. But this [costume] suited Klemperer's kind of production, design, acting style and musical approach – it was, in effect, a severe Ur-*Höllander*."[23]

What was new here was that an exponent of *Werktreue* like Klemperer should have sought to maximize the drama as a whole by giving the stage action whatever freedom it required, consistent only with the music being given full value on its own terms. And of course Klemperer and his team were not just picture-cleaning, they were also projecting their own concerns and images into the work. The creators of the production presented an un-mystical, story-telling Wagner, a Feuerbachian utopian instead of a Schopenhauerian doom-monger, a republican revolutionary who mirrored their own impatience with burdensome cultural tradition, an angry republican tossed around by the tempests but with his feet never far from firm anchorage. That was the *actualité* of the performance. It was inevitable that it should offend those who preferred to have the explosive power of Wagner's work defused into an agreeable aesthetic experience by sanctimonious tradition. Before Klemperer's production, the critical reformers had largely sought stagings that would help the musical drama speak more eloquently, more directly, than adherence to Wagner's own stage rubrics allowed. Klemperer and his team had, perhaps even to their own surprise, shown for the first time that the myths and metaphors could, with gain rather than loss, be interpreted as of contemporary relevance.

The Krolloper's repertoire and productions were not what most of its audience would have chosen themselves; like most opera audiences of the day, as Klemperer later said, they only wanted "big singers, big arias, big applause and so on."[24] The Krolloper excited the Republic's artists and intellectuals while increasingly incurring the wrath of those who saw in it only the betrayal of the highest values of German culture. The institution became a stalking horse for rightist attacks on the Republic. Klemperer fought hard to save it but became engulfed by the political tide of conservative nationalism and the theatre was eventually closed down on 3 July 1931. He joined Leo Blech and Erich

Kleiber as one of the three principal conductors at the Berlin Staatsoper (where in 1933 he conducted a *Tannhäuser* in "Kroll" style as part of the celebration of the fiftieth anniversary of Wagner's death), fleeing first to Switzerland then to the USA when the Nazis seized power. As for the Krolloper itself, it suffered the ironic ignominy of becoming the temporary home of the Reichstag after the fire of 27 February 1933 and was later razed to the ground by the Allies.

Bayreuth 1939–59: the theatrical realism of Wieland Wagner

Despite the rampant nationalism at Bayreuth in the 1930s, it could not resist the Europe-wide trend away from cluttered, over-illustrative production. In these dark years Emil Preetorius produced many elegantly stylized designs for Bayreuth, including settings for Heinz Tietjen's 1939 staging of *Der fliegende Holländer*, conducted by Karl Elmendorff. Only a part of Daland's ship was represented, not the whole boat as previously, while the Dutchman's vessel was visible only as a spectral silhouette of its bow. The impressionistic images of the coastline, sea and sky were deliberately contrasted with the simple, log-cabin living room of Daland's house.[25] The cast was notable for the intensity of Maria Müller's Senta.

For opera houses finding their feet after the Second World War the *Holländer* was a safe choice as it had remained relatively unsullied by the Third Reich's nationalistic appropriation of its composer. Most performances were unexceptional in style. But the political and social upheavals instigated by the war induced a more questioning attitude.

When in 1951 the Bayreuth Festival resumed, the composer's grandsons Wieland and Wolfgang put a huge aesthetic distance between their productions and everything that had previously been seen on that stage. There were obvious political reasons why such a break with the past was essential, but theatre can never stand still, and the Wagner grandsons were determined that Bayreuth should begin to build on the theatre-reform movement of the earlier part of the century. They were especially keen to make creative use of the latest lighting technology to carry through Adolphe Appia's argument that the literal interpretation of Wagner's scenic prescriptions did the music no service as these were effectively tautologous. Appia had seen the task of staging as the creation of spaces which would grow out of the music and focus attention on the singing actors. This could best be done using the simplest solid shapes and forms, a cyclorama and the imaginative use of lighting. The lighting was to take its cue from the music so that the stage picture would be "the opened eye of the score." Hence the birth of the so-called *Lichtregie* or "direction through lighting," and in Paul Eberhardt the Wagner grandsons found an artist-virtuoso of the lighting console to help them realize this vision.

Four years later this was the guiding principle of Wolfgang Wagner's 1955 production which drastically simplified the Act I setting into a forestage barely suggestive of the deck and sloping gunwale of Daland's ship, with a counter-sloping platform behind on which the Dutchman appeared. The huge open space to the rear was taken up by a cyclorama canvas on which the lighting painted the moods of the sea and the sky. "The sea," wrote Ernst Thomas, " had a major role; it dominated the whole opera. Wagner's overwhelming musical vision of Nature's power here found its scenic equivalent."[26] The arrival of the Dutchman's ship was a projected image of black mast and red sails which seemed to expand out into the audience before suddenly collapsing, leaving behind on the stage the dark figure of the Dutchman. To minimize the risk of any distraction from the central figure, the Helmsman and chorus sang from off stage. Act II was a box-like room with a plain wooden bench round the walls. There were business-like spinning-wheels, but extraneous picturesque and folkloristic elements were banished. Characterization and costumes were earthy and anti-heroic. For the final apotheosis the projected contours of the Dutchman's ship dissolved into the dawning light of day.

This production was characteristic of the early years of "New Bayreuth" – an austere, disciplined beauty of the strongest, simplest shapes and a visual symphony of light, space and air celebrating liberation from the past. Three years later (in 1959) it was Wieland Wagner's turn and in a famous production he stepped back from the spiritualizing abstraction evident in Wolfgang's production into a theatrical realism where character and physical movement were of central importance.[27] In Act I there was no shore but simply the planked deck of Daland's ship with its guard-rails and rope ladders vanishing aloft. At the climactic chorus, "Mit Gewitter und Sturm," the men were clustered round the wheel in a tight protoplasmic ball, lurching and swaying together – an extraordinary image of a ship driven before the wind.

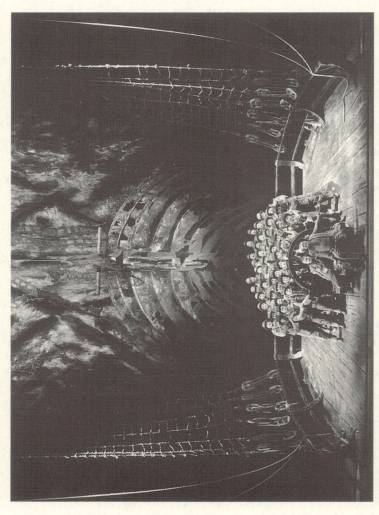

5.7 The "Südwind" chorus at the end of Act I in Wieland Wagner's Bayreuth production, first seen in 1959 but pictured here in 1961

The Dutchman's ship was once more a projection, this time emerging from the darkness enveloping Daland's deck, its prow a monstrous rib-cage with the Dutchman pinioned upon it – no pale ghost but a wild man. It was as though the blood-red firmament had broken open and thrust the cursed vessel to shore – a magical image of extraordinary power.[28] Unforgettable was the moment in Act III ("Seeleut'! Wacht doch auf!") when, in response to the sailors' challenge, the masked figures of the Dutchman's crew rose up like grey lemurs out of the sea behind the maniacally dancing Norwegian sailors, singing full out to the audience and, spectrally phosphorescent, trampled them to the floor while advancing threateningly towards the audience.

Wieland used the original 1843 Dresden version of the score, but with some softening changes and short pauses inserted between the three separate acts. Daland sported a vulgarly striped sailcloth suit and a rakish top-hat. Wieland saw him as avarice personified, like a character from Balzac. In action he reminded Walter Panofsky of "a performing bear, a malevolent clown, even a nordic descendant of Pantalone."[29] If this should suggest the caricature that Wagner specifically warned against, in Josef Greindl's performance Daland emerged as a figure scarcely less powerful than the Dutchman. For K. H. Ruppel the overall effect was poised somewhere between the grotesque realism of Dickens and the expressionist coloring of Nolde. With George London (initially) as the Dutchman, Anja Silja joining as Senta in 1960 (in Panofsky's words "a somnambulist harboring a secret animus in her heart"[30]) and Wolfgang Sawallisch conducting, this staging transported the opera to a wholly new plane of seriousness and importance. It was rich in comedy, and pointed the way towards demythologizing productions which were later to treat the opera as a drama of social realism.

Wieland's characterization of the roles followed Wagner's own, often ignored injunction: that once touched by love for Senta the Dutchman "becomes truly human," being every bit as much concerned to save her as she him.[31] In the words of Wieland's friend, Walter Erich Schäfer, the opera became less the ballad of the damned Ahasuerus than a didactic piece (*Lehrstück*) about the impossibility of masculine, questing restlessness being pacified by womanly self-sacrifice.[32] For William Mann, critic of the London *Times*, the production ranked "among the greatest operatic realizations of our time." At the end Senta disappeared into the shadows (considered a

5.8 Anja Silja as Senta in Act II of Wieland Wagner's production, Bayreuth, 1960

fudge by some commentators), after which the Dutchman collapsed before he could reach the gangplank of his retreating ship. The harsh truths of myth were not to be mollified by mystic apotheosis.

Komische Oper, Berlin 1962: Joachim Herz's social realism on stage and film

Wieland Wagner's rare foray into theatrical realism brought him close to the "music-theatre" aesthetic of the Berlin Komische Oper.[33] Founded in East Berlin in 1947 by Walter Felsenstein, the Komische Oper had inherited something of the Krolloper's mission to perform opera as theatre and thus now to make it enjoyable across all strata of the audience of the so-called democratic socialist state of the German Democratic Republic (DDR).

Felsenstein himself had produced six Wagner operas between 1927 and 1943, but an antipathy to the composer, doubtless nurtured by the experience of Nazi Wagnerism, kept his works off the Komische Oper stage until 1962. The natural choice for the company's populist ethos and modest theatre size was *Der fliegende Holländer*. Felsenstein entrusted its staging to one of his most gifted protégés, the thirty-eight-year-old Joachim Herz who since 1959 had been director of the Leipzig Opera. He had opened the rebuilt Leipzig theatre in 1960 with a production of *Die Meistersinger* which, turning its back on Nuremberg nostalgia and nineteenth-century Romantic naturalism, adopted an almost Brechtian "let's pretend" approach to the action.[34]

Herz brought an equally fresh approach to *Der fliegende Holländer*, so successfully that he re-created the production in his own Leipzig theatre, was invited to direct it in Moscow, and ended up making a film version which appears to have been the very first of a more-or-less complete Wagner opera. Here was a work by the revolutionary young Wagner which offered, inter alia, a brisk wind to blow away misconceptions about the composer's political viability, a critical view of bourgeois existence, and a heroic view of an individual in quest of self-realization. Herz sought to make the fable as tangible as possible – "a 'real' situation into which phantoms from another world break in."[35] He depicted Daland and his family as a prosperous 1840s ship-owner's household with a finely furnished parlor with a boudoir grand piano, striped wallpaper and candelabra. Senta and her companions were well-to-do young ladies in tea-gowns, spinning to pass the time while singing favorite songs (things they enjoyed rather than with which they identified). Senta, however, whose fantasies have been nurtured by the nautical memorabilia tastefully displayed in the room – model ships in glass cases, charts, a small portrait of the Dutchman on the wall – identifies totally with her Ballad. As she sings the walls become transparent and the sea is seen to roar and rage outside. She conjures it into becoming her new, liberating reality. Daland's ship was no rough fishing vessel, but a sleek schooner with auxiliary steam-powered paddle-wheel. The Christian notions of "damnation" versus "redemption" were interpreted as bourgeois constraint versus freedom to break out into a life of one's own. In Berlin, Herz followed Klemperer in using the original 1843 ending. In Leipzig, however, the Tristan-style epilogue of 1860 with the two harps and the transfigured "Senta" motive was played, from which Herz distanced himself by refusing to show any representation of the lovers' physical apotheosis and offering only the projection of an abstract image.[36]

Plainly such an interpretation fitted well with social aspirations in the DDR in the early 1960s and with the cultural climate in Moscow. Herz's production there on 14 May 1963 commemorated the 150th anniversary of Wagner's birth.[37] It was the first *Holländer* at the Bolshoi since the 1904–05 season, and the first Wagner production to be given there since Eisenstein's staging of *Die Walküre* in 1940, as well as the first time a foreigner had directed an opera at the Bolshoi. Herz was allowed an incredible eleven weeks of rehearsal time. At the Bolshoi the conductor, Kurt Sanderling, had wanted to eliminate the "angel" from the Russian translation in which the opera was sung, a move successfully resisted by Herz. (Socialism, the director commented wryly, had no problems with Satan.) What the company lacked in Wagnerian stage experience it had made up for in real life: quite a few members of the male chorus had served in the Soviet Navy. Primitive scene-change technology (and an appetite for ice-cream and *shampanskoje*) meant two intervals, not the continuous "Bayreuth" version given in Leipzig.

Herz's conception of the opera had its apotheosis not on the stage, however, but in the black-and-white film version he made for DEFA (the DDR's state film company) in 1964, the composer's score being fairly painlessly shortened to the ninety-seven-minute span of this *Film nach Wagner*. Four weeks were spent pre-recording the music with the Leipzig Gewandhaus Orchestra and Leipzig Opera Chorus

5.9 Anna Prucnal as Senta (sung by Gerda Hannemann) and Fred Düren as the Dutchman (sung by Rainer Lüdeke) exploring the coastline during the Act II duet in Joachim Herz's 1964 film version of the opera

under Rolf Reuter, with each singer's voice on a separate track. In anticipation of the needs of production filming, alternative takes were made at different tempi. The use of four-channel stereo sound (for the first time in European film-making, says Herz) enabled the "voices" to issue from the separate cast of miming actors, wherever they happened to be in screen-space. The Dutchman's ghostly crew was heard as though from the rear of the cinema. An even sharper visual separation between Senta's prison of her real world and her fantasy life was accomplished by using normal screen size for the former, the image broadening out into wide format as Senta's dreams take wing.

When the film begins, Senta is reading the legend of the Flying Dutchman to herself from an old book. A door mysteriously creaks ajar (there is an ominous ghost-story atmosphere). Senta presses her face to the wooden shutters, listening to the wind, its whine rising in pitch until it blends into the D-minor music of the overture which breaks in like the seas raging within her. As she begins to dream, the eye of the camera takes us in cinemascope out through the shutters into the waves beyond. It pulls back into the reality of the prosperous, bluff Daland confronting his preoccupied daughter who retreats back to her room with the small portrait of the Dutchman she has taken down from the wall. As the Dutchman's theme is heard in the orchestra the camera closes in on the portrait, the image dissolving into the sea and sky, then capturing the silhouette of the Dutchman's ship with its tattered sails driven before the wind. Once again a close-up of the portrait, and a cleverly patched transition from the overture into the middle of the Dutchman's monologue ("Wie oft in Meeres tiefsten Schlund") as a voice-over. We soon see him, an unheroic, rather slight figure, pulling on ropes and anxiously bustling about because his crew – incapacitated by fatigue or disease – are little better than corpses lying below decks. At times he is seen to sing, at times his voice is heard only on the soundtrack (as inner soliloquy). When the monologue ends the screen image is again that of the portrait, which Daland snatches from Senta as the Dutchman's torpid crew are heard echoing his despair.

Thenceforth the film moves cleverly between Senta's home life and her fantasy, the transitions marked by such expedients as Senta being transported by what she sees reflected in water or in the flames of the huge stone fireplace. Reality and dream modes are chillingly juxtaposed when in Act III the members of the Dutchman's crew, eventually goaded from their sleeping sickness, rise up like Golems to stare in through the windows at the Norwegians' celebration party for Senta's betrothal. With its low camera angles and chiaroscuro lighting the film owes as much to the 1920s films of Murnau and Pabst as it does to those of Bergman, not least *The Seventh Seal* (1956).

Senta dreams the story through to the bitter end of the Dutchman's departure. As his ship sinks beneath the waves she is seen running out along a jetty; there is no jump but her image dissolves into the foaming sea and the film returns to reality. She awakens from her dream-death lying in front of the cold hearth whose flames had once fired her fantasy. What she has experienced in the dream gives her the courage to change her life.[38] As the harps of the 1860 version are heard in the orchestra, she once again takes down the Dutchman's portrait from the wall, leaves the house and – with the sun catching her smiling face – walks cheerfully out along the beach with new-found resolution.

Herz's aim was to make a real film (i.e., not to film a stage performance but to make a film from Wagner's text and music) that would open up opera "to people who have a horror of it."[39] "We hope," he said, "to have shown Richard Wagner was a born film composer."[40] What it certainly did show was that a visual realization of *Der fliegende Holländer* could remain rooted in the music and communicate the drama affectingly to audiences with very different expectations from those of the 1840s. His approach to the opera – on stage and screen – was the forerunner of many productions by himself and others which have introduced Wagner's own life and the political and social horizons of his time as ingredients in the staging. Herz's emphasis on Senta's dream-world as a key element in the interpretation was widely copied. In 1975 in San Francisco Jean-Pierre Ponnelle offered a variation on this theme, staging the principal events of the opera as dreamt by the Helmsman.

San Francisco, 1975: Jean-Pierre Ponnelle and the Helmsman's dream

Ponnelle's strategy had at least an initial advantage in connecting the sweetheart of the Helmsman's fitful dream with Senta, his captain's daughter. But what to do with him thereafter? Ponnelle leaves a double asleep on the stage, freeing the singer to participate in the "dream" both as his real self and, in a typical Ponnelle gambit, transmuted into Erik, an alter-ego striving to win her against impossible competition from the devastating Dutchman. At the end of the opera the Helmsman awakens hugely relieved from a dream whose final, Hollywood-style image had been that of the Dutchman retreating whence he came with Senta enfolded in his arms. Her would-be suitor rubs his eyes and smiles, doubtless glad for the warning against such a crazy woman.

Once again, realism flows in to annihilate fantasy. Idiomatic unity of time and place was secured by use of a single setting, essentially that of the rear deck of Daland's ship with the wheel downstage center. It transformed itself into the Dutchman's ship by eerie red lighting and the presence in the rigging of cobwebbed, corpse-like figures who were to be imagined as either the Dutchman's victims (former wives?), his crew, or maybe both. In Act II the deck welcomed the girls aboard, each of whom had her own ship's wheel to set a-spinning. Such ingenuities could not disguise the dramaturgical nonsense of framing the central conflict within the specious gambit of a tangential character's infatuation with Senta. (The transmutation of the Helmsman into Erik also flatly ignores the fact that the latter, "a hunter," is explicitly characterized as an outsider to the seafaring community.) The Ponnelle production was restaged in 1979 at the Metropolitan opera, where it caused a fair degree of outrage, although it gave US audiences a relatively easy introduction to production as interpretation – as real theatre and not just a concert in costume.

Kassel 1976: Ulrich Melchinger unmasks a Dr Jekyll of depravity

Back in Kassel (West Germany), in 1976, Ulrich Melchinger went to the furthest frontier of productions seeking to unmask the "redemption" thread as humbug, or in this case the encoding of a sexual perversion. Here the Dutchman was the only sane man in a sea of lunacy and hysteria. In the minds of those fantasizing about him, this respectable Mr Hyde becomes a Dr Jekyll of depravity, "a miscreant, a sinner and a kind of Marquis de Sade, scandalously embodying the sexual repressions of bourgeois society."[41] His monologue was a Black Mass dreamt by the Helmsman, the vestiges of his ship barely visible behind a huge skull and various skeletal figures. All this was a crude but by no means impossible reading of the Dutchman's lines:

> 'Wie oft in Meeres tiefsten Schlund
> stürzt ich voll Sehnsucht mich hinab:
> doch ach! Den Tod, ich fand ihn nicht!"

> [How often into the ocean's deepest cleft
> I hurled myself with deepest longing:
> But ah! I could not die!]

Attended by scantily clad girls, the Dutchman was a satanic priest sacrificing a naked virgin. He killed a cock and poured its blood over her before dispatching his victim with a sword though her vagina. Mass hysteria broke out in Act III and Senta, who had thrown herself between the Dutchman and Erik, was stabbed to death by the latter, the Helmsman suffering a similar fate. Mr. Dutchman–Hyde counted himself fortunate to wash his hands of the whole business. Not surprisingly this production excited even its well-schooled German audience into hysteria and tumult.

5.10 The Dutchman's Act I monologue treated as a Black Mass in Ulrich Melchinger's Kassel production, 1976, with designs by Thomas Richter-Forgách

Bayreuth 1978: Harry Kupfer springs the walls of Senta's prison

Two years later (Bayreuth, 1978) the Dresden-based director Harry Kupfer had an immense success with a "Senta's dream" production that was greatly indebted to Herz's concept. Kupfer's early work had been much influenced by Wieland Wagner ("I was swimming in his wake . . ."), but he had subsequently moved towards the music-theatre approach of Felsenstein and Herz, to which he had added his own ideas about psychological truth in acting and up-to-the-minute scenic technology. Ibsen was again a palpable presence, but with a new infusion of utopian idealism from Ernst Bloch, whose ideas had earlier fed into Klemperer's 1929 staging and into Wieland Wagner's Bayreuth.

Where Herz had chosen Stanislavsky-style realism for Daland's bourgeois milieu, Kupfer and his designer Peter Sykora used constructivist, surrealistic, even expressionist means to move swiftly between Senta's real and fantasy worlds. The walls of her prison flew asunder or reassembled in the twinkling of an eye. Senta was on stage from the very beginning of the overture. The Dutchman's picture suddenly fell off the wall. Clutching it to her, Senta climbed a metal stair to a vantage point by a window from where, in constant view of the audience, she observed the dream-action as it rapidly unfolded. The fantasy Dutchman conjured up by Senta was her dark counterpart. But the chains from which he hung inside the cradling fingers of his vessel were (unlike hers) self-forged; through Senta's power he cast them off and stumbled ashore to tell his tale.

At the beginning of Act II, still clutching the picture of the Dutchman, she stepped down from her platform into the real world of the spinning session. The crucial moment was that of her father's arrival with a stranger, the light streaming in so powerfully from behind him that she could not tell who he might be. As in Heine, she anxiously kept checking the portrait in the hope that *this* could be him. As the stranger moved forward, the red-sailed ship loomed up again and it was the Dutchman who stepped down from its prow to take the stranger's place in the room and in her imagination. Fantasy and reality had become interchangeable. The ship remained, transforming itself into a love-bower, its rigging strewn with flowers.

In Act III Erik's protestations suddenly made it clear to her that her fantasies were a neurosis and that she'd put herself beyond all chance

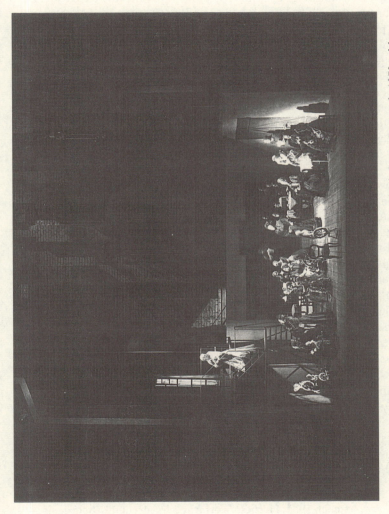

5.11 The opera staged by Harry Kupfer as the dream of a psychotic Senta, Bayreuth, 1978, with designs by Peter Sykora

of future happiness with him. Leaping from her high window she crashed to her death on the ground, still clutching the picture. A small group gathered uncomprehendingly around the body – Erik was the only one to kneel to mourn her. Kupfer explained the tragedy as the triumph of the mundane over the dreams and fantasies that spring up in protest against it. "Whether she jumps from a cliff or from a window is immaterial – the only important thing is that there's no longer any role for her."[42]

Kupfer's reading of Wagner is that the lure of the transcendent – whether the ecstatic swan-paradise of Lohengrin, Tannhäuser's vision of Venus, the song of the Flower-maidens or the celestial choir of the Grail in *Parsifal*, the hope of "one freer than I, the God" in the *Ring* – is always defeated by the irredeemable facticity of the world: "escape from reality is a fiction, in the end reality wins through just like chunks of plaster which crash down on you."[43] Much of the power of Kupfer's production (also captured on video) lay in exceptionally swift transitions between reality and dream modes – and in fostering a Pirandello-like sense of ambiguous suspension between the two modes. At the narrative level the production never lost touch with the music. Modern stage technology and psychological insight had been harnessed to create an extraordinarily powerful dream interpretation.

Kupfer's use of stage-wizardry was a modern means of realizing Wagner's own intentions for the work as a "dramatic ballad," effecting cuts of filmic rapidity between scenes and within scenes, thus (correctly) denying that the work is a developmental drama based on the working out of conflict. The sheer verve of Kupfer's production, its psychological acuity and the magnetic performances by Lisbeth Balslev and Simon Estes made this a staging which deservedly attracted a huge wave of critical approbation.[44] Inevitably the bleakness of Senta's suicide, however logically justified, was not to everyone's liking; but, as Kupfer said, he was not in the business of providing the audience with the "untroubled pleasure of an apparent catharsis."[45]

Munich 1981: Herbert Wernicke's irredeemably bourgeois Dutchman

Herbert Wernicke's 1981 Munich production turned the spotlight back on the Dutchman. This time he was after not just a faithful

5.12 Franz Ferdinand Nentwig as the Dutchman in Act I of
Herbert Wernicke's 1981 production at the Bayerische Staatsoper, Munich

woman but the comforts of bourgeois existence. Daland thus became
an even more prosperous burgher than any yet shown – clad in fur-
collared greatcoat and the inevitable top-hat – with all three acts
being set in his drawing-room. The arrival of the Dutchman's ship
was signaled by its landing ramp thrusting in through a large
doorway to the left, but he sang his monologue as an outsider looking
in through one of the two large window-frames at the rear. The
tragedy sprang from the clash of the two parties' entirely different
expectations of the relationship, Senta wanting only rescue by an outsider, the outsider wanting only to be an insider. Bitterly aware that
the fashionably dressed suitor had nothing in common with the
Dutchman of her dreams, the cry of "Treu bis zum Tod" was despair-
ingly sworn only to the image in her picture before she takes hold of
Erik's hunting knife and stabs herself. The Dutchman's response was
to drop anchor in his fireside chair.

This production, of course, created quite a storm (of which, incidentally there was apparently no visible sign in the staging, nor of the
sea). Its central flaw was its attempt to swim so determinedly against

the musical and verbal characterization of the Dutchman by insisting that this was a man aspiring to nothing better than the respectability of a bourgeois marriage and the deep, deep peace of the marital bed. If this could be construed as one form of the "death" for which the tormented navigator is longing, it is surely the last kind of redemption that Wagner had in mind. No question that there was a part of the composer that longed to throw off the Faustian torment of a creator's life, but at no period would he have done so for any kind of petty bourgeois existence – indeed he fought continually against Minna's wish that he renounce his creative ambitions and settle down to that kind of security. Wernicke was fighting both the essential substance of the opera and its projection of its creator's personality.

Bregenz 1989: David Pountney puts the Dutchman to sea without a ship

The aim of Wagner and the early stage directors had been to bring the wind and the waves into the theatre. They might have felt that their problem could finally be solved by taking the opera out into the elements on the "floating" stage, first built in 1948 in Bregenz at the eastern end of Lake Constance. In 1973 this was attempted in a full "ships and all" style. Its aesthetic and practical limitations were exposed in a later, anti-naturalistic, production in 1989 by David Pountney, with designs by Stefanos Lazaridis. By now the theatre had been rebuilt as a shore-based classical amphitheatre seating 4397 and looking west across a strip of water to an enlarged *Seebühne* (lakestage) of some 3600 square meters with the lake and sky beyond.

The Pountney/Lazaridis staging had a quite specific nineteenth-century industrial resonance. But its significance, paradoxically, lay in its anti-naturalistic response to the beautiful setting. Not for Pountney the hubris of imagining that nature would consent to dance to the tune of Wagner's drama. In Pountney's own words, the first thing he knew was that "as it's set on water, the one thing we can't have is ships of any kind. If the water is playing a naturalistic part in the drama it would constantly contradict you. It would either be calm when it's meant to be stormy, or stormy when it's meant to be calm."[46]

Pountney's response to the huge stage and the possibility of creating satellite "islands" around it was to abjure any attempt at close-encounter relationships between the characters, and to emphasize their tragic isolation from one other by giving each a distinctive space.

5.13 Satanic mills for *Der fliegende Holländer* on the floating stage at Bregenz on Lake Constance, 1989. Designs by Stefanos Lazaridis, production by David Pountney

The watery ambiance was treated as an image of the subconscious. Senta was the spirit of the lake, symbol of life emerging from the waters and returning to them at the end. "Her world," says Pountney," was dreamlike, always associated with the water." She floated into view during the overture, draped in a white evening dress on a chaise-longue reading in her book the story of the Flying Dutchman (an idea also used in Herz's film). In Act II of Pountney's continuous version the metallic grid floor of Daland's house (in effect more of an industrial complex than a home) rises up from under the water to beach Senta's chaise-longue and her floating grand piano on the terra firma of her father's world of capitalist fantasy. But not quite terra firma, for the water is always lapping at her feet and at the end of her Ballad she falls to her knees in it.

"She was," says Pountney, "constantly in this rather unstable state – living on the edge of a firm grip on reality." The only character who had this grip was Erik who had a dry little island all to himself, complete with grass, flowers and some real live ducks. The main stage was Daland's domain with its spinning jennies and chrome-plated engine-room machinery. The spinning girls themselves were factory hands who challenged Mary's orders by turning revolutionary and brandishing red flags. Daland was a man more than happy to barter his daughter as bride. To initiate the betrothal celebrations he threw a great lever lighting up the dark Satanic mills with festoons of fairy lights and during the dancing he laid on a firework display over the lake.

For the Dutchman, no ship but a cube-like three-storey tenement block that remained shrouded in black silk until his arrival. Behind its bare window-openings fluttered red curtains, maybe a reminiscence of the "red sails" of the Dutchman's mythical vessel. The front of the structure hinged up to reveal a desert inside. In the love-duet Senta tried to bring light and warmth by kindling a fire in the building. In the third act the Dutchman's crew appeared at the windows while the structure revolved on a central axis. At the very end, with the help of courageous doubles, Senta ran to the top of the thirty-meter-high lighthouse that had dominated the rear of the stage and hurled herself down into the water. The apotheosis was suggested by a cone of green laser-light projected up into the infinity of the night sky.[47]

The unseen orchestra, conducted by Ulf Schirmer, played in a space beneath the stage, its amplified sound following the singers around the stage from loudspeakers built into the set, and from there also directed out across the water to the audience in the amphitheatre.

Because of the large number of consecutive festival performances the principal roles were multi-cast, Robert Hale's Dutchman and Rebecca Blankenship's Senta outstanding among them.

Doubtless the most ambitious large-scale staging of the opera ever attempted, the production was a great critical success. The not-easily-impressed London critic Max Loppert wrote that it "counts high among the most thrilling and dazzling pieces of lyric-theatre spectacle of my entire opera-going experience." (*Financial Times*, 7 August 1989). The opera had been exposed to the very elements from which it had sprung (albeit in the domesticated locale of an inland lake) and survived with its vigor undiminished, Pountney and Lazaridis not deploying spectacle for its own sake but using it for a richly imaginative reinterpretation.

The voyage in retrospect

Some general patterns of change in interpretation are discernible. Between Wagner's death and 1914 most performances took the work at face value and presented its three-act form. The huge improvements in stage technology following the introduction of electric lighting in the 1880s made it easier to realize Wagner's Romantic naturalism. Unexpectedly it also helped to undermine it. Effects that had worked well enough in the soft glow of gaslight were exposed under electric lighting as clumsy artifice. The well-lit arrival and departure of dummy-ships manned by actors only emphasized discrepancies in scale and perspective between the human figures and the ship-models; waves and storm-driven clouds on painted flats and drops were unmasked as painterly fancy not the faithful representations of nature they purported to be. At Bayreuth, Cosima continued along this route with her scrupulously Norwegian staging of 1901. Elsewhere, those of the younger generation who were caught up in the theatre revolution that had taken wing in the 1890s (Appia, Craig, *et al.*) were weaning opera away from the old picturesque aesthetic, concentrating the visual aspect into its essentials and insisting on psychological and dramatic truth. These were the aims of Mahler and his designer Alfred Roller in Vienna, and they carried through into the *Holländer* produced there in 1913, six years after Mahler's departure and two years after his death. It was, however, not until Klemperer's Krolloper production of 1929 that the traditional way of staging the opera was seriously challenged.

After the Second World War this critical approach was developed in the name of music-theatre, and from it sprang new questions about what the characters in the opera had meant to Wagner, and what they could most powerfully mean to a generation with very different ideas about the relationship between men, women, and society, and for whom notions of "redemption" and "transfiguration" were either deeply suspect or meaningless. Thus the trend was to relocate the legend in the Ibsenesque drawing-room, to color the Norwegian fisher-folk as a bourgeois community cramping to the woman of the future as much as to the Promethean artist – or even as workers exploited by the capitalist Daland.

Utopian socialism could see Senta putting the opera behind her and walking off into a better future, symbolized by sunrise over the seashore, or hand-in-hand with her man gazing up at the splendor of the Aurora Borealis. To a new age, born of Freud and surrealism and saturated with the realistic aesthetic of film, the balladesque shifts between irrational longings and mundanity could best be made comprehensible by a variety of "dream" strategies, usually moving between the tangible reality of Daland's world and the escapist dreams of his daughter. Senta's progress from saving angel to sacrificial victim has done no more than make explicit what had been implicit all along, although it needed an awakened conscience about man's immemorial subjection of women before this could be safely shown. Maybe the time has now come to tip the Dutchman from his easy-chair and send him off again on his travels. There is far too much of Wagner's own restless spirit in his soul for him to be allowed early retirement. It is only surprising that, so far as I am aware, producers who have happily given us Wagner-Wotan and Wagner-Sachs have yet to project the composer directly into the figure of his Flying Dutchman.

6 Der fliegende Holländer
in performance

DAVID BRECKBILL

Wagner did not live to complete a thorough revision of *Der fliegende Holländer*, even though at the end of his life he wanted to sharpen its dramatic focus, make it less noisy and repetitive (*CWD*, 8 September 1881), and allow numerous features of its writing to profit from the skills he had gained in a lifetime of honing his craft. In the absence of such a facelift, assurances from Wagner (and subsequent Wagnerians) have failed to convince all observers that the *Holländer* fits entirely comfortably into the canon of true Wagnerian music dramas (see Chapter 7). In no respect is this awkwardness more apparent than in the regular application to the *Holländer* of a long-standing Wagnerian performance style developed primarily for the needs of the later works. This chapter aims to provide a survey of the performance history of the *Holländer* by describing and evaluating three leading musical approaches to the work; to examine several important passages against the background of both Wagner's ambiguous instructions and well-entrenched traditions of interpretation; and to propose a potentially productive new perspective on the performance and understanding of the musical component of this drama.

The three approaches I wish to identify developed in stages over the course of the *Holländer's* performance history. The first has its roots in the nineteenth century, when, in the wake of the runaway popularity of Wagner's subsequent operas, *Tannhäuser* and *Lohengrin*, *Der fliegende Holländer* also became a repertoire work (by the end of the century it was generally the third-most-performed opera in Wagner's output). The Bayreuth production of 1901, a painstaking and thoroughly considered effort through which Cosima Wagner aimed to refashion the *Holländer* as a music drama, inaugurated the second treatment of the opera, and was extremely influential for increasing the prestige of the work. But the view it proposed, which became entrenched through the hardening of the Wagner canon, inevitably invited a reaction that came in the form of the Berlin Krolloper's 1929 production. This third approach, which used the brash ending and scoring of the original version, downplayed the *Holländer*'s connections to the later Wagnerian canon, and insisted rather on the natural energy of the score as a characteristic virtue. Since then (and particularly since Wieland Wagner's Bayreuth production of 1959, a still more influential attempt to perceive the essence of the work through the original version), these three approaches to *Der fliegende Holländer* – as repertoire opera, music drama, and early Wagner opera – have alternated and intermingled freely. The continued popularity of the work suggests that each approach contains its share of validity.

1

Wagner's own account of the initial Dresden production remains the most colorful and informed comment on the subject (*ML*, 241–42, written nearly a quarter-century after the event). The picture Wagner paints of the famous and inspirational prima donna, Wilhelmine Schröder-Devrient, absorbed in learning her new role from the young composer himself, sinking herself into it as a means of turning turbulence in her love life to artistic account, and then, when faced with a physically unsuitable Dutchman, only being able to summon the requisite emotion when singing to her new flame, planted in a prominent location in the stalls – all this sounds like a tale improved by the telling. But Wagner's letters of the time at least confirm the detailed rehearsals. Writing to his friend the painter Ernst Benedikt Kietz, he insisted that his collaboration with Schröder-Devrient "was extremely notable; a whole book could be written about our work on Senta" (6 April 1843; *SB*, vol. 2, 228–29). One can only regret that no early equivalent of Heinrich Porges, who later chronicled preparations for the *Ring* at Bayreuth, was on hand to report on the sessions between Wagner and Schröder-Devrient, since their apparently time-consuming rehearsals (the singer did not learn new roles easily) undoubtedly weighed many shades of expression and meaning in the role. The specifics of Wagner's achievement with so powerful and emotional an artist must, alas, remain a source of speculation. Interestingly, none of his comments on Schröder-Devrient's performance mentions a quirk about which Berlioz complained when he saw the production, namely her tendency to interject spoken comments and asides.[1]

Wagner afterwards voiced his dissatisfaction with the first *Holländer* production,[2] which survived for only four performances; but at the time he was enthusiastic, and portrayed it as a success (see the letters included in Appendix B). His pleasure at having the opera praised by Louis Spohr, who assembled a locally popular and accomplished cast for a production at Kassel just a few months after the Dresden première, recurred as a frequent leitmotif in subsequent letters of 1843 (and persisted throughout his life – see *CWD*, 4 April 1879). Although he was dissatisfied with the arrangements for the Berlin première in January 1844 (he himself conducted the first two performances), this did not prevent his taking pleasure in the enthusiasm and achievement of that cast (*ML*, 262–63). Indeed, he cited that achievement as a selling point when corresponding with Johann Kittl (31 January 1844; *SB*, vol. 2, 360) in an unsuccessful attempt to bring about a production at Prague, where the *Holländer* ultimately did not appear until 1856.

The opera did not enter the standard German operatic repertoire with a dense flurry of new productions, as was the case with *Tannhäuser* and *Lohengrin* in the early to mid-1850s. *Holländer* arrived at most theatres in the wake of (or even well after) those more popular operas, and thus found a home because of its composer's fame rather than primarily for its own virtues. Exceptionally, it was the first Wagner opera performed in England: the 1870 performance at Drury Lane, conducted by Luigi Arditi and with Charles Santley in the title role, was sung in Italian (it would be another seven years before it received its Italian première at Bologna). This was followed by an 1876 production in English under the direction of Carl Rosa, and finally by the first performance in German, a part of the Pollini season of Wagner at Drury Lane in 1882. The musical side of this production was reportedly excellent, with Hans Richter conducting a cast headed by Rosa Sucher and Eugen Gura, but scenically it nearly ended in catastrophe. Sucher noticed at the last moment that the area into which she was to throw herself when leaping from the cliff had been left open to the cellar beneath the stage (a contretemps attributable to the language barrier between director and stagehands); despite Richter's furious gestures from the podium, she exited into the wings rather than sacrifice her life for dramatic effect.[3]

A sudden spate of productions brought *Holländer* to the American stage in Italian (Philadelphia, 1876), English (New York, 1877), and German (New York, 1877). The second of these was presented at the Academy of Music in New York by the opera company of Clara Louise Kellogg, who portrayed Senta. Kellogg's memoirs document one of the (apparently) few instances in which Wagner's essay "Remarks on the Performance of the Opera *Der fliegende Holländer*" (hereafter "Remarks"; translation given in Appendix C) was consulted by performers. Kellogg and her conductor could make nothing of how the singers were meant to act during the music following Senta's and the Dutchman's first glimpse of one another, and moreover could find no one who had seen the opera in Germany for guidance. Thus they were reassured to find that Wagner's pamphlet encouraged them to remain absolutely motionless during that passage (although this was apparently an unprecedented demand on their concentration as actors).[4] A German production followed in New York within the year, but the first Metropolitan Opera performance did not occur until 1889 (the *Holländer* was the last of Wagner's operas to be produced there save *Parsifal*, which received its controversial Met première in 1903). It was the opera chosen for the opening night of the 1889–90 season, when it featured Theodor Reichmann (the first Amfortas and a Vienna favorite) in the title role, but one suspects that it was added to the repertoire primarily so that it could fill its place in the complete cycle of Wagner's operas from *Rienzi* to *Götterdämmerung* being presented that season. Thereafter the *Holländer*'s Met career was hardly hardy; it received a mere twenty-four performances in six seasons through early 1908, and was not in the repertoire again until 1930, when Friedrich Schorr's classic portrayal of the title role (and later Kirsten Flagstad's Senta) gave it a new lease on life during four seasons in the 1930s. Another fine Dutchman, Hans Hotter, was the motivation for a new production in the 1950–51 season, but this was not revived until 1960, when the famous Senta–Dutchman team of Leonie Rysanek and George London, which had triumphed at Bayreuth in 1959, made the work a greater staple in the 1960s. In short, the *Holländer*'s career as a repertoire opera, in which a star in one or both of the two leading roles was a main criterion both for performance and for success, made it something of a weak link in the Wagner canon. Not until the late 1970s, when new production emphases came to the fore (see Chapter 5), did the *Holländer* gain wide acceptance for its own merits rather than on the basis of its composer's fame.

Operas understood as repertoire works were frequently subjected to cutting. Although today we are rarely subjected to the drastic abridgements once customary in Wagner's later works, some of those which have become customary in *Holländer* show little sign of falling into disuse, especially in the theatre. From a strictly musical perspective these cuts are rarely improvements. In the Dutchman–Daland duet in Act I, for example, Wagner's design, which allows the reprise of Daland's "Gepriesen seid, des Sturmes Gewalten" to achieve a stretto-like effect when heard after its first, more balanced presentation, is foiled by the standard cut which allows only the stretto version to be heard. The trio just after the entrance of the Dutchman in Act III is often abbreviated in a similar way. The persistence with which these cuts continue to be adopted does suggest, however, that Wagner's music does not match conductors' or directors' sense of ideal dramatic pacing.

Another passage often abridged is the final trio of Act II (several different abbreviations have been proposed here); less frequent nowadays are cuts in Erik's Cavatina "Willst jenes Tag's" and the choral scene in Act III. Wagner himself permitted cuts in this latter passage when discussing the first Weimar production with Franz Liszt, who led it (letter of 3 March 1853; *SB*, vol. 5, 211), and even though it seems that Wagner reinstated all generally cut material when he oversaw the Munich revival in 1864, cuts in that scene continued to be heavy throughout the nineteenth century. Thus a reviewer of the 1901 Bayreuth production observed that the performance of the choral scene "offer[ed] quite unexpected beauty in passages that are otherwise mostly cut."[5] Further cuts are likely to have been introduced over the years. (In his "Remarks," Wagner insisted that the orchestral passage following Daland's aria in Act II "must be played in its entirety," demonstrating a fear that it would be seen as superfluous by some performers.)

A glimpse of the *Holländer* as an old-style repertoire opera can be found in a recording of the 1936 performance from the Teatro Colón in Buenos Aires (released in 1992 by Pearl). Conducted with feverish haste by Fritz Busch, including one or another version of all the documented cuts mentioned here, and featuring a German-singing cast backed by a Spanish-singing chorus, this account reveals how the opera sounds when painted with a broad brush, relying on memorable moments for its effectiveness rather than presenting a considered exposition of the drama. In such an environment, exaggerated temperament is all-important, so that Marjorie Lawrence's unusually energetic interjections as Senta during the Spinning Chorus are perhaps less her own preferred reading than one she felt was demanded by the circumstances. On the other hand, the little-remembered journeyman Fred Destal as the Dutchman capitalizes on the advantages of observing the *mezza voce* prescribed for "Wie aus der Ferne" in the Act II duet. By murmuring the beginning of this passage quietly, he effectively marks it out as an important moment within this otherwise scrappy and aggressive performance.

The most "operatic" commercial recording of the *Holländer* features the already mentioned Senta–Dutchman duo of the late 1950s and 1960s: Leonie Rysanek and George London, under the direction of Antal Dorati. Although of lasting value on numerous counts, this performance is especially memorable for Rysanek's great moments. Her final cry of "Preis deinen Engel und sein Gebot! Hier steh ich, treu dir bis zum Tod!," detained and made unabashedly emphatic and exalted, seems to be the crux of her conception of the role, a grand clarification of the character. Other singers may match her intensity here, but her floating sound and utter confidence add a further, unique dimension. (By comparison, her strengths seem hemmed in by the musical and dramatic approach of Wieland Wagner and Wolfgang Sawallisch in the 1959 Bayreuth production.) *Der fliegende Holländer* can still function as a vehicle for fine singers, if they are given latitude to bring their own perceptions into play. But in the course of the twentieth century other approaches to the work have generally taken precedence: those treating it as "music drama" or as a work of raw, youthful vitality.

2

Since it had been one of Wagner's ambitions to present model productions of his works from *Holländer* on at Bayreuth, this desire was inherited by his widow Cosima as well when she began to look to the future after a period of intense mourning following Wagner's death on 13 February 1883. Early in her planning – probably as early as autumn 1883 – she envisioned an overly ambitious schedule for the future of the Festival according to which the repertoire was to be cumulatively augmented by an opera a year through 1889, when all the canonical works save *Die Meistersinger* would be performed in a single season.[6] (In the end, during Cosima's tenure as head of the

Festival through the summer of 1906, no more than six works – counting the *Ring* as four – were heard at Bayreuth in a single year.) Of interest for our purposes is the fact that *Holländer* appeared so early in her plans (it was to be preceded only by the existing *Parsifal* production and *Tristan und Isolde*). Its prominence at this initial stage can probably be explained by Cosima's special love for the work, which had deep personal resonances for her, since she understood herself as the Senta who had rescued Wagner from life's turmoil. As events were to unfold, however, Wagner's earlier "Romantic operas" (reconceived as music dramas) were to be among the last, not the first, of Cosima's model productions. *Tristan* appeared in 1886, *Meistersinger* in 1888, *Tannhäuser* in 1891, *Lohengrin* in 1894, a restaging of the *Ring* in 1896, and finally it was the *Holländer*'s turn in 1901, a full quarter-century after the opening of the Festival Theatre.

The means available for transforming the *Holländer* into a music drama were at first glance not very extensive. The most remarkable change was Cosima's decision to present the work in a single act, which corresponded to the composer's original intention even though it was never realized in any of the productions he supervised. The final product, with scene changes during orchestral transitions, resembled *Das Rheingold* in length and format. From a textual standpoint, Cosima generally settled on the latest versions of variants in the direction of Wagner's mature style: thus the Tristanesque redemption music at the end of the overture and opera (composed in 1860) was *de rigueur*, as were numerous passages in which the original orchestrations had been toned down. The text she employed was that found in the Weingartner-edited Fürstner score published in 1896 for which she had been a consultant,[7] but in the years leading up to 1901 she personally consulted all relevant scores and parts she could locate in an effort to base her production on a text she considered authoritative.

An insight into the level of detail Cosima addressed may be derived from the recordings of Senta's Ballad made by Emmy Destinn, who was in her early twenties and just beginning to be known on leading stages when she performed the role at Bayreuth in 1901–02. In the standard version of Senta's dreamy introduction to the Ballad , the syllables sung in the third phrase are (rather implausibly) "Ho-ho-hoe." Isolde Vetter's edition of the 1841 score (in the new *Sämtliche Werke* published by Schott) gives instead the syllables "Ho-jo-hoe." Interestingly, in her two 1906 recordings of the Ballad for Odeon and

G&T (the Gramophone and Typewriter Company, Ltd.), Destinn adopts the 1841 reading of this third phrase – the only recordings from the acoustical era to do so (except for Destinn's 1911 Odeon recording, which blunts this point by additionally reversing the first two syllables of both the first two phrases). It is tempting to attribute this variant to Cosima's editorial work.

Cosima's correspondence gives rise to speculation as to whether she attempted to finesse the text even further in the direction of music drama. In a letter of 2 August 1900, while attempting to induce Ernest van Dyck (a celebrated Bayreuth Parsifal) to study the role of Erik for the forthcoming production, she admits that the tessitura of the role is too high for him, but proposes having him sing it with a downward transposition, "particularly since permission for this has been granted in the 'Remarks'."[8] Wagner's comments in that essay (see Appendix C) do not specifically mention transposition, but Cosima's reverence for Wagner's text did not permit her to rewrite the vocal line in order to avoid high notes, and so transposition became her preferred option (Einhard Luther reports that in 1901 Cosima's eventual Erik, Ernst Kraus, transposed "Willst jenes Tag's" down a semitone, a modification which brought the upper reaches of the role into Kraus's range).[9] Cosima's practice may have served as precedent for the transposition, now amounting to a whole tone, heard in the 1942 Bayreuth production. Again in this case the transposition may not have been ideologically motivated, since Franz Völker's voice seems to be in an especially tired and overused condition. Nevertheless, it seems clear that in old Bayreuth the transposition of the Cavatina was a necessary practicality given the sort of singers available, and that this practice was justified as a preemptive defense against the misconceptions of Erik about which Wagner warned in "Remarks."

When it came to vocal ornamentation, however, Cosima seems to have been more willing to wield the red pen. In another letter from 1900, this one to the conductor of the production, Felix Mottl, she inquired: "Do you know on what occasion Erik's cadenza was removed? Did Bülow tell you? I do not remember whether Schnorr sang it [at the Munich performance in July 1865]."[10] The first question of course implies that Wagner himself had suppressed the cadenza in an actual production (i.e., more tangibly than he did in the "Remarks"). In any case, Cosima's willingness to consider these alternatives was most likely an attempt to resist the "operatic" tendencies of the *Holländer*, or at least to provide a considered riposte to traditional performances of the work. In the aforementioned 1942 recording of the 1939–42 Bayreuth production (which undoubtedly shows the music drama treatment at a more established stage), Völker sings a heavily abbreviated cadenza in his transposed Cavatina, and Ludwig Hofmann as Daland cuts most of the cadenza in the middle of "Mögst du, mein Kind" (as he does in a recorded excerpt from a performance in the 1939 season – see below). It must be admitted that the recorded evidence from the singers cast as Erik and Daland in 1901–02 does not support any suspicion that these changes were introduced at that time.[11] But as the music drama approach to the *Holländer* gained acceptance, non-Bayreuth singers also occasionally abbreviated these cadenzas (as in Peter Anders's 1939 Telefunken recording of "Willst jenes Tag's").

Not only did the 1901 production consider or adopt the least "operatic" textual alternatives as a means of remaking the *Holländer* into a music drama, but the performance approach, too, was calculated to transform the work into something more profound and idealistic than emerged in most productions of the time. Toward this end Cosima relied on the thorough realization of details. For example, in the letter to Felix Mottl already cited, we find her remarking: "Just now I'm working through Erik with Ernst Kraus . . . On this occasion Kniese [Julius Kniese, Cosima's primary musical assistant] drew my attention to the orchestral accompaniment of the 'Dream' and opined that this delicate nuancing of presentation has never yet been realized. I guaranteed him that under your leadership it happens." And Otto Neitzel praised Destinn's behavior as Senta when first glimpsing the Dutchman: "She possessed the good taste – which can never be praised highly enough – to spare us the usual prima donna's scream, shrill like a locomotive whistle. Her cry remained stuck in her throat, as though she believed she had seen a ghost."[12]

For Cosima there were no minor roles. Anything that could disturb the overall dramatic effect was to be avoided, and so she took uncommon care to match the talents of her singers to the most appropriate roles.[13] Recorded evidence suggests that the inverse assertion, that certain roles demand certain characteristics, seems to have been betrayed in *Holländer* only by Cosima's casting of Daland. The singers who alternated in that role in 1902, Max Lohfing and Paul Knüpfer, both left recordings of excerpts from it. On the basis of his recording of the Act I duet with Cornelis Bronsgeest as the

Dutchman, it is difficult to imagine that Lohfing was ever drilled to within an inch of his life in this role – his rhythms are coarse, his sound tubby and folkish. By contrast, Knüpfer excelled in "singing" roles (Meyerbeer, Verdi) as well as Wagner during his long career in Berlin, and his 1915 recording of "Mögst du, mein Kind" is in a different league from Lohfing's where vocal and expressive sophistication is concerned: for example, the last syllables of "fernen, weiten Reisen" and "Vaterland verwiesen" are nicely tapered, while the cadenza is dispatched with ease and elegance, if little apparent interest. Indeed, the whole reading seems restrained and smooth in a way at odds with the perspective Lohfing brings to the part. The Dutchmen are less different. Cosima was quite shattered by the emotional intensity her protégé Anton van Rooy brought to the role.[14] The only recorded memento of his impersonation, a 1906 Edison cylinder of "Nur eine Hoffnung," shows the vociferous end of his expressive range. Although his performance is vocally raw in places, the intensification of vibrato for the first word of the final phrase, "Nimm mich auf!," prepares the final ascending leap while also enriching the point of the utterance (most singers give primary attention to the high note). Theodor Bertram offers similar visceral force but his rhythms are less tightly sprung, and thus he makes a more generalized effect than van Rooy. Bertram made recordings of four passages from the role, including four separate versions of "Wie aus der Ferne." All are deeply felt and the words are lived in each, but his precipitous vocal decline (his imposing sound often turns hollow and becomes infected with wobble, especially at softer dynamic levels), exacerbated by *Trunksucht* after the death of his wife in 1905, combines with his vague rhythms to make a lugubrious impression in some of the recordings, particularly in "Weit komm ich her."

Along with van Rooy, Czech soprano Emmy Destinn was the great star of Cosima's production, the only Senta at the ten performances spread over successive festivals. A British critic described her Senta in 1913 as "singing with great vocal beauty as well as dramatic intensity,"[15] and that can stand as the quintessential review of Destinn in this role. Her three recordings of the Ballad show more of the intensity than of the vocal beauty, although the clarity and focus of her sound are qualities not conspicuous in the work of her German contemporaries. Ernst Kraus alternated as Erik in both 1901 and 1902; his 1911 recording of the Act II duet with Melanie Kurt shows him inflecting his dry, nasal, often roughly used voice rather more than on some occasions.[16] Daland apart, these were all in all typical Bayreuth casts for the period in that they favored distinctive views of each role over homogeneous vocal attributes.

These first performances to view the *Holländer* as a music drama can be recovered only incompletely because of our inability to recall the work of their conductor, Felix Mottl – and responsibility for much of the "music drama" approach must stem from the podium. Apart from a modified, critically unsuccessful revival of this production in the war-shortened festival of 1914,[17] which under Siegfried Wagner's baton seemed complacent but flowing, the next Bayreuth performance of the *Holländer* took place in 1939 in a production that ran for four consecutive summers. Recordings show that the music drama approach was well enshrined as a performance style (maintaining the textual changes already mentioned). Conductor Karl Elmendorff was the mainstay of Bayreuth between 1927 and 1942 while various stars – Arturo Toscanini, Wilhelm Furtwängler, and Richard Strauss – came and went. Elmendorff's conducting continues the tradition of Bayreuth's long-time *Parsifal* guru Karl Muck by fashioning continuity and coherence with an exceptional ear for a seamless stream of sound and pacing. Although there's much to admire in his abridged Columbia recordings of *Tristan und Isolde* (1928) and *Tannhäuser* (1930), it could well be argued that his finest surviving memento is a snippet from the 5 August 1939 Bayreuth performance of the *Holländer*, which begins during Daland's aria in Act II and continues into the early pages of Act III. The billowing flow as the first great climax of the Senta–Dutchman duet unfolds is inexorable; Elmendorff's approach in this passage makes explicit the kinship of "Versank ich jetzt" and "O sink' hernieder" in Act II of *Tristan*. He also offers considerable character in the heavy phrasing and tempo of the Sailors' Chorus. This manifestation of controversially heavy "Bayreuth tempi" seems justified due to Elmendorff's effective integration of it into its surroundings; further, he succeeds in making it sound purposefully weighty, not merely turgid.[18]

A more widely available recording that promotes the music drama approach is under the direction of Hans Knappertsbusch, made at the first performance of the *Holländer* at the 1955 Bayreuth Festival. (A commercial recording was made by Decca in the course of the same festival, but it is conducted by Joseph Keilberth, who led most of the performances; the singers generally seem to prefer Keilberth's more vigorous tempi.) Knappertsbusch's pacing is consistently slower than Elmendorff's when heard in isolation, sometimes breathtakingly so: for example, Knappertsbusch quashes any sense of organic momentum at Daland's entrance at the end of Act II. But the Bayreuth sense of seamless continuity and sonority is usually in evidence, and Knappertsbusch generally ensures tension by giving rhythmic integrity to notes often treated as passagework (as in the Dutchman's opening monologue). Ponderous if sometimes flowing tempi also characterize later recordings led by Herbert von Karajan (1981–83) and James Levine (1994). Slow tempi and seamless textures are the chief musical features of the music drama approach, with results that often do not show the work to its best advantage.

3

Once the possibility of viewing the *Holländer* as a music drama took root, the canon of Wagner's works attained its definitive form. *Rienzi*, which everyone recognized as ineligible for performance in the Festival Theatre, became even more of a rarity in the years just after the first Bayreuth *Holländer* production. Although after 1914 Bayreuth did not present the *Holländer* again until 1939, the orthodoxy that perceived the work as part of the Wagner canon was well entrenched when the Krolloper in Berlin staged it in January 1929, employing the original scoring (much brassier, for example, in the Dutchman's "Erfahre das Geschick" at the end of the opera) and the original, blunt endings of both overture and opera. Otto Klemperer, the conductor of this production, made a recording of the opera in 1968 in which the endings follow the revised version until the final, transfigured statement of the redemption theme is to appear, upon which he substitutes some loud tonic chords that do not precisely correspond to those in the original version. It seems likely that this synthesis postdates the 1929 production; Klemperer appears to have used or at least to have worked from the score Wagner himself used for the 1844 Berlin première.[19] Although the radical staging was the most controversial aspect of the production (see Chapter 5), the decision to use the original scoring and endings did not go uncontested. Indeed, "the dramaturg of the Krolloper had . . . to justify [the use of the original ending] to the Prussian parliament."[20] The use of the original was selective, however: since the music drama approach had appropriated the one-act layout, Klemperer opted for the traditional three-act division.[21]

Three decades later came a more influential production along the same lines. Wieland Wagner's 1959 Bayreuth production reverted quite thoroughly to the original score for the first time at Bayreuth (while still incorporating the standard cuts in the trios of Acts II and III). The most interventionist touch was the omission of the orchestral introductions to Acts II and III, which duplicate material from the ends of the previous acts (like Klemperer, Wieland Wagner preferred the three-act division). As mentioned in Chapter 3, these passages (especially the first one), when heard as interludes in a one-act performance, demonstrate Wagner's early mastery of the "art of transition." But Wieland apparently found this hint of Wagner's later style incompatible with his desire to demythologize the *Holländer*. Consequently, he began Act II directly with the Spinning Chorus and Act III with the Chorus of the Norwegian Sailors. Wieland's conductor, Wolfgang Sawallisch, made several other adjustments as well: he omitted the two measures of orchestral transition at the end of Erik's Cavatina, allowed the chorus to crescendo into Senta's outburst ("Ich sei's, die dich durch ihre Treu' erlöse!") at the end of the Ballad (turning to expressive account a notational inconsistency in the original manuscript), and followed the autograph and the early Meser full score in giving Erik an extra "Senta!" at his entrance in Act II.[22] At some point after Anja Silja joined the cast as Senta in 1960 another feature of the original score was reinstated: the Act II Ballad was sung in A minor rather than in the G-minor transposition (favored by Leonie Rysanek in 1959) which Wagner had authorized for Schröder-Devrient's convenience and then carried over into the published scores. The 1961 Sawallisch recording (Philips) is thus of considerable interest as the only commercial recording to adopt this authoritative textual option. Senta's recapitulation of the redemption theme just before the Dutchman appears in the doorway later in the act was originally in C major to correspond with its key in the Ballad; unfortunately, Sawallisch and Silja neglect to transpose this back from the published B-flat major. Even so, and despite the cuts, this is the recording that most thoroughly incorporates the original 1841 readings.

From the standpoint of performance style, however, the recording which most fully realizes the alternative view provided by the earlier version is a later Philips recording (released both as a sound-only version and on video formats) made in 1985, in the final season of Harry Kupfer's Bayreuth production first unveiled in 1978. Conductor Woldemar Nelsson suffuses the score with highly charged intensity, giving the impression of brisk tempi (even where they are no faster than usual). Most of the leading cast members reinforce this approach with vibrant tone and delivery; the exception, Simon Estes as the Dutchman, has a powerful voice but lacks the incisiveness of rhythm and diction that would make his portrayal more multidimensional. Although some regard Estes's performance as a "pretty significant vacuum" in an otherwise laudatory recording,[23] the Nelsson account seems more consistently responsive to the dramatic issues of the opera as a whole than any other in my experience. At the beginning of Act I (to cite just one example) the way in which Nelsson causes the orchestral echoes of the sailors' three-note cries of "Hallojo!" to crowd in on each other captures the feeling of the stormy setting and the sailors' bustling activity. (For an extreme contrast, hear Klemperer's deliberate, desiccated treatment of the passage.) Nelsson's performance offers many similar telling dramatic gestures, offering suggestive opportunities for those who wish to project a different conception of the drama.

4

By the time Wagner began editing the *Holländer* score for publication during the first half of 1844 he had conducted the opera not only in its four performances in Dresden in early 1843 but also the general rehearsal and first two performances of the Berlin production almost exactly a year later. These experiences with the work in performance must have influenced some of the variants and alterations first introduced in the 1844 Meser vocal score and the lithographed orchestral score(s) issued a year later. The differences in detail between these two published editions, and in turn between them and the original manuscript, are quite extensive.[24] A few of them have already been mentioned, but a particularly obvious one is the inclusion of metronome markings in the vocal score but not in the full score. This discrepancy is surprising given the order in which these scores were published, but in any case the metronome markings contained in the vocal score have become a standard feature of most subsequent editions, including the Fürstner edition by Felix Weingartner. Their inclusion there shows that Weingartner and the Wahnfried establishment knew (or believed) them to stem from Wagner himself. (Since they appear to have been determined in 1844, they do not appear in the 1841 score published in the new *Sämtliche Werke*.)

When considered against the background of performing traditions that have grown up around the *Holländer*, some of these metronome markings seem implausible. They sometimes occupy a rather narrow range of practically imperceptible gradations – one comes to feel at times that Wagner has merely adjusted the metronome marking a notch or two to suggest changes in tempo rather than carefully determining the tempo he really desires. At other spots, the tempi represent a challenge of some sort: few conductors, for example, attempt (and even fewer achieve) so precipitous a tempo as Wagner's prescribed ♩ = 100 in the maidens' second chorus of Act II ("Das Schiffsvolk kommt," end of No. 4). Other tempi seem surprisingly slow – in the Act II duet, ♩ = 88 for the Dutchman's "Du könntest dich für ewig mir ergeben" and ♩ = 56 for Senta's "Wer du auch sei'st" are both below, sometimes well below, the tempi traditionally adopted. On the other hand, ♩ = 112 is a very accurate approximation of traditional tempo for Daland's "Mögst du, mein Kind."

Two of the most famous passages of the opera, passages which contain musical material central to our understanding of the nature of the work, bear metronome markings that confound and contradict traditional practice: the overture and Senta's Ballad. Both involve interaction between the stormy Dutchman music in some sort of Allegro and a statement of the redemption (Senta) theme. Not only do Wagner's metronome markings imply a very different sort of relationship between the two than that which has become customary, but the metronome marking for the Dutchman material seems to be misaligned with the corresponding tempo indication.

The problem in the overture is unwittingly posed by a blast from George Bernard Shaw. In praising an 1894 London concert performance, he states that Felix Mottl's "*allegro . . .* was a true *allegro con brio*, as marked, and not the customary *allegro pomposo*."[25] Intriguing as this observation is regarding Mottl, who during precisely this period was generally identified with *slow* Bayreuth tempi, it disguises the fundamental issue of disagreement between tempo indication and metronome marking. Indeed, on the basis of the evidence provided by over fifty recordings of the overture, led by more than forty conductors, it can be confidently asserted that Wagner's "Allegro con brio (♩. = 72)" is a musical oxymoron. Only a handful of conductors spend any significant part of the first forty-five measures in the ♩. = 70s area; they mark the extreme slow end of the spectrum. The remaining recordings are distributed evenly along a continuum

144 *David Breckbill*

from 80 to 104, with Fritz Busch (from the 1936 live complete recording) operating at 108. Considering the range of tempi represented, those in the 80s would seem to attempt a compromise between tempo instruction and metronome marking, since over half of the performances in my sample move at 92 or faster.

Once established, this tempo is meant to contrast decisively with that for the following "Andante (♩ = 100)." Wagner's own metronome indications suggest no obvious proportional relationship between the two tempi: ♩ = 100 rounds to ♩. = 33, not far under half the Allegro's metronome marking (although the compound meter mitigates against such a relationship being very apparent even if it were more precisely calculated). In practice, however, just as 72 is at the extreme lower edge of tempi adopted in the opening section, ♩ = 100 is at the upper edge of tempi for the Andante: only a handful of conductors on my list take it that fast or even more quickly. (It should be noted that these measurements apply only to the opening four notes of the theme, and that the general tendency is for conductors to allow the tempo to run more quickly in at least some of the quarter notes that follow.) The performances that do approximate the metronome marking at this point, however, adopt a tempo for the opening (Allegro) section within a notch or two of ♩. = 100, thereby creating a 1:3 relationship with the tempo of the Andante. Most conductors closely approximate this proportion even if their basic pulse is slower. (Since the two tempi are not directly juxtaposed – many conductors relax the tempo in the closing measures of the opening section – and since there is considerable flexibility in the way the Andante theme is phrased, any minute differences are not clearly apparent.) About a dozen conductors, however, select a tempo in which the ♩ in the Andante is markedly slower than their Allegro con brio ♩., while only three choose tempi for the Andante ♩ that are two or more notches faster than the Allegro con brio ♩.. (Particularly quirky here is Roger Norrington: although one of the few to adhere roughly to the metronome marking for the Allegro con brio, he far exceeds the suggested tempo for the Andante, beginning at around ♩. = 52!).

As the overture approaches its coda, the relationship between the two tempi becomes more explicit as three-measure units of the Senta theme (generally marked *ritenuto*) punctuate the faster basic tempo featuring Dutchman material. Again, most conductors assume a 1:3 ratio as the starting point, even though in this situation most

conductors feel the need for flexibility, thus rejecting a precise obser-
vance of the 1:3 proportion (Toscanini is among the few to maintain
the pulse without modification). But should the pulse slow for the
Senta material (that is, should it become *more* than three times slower
than the Dutchman material)? Or, if one recognizes that the Senta
theme is already three times slower than the main pulse (if the traditional proportion is maintained), should the pulse increase during
these three-measure units? Different conductors see this issue in
different ways, and at least one of them has reversed his opinion over
time: in 1939 Karl Böhm interjects ♩ = 96 Senta material into a prevailing tempo of ♩. = 84, while in 1971 the prevailing tempo is 96, the
interjections 84. In this regard, it is interesting to return to Shaw:

Again, take the Flying Dutchman overture. In the second half of this, the
contrast between the furious raging of the storm on the one hand, and the
consolation of the salvation theme on the other, should be so obvious, one
would think, to any ordinarily imaginative conductor, that Wagner thought
it sufficient to indicate the necessary changes of tempo by such hints as
ritenuto, *stringendo*, and the like, depending on their apparent inevitability
for their full comprehension. Yet we are accustomed to hearing our bands
dragged tearing through the salvation theme at almost the same speed as
through the storm, some attempt being made to strike a balance by taking
the one too slow and the other too fast. Mottl varied his speed from *allegro*
to *adagio*, managing the transitions with perfect address, and producing the
full effect of which everybody except our conductors knows to be what
Wagner intended.

Without hearing the performances to which Shaw was accustomed,
and to which he so pointedly objects, I deduce that he expected (and
preferred) to hear the Senta material with a quarter-note pulse slower
than that applied to the dotted half in the Dutchman material. Surely
no performance I have heard comes anywhere close to maintaining,
or even "almost" maintaining, the "same" tempo in these adjacent
passages.

If the case of the overture justifies the overriding of Wagner's
metronome markings (whether in the interest of proportional tempi
or of Wagner's own expressive markings), those for the Ballad represent an intriguing challenge to tradition. The tempo issues are similar
to those in the overture, although here the specific figures are Allegro
non troppo (dotted ♩. = 63 – that is, Dutchman material even slower
than in the overture) and *più lento* (♪ = 100). What makes this passage

more complicated is the fact that the Ballad theme itself – the four phrases Senta sings at the beginning of each stanza – and the Dutchman/storm music that follows it are traditionally performed in widely contrasted tempi. Indeed, in most performances the pulse for the Ballad material is more easily felt at the eighth-note level (i.e., much more slowly than the metronome marking), while the storm material is taken more quickly than the metronome marking (as in the overture).

This fact might have to do with attempts to turn the Ballad into something worthy of what Wagner later (disingenuously) described as the kernel out of which the opera grew. But certain entries in Cosima's diary from near the end of Wagner's life suggest that the composer would not have sanctioned such a treatment of the music as it stands. On 7 September 1881 the conductor Ernst von Schuch visited Wagner a day after he had conducted the *Holländer* in the composer's presence during the latter's visit to Dresden. During their chat, Wagner "was able to put him right on the tempi . . . particularly in the Ballad (beginning too slow, continuation too fast)." "Continuation" is of course vague – does it refer to the storm music or the Senta/redemption theme? But there can be no question that Wagner wanted Schuch to lighten the tempo in Senta's first lines. Several years earlier Cosima recorded that "he is also thinking of revising Senta's Ballad, the beginning of which he finds is quite properly like a folk song, but not characteristic of *Der Holländer*" (*CWD*, 17 October 1878). In short, Wagner wrote and conceived the Ballad as a folk song that needed to move nimbly. By the end of his life he was beginning to have second thoughts about how appropriate such a treatment was for this moment in the work and would have liked to revise it in the direction of the dark, serious tone of the opera as a whole – but he objected to using heavy tempo as a means of effecting such a revision.

How would the first part of the Ballad sound at ♩. = 63? Alas, I have encountered only two scrappy acoustical recordings, sung by Gertrud Kappel (Favorite, 1911) and Gertrude Runge (Favorite, *c.* 1907–08), that achieve such a tempo; in those cases the haste seems determined by an attempt to fit two stanzas onto one side of a ten-inch record. The more considered performances that come nearest to this metronome marking are those made in 1976 by Sir Georg Solti (in his complete recording, with Janis Martin as Senta), and in 1978 by

Dame Joan Sutherland, who includes the Ballad on her recital of Wagner arias in collaboration with her husband Richard Bonynge. Martin/Solti move at 52, Sutherland/Bonynge at 54–56. The latter treatment is particularly interesting for its lightness (Martin and Solti are more emphatic and dynamic) and for its long silences before the beginning of each stanza, and because it is among the few modern performances to exceed the metronome marking in the redemption theme ($\downarrow$ = 108–112 in the early stages, quicker yet beginning in the third phrase). Solti, by contrast, helpfully minimizes the difference in speed between sections – his introduction and storm tempo are only in the 70s, whereas Bonynge's introduction is 96, the storm in the 80s.

I am convinced that Wagner's metronome marking deserves to be taken seriously for the opening phrases of the Ballad. This conviction is due neither to pedantry nor to a yearning for unified tempo, however, but from long-standing dissatisfaction with the way in which traditional ponderous tempi destroy the narrative quality of the Ballad. Aside from the metronome marking, the tempo should be guided by the instructions *poco riten.* and *più ritard.* for the third and fourth phrases of the third stanza, culminating in a Lento marking in the final measure (and incorporating a fermata over a melodic note). How much can one detain this final phrase without compromising the sense of the text? If one permits such a consideration to determine the speed of the final measures, the basic tempo would be in the vicinity of 63 or even faster. Hearing the Ballad delivered at that pace, unhurried but with a pronounced rhythmic profile, would be a welcome antidote to so many elephantine performances featuring an etiolated lingering between phrases.

Metronome markings are not everything, of course, and there are effective performances of the Ballad that adopt tempos falling within the traditional range. Although I have heard and studied many dozens of recorded, broadcast, and live performances of this passage, the solutions offered by Maria Müller (the Bayreuth Senta in 1939–42) in her 1943 radio recording seem to me to represent a touchstone. Her sound has matured and loosened a bit here from its prime, but it nevertheless remains centered and forceful, and her confident manner gives her Senta a tone of ecstatic *naïveté*. What makes Müller's realization exemplary, however, is her diction, which seems to create the vocal line rather than being grafted onto it. For once the Ballad tells a story that grips the listener from beginning to end. A listing of Müller's points of excellence suggests some of the challenges this aria poses, which many other Sentas too often fail to meet:

(1) Marked dynamic variety does not tempt her to offer a purely musical response in the vocal introduction.

(2) Although she vigorously accents the high anacrusis in the opening phrases of each stanza, these notes are integral parts of the phrases they launch.

(3) The space between phrases points forward rather than marking a point of repose.

(4) The storm material ("Hui! Wie saust der Wind!," etc.) is vividly enunciated and thus the "Hui!" is made properly onomatopoeic.

(5) In "dass bald ein Weib Treue ihm halt'!" (at the end of the first two stanzas) the accents on the first three words are understood as an invitation to make enunciation emphatic, and the placement and stress of "Treue" for once has the rhythmic integrity to create a grinding syncopation against the accompaniment.

(6) The progressive slowing in the third stanza is an inflection of momentum rather than a disruption of it.

(7) There is no trace of hesitancy in beginning her outburst at the end of the third stanza.

(8) The concluding cadenza has shape and dramatic urgency instead of resembling a clumsy or meandering vocalize.

Other Sentas have offered fine performances of the Ballad, but none I know of matches the resourcefulness of Müller's in detail and in meeting the Ballad's overall vocal and dramatic challenges.

Such resourcefulness is even more vital for those attempting the Dutchman. "His interpretation was greater than the music . . . Wagner could give him in this early Romantic score" wrote Olin Downes of Hans Hotter's first Dutchman for Metropolitan Opera.[26] Although this evaluation of the music seems to smack of condescension, extended exposure to various interpretations of this role convince one that it requires uncommon inventiveness to be truly effective – a coupling of psychological or analytical insight with powerful musical instincts and exemplary control of both voice and diction. The vocal challenges alone are immense. First is the issue of range: the sound must be reliably and fully produced over nearly two octaves (F# to f'). The voice must be able to contend with a brassy orchestration, but at the same time the vocal writing contains many chromatic passages in which precise intonation is mandatory. The ability to give life and variety to declamatory passages demands scrupulous and instinctive differentiation of rhythms. The ideal singer of the role also needs to be able to range freely across the dynamic spectrum, and from smooth cantilena to the most vociferous declamation if he is to project the extremes of joy and despair, of hope and torment, which the character expresses. Even the best performers cannot be expected to meet all facets of such a demanding job description.

Wagner's "Remarks" focus on this role more than on any of the others, and while the essay is revelatory concerning Wagner's conception of how the performer should portray the action visually and in relation to the orchestral music, its value for the singer is less obvious. David Hamilton's survey of the challenges in the opening monologue (geared closely to Wagner's instructions in the "Remarks") and the ways in which recorded singers up to 1979 have coped with them continues to be a valuable piece of work.[27] But he overlooks the largest pitfall of this role by dealing with the challenges one by one, as Wagner's instructions concerning the delivery of certain lines might tend to encourage. By suggesting so often that lines be sung with intensity, Wagner forces singers to resort to physical gestures for creating high points (not a usable strategy for singers making recordings or attempting to create a complex character in sound as well as in sight). Singers who can provide a vast but precisely gradated dynamic range have found that the role has a great deal to offer. Indeed, this is one of the keys to the success of Hans Hotter's portrayal on the Clemens Krauss recording – his imposing voice makes only sparing use of the greatest force, thereby causing the emphases and colorings adopted for other lines to gain dramatic contour, variety, and depth.

Some singers who lack the vocal resources to convey a large scale of variety have nevertheless achieved success here. Despite its many beauties, Dietrich Fischer-Dieskau's voice is hardly the ideal instrument for the Dutchman, lacking both the requisite depth and power. Yet his resourceful treatment of diction, articulation, and rhythm makes his recorded portrayal an enormously stimulating one. After hearing him, one awaits a Dutchman capable of combining the variegated declamation and vocal subtlety of this experienced Lieder singer with the vocal amplitude of a powerful bass-baritone. Whether Bryn Terfel will develop into the next great Dutchman remains to be seen, but he seems to have the wide range of both pitch and dynamics, the spontaneous temperament, and the variety of vocal colorings to make this role his own.

And that is precisely the challenge of this role, and of the opera as a whole. *Der fliegende Holländer* was written in an age of performer's music. Wagner's comments in "Remarks" on how to project the music demonstrate both the intensity at which he aims and his inexperience in writing vocal parts that endow important characters with multiple dimensions and contours. In his later works he developed characters whose essence can, in conjunction with the orchestra, be approximated by a correct realization of the part as written; but to perform the *Holländer* as though it were a later work is to expose the younger Wagner's inexperience. Paradoxically, in order to deserve equivalent status with its partners in the Wagner canon, *Der fliegende Holländer* requires performers whose temperament, spontaneity, and technique can bring out the fresh, vigorous qualities that set this opera *apart* from the later "music dramas," instead of assuming that a uniform performance style based on the later works will bring the *Holländer* closer to them.

7 Canonizing the Dutchman: Bayreuth, Wagnerism, and Der fliegende Holländer

STEPHEN MCCLATCHIE

Der fliegende Holländer was not performed at the Bayreuth Festival until 1901, a quarter-century after the *Ring* and almost twenty years after *Parsifal*. It has always been something of a "poor relation" within the Wagnerian pantheon: less performed and discussed than other of Wagner's works, especially at the height of Wagnerism at the turn of the century, likely owing to the unmistakable "operatic" aspects – a score divided into discrete numbers (albeit blurred), choruses of generic characters (spinning women, sailors, etc.), and characters with clear prototypes in German Romantic opera (hunter tenor and supernatural baritone). An examination of Bayreuth's treatment of the work, both in terms of performance and propaganda, over these same years reveals a process of canonization: the fitting of *Der fliegende Holländer* into the larger, "unified" Wagnerian canon. At first this happens stylistically and ideologically by giving the work in a single, unbroken act and performing it according to the edicts of Bayreuth style, while simultaneously using the Bayreuth publicity machine to dictate the terms according to which the work should be understood. Later, *Der fliegende Holländer* becomes part of a broader attempt to demonstrate the unity of the canon in music-analytical terms as well. This process may be further illuminated by contrasting material stemming from Bayreuth with that by Wagnerians of a more independent stripe, such as Guido Adler. Since the *Holländer* remains fundamentally resistant to such a reception-based approach, this examination also provides an index of the workings of ideologies in Wagnerian scholarship in the years between Wagner's death and the end of the Second World War.

While full canonization of *Der fliegende Holländer* occurs only in the wake of the 1901 Bayreuth performances, the initial work was begun by Wagner himself. His well-known propensity for myth was not restricted to his musical works, but extended to his life as well.

Indeed, until quite recently the reception of *Der fliegende Holländer* has largely been shaped by Wagner's own retrospective myth-making about the work and its position within his compositional output: its autobiographical origins and place as the first music drama.[1] Wagner's writings, however, repeatedly reveal a tendency to recuperate his earlier works in relation to his later prose writings. For *Der fliegende Holländer*, this idealizing process begins almost contemporaneously with its première. An early account, already tendentious in its details, is found in Wagner's letter to Ferdinand Heine, published as part of an anonymous article on the work in the Leipzig *Illustrirte Zeitung* of 7 October 1843. Here Wagner speaks of the "quite special colour and character" of the subject matter, the "aura" of which "spread unchecked over the entire piece," and he offers some specific observations about the music (which will seem counterintuitive to those who know the score):

From the outset I had to abandon the modern arrangement of dividing the work into arias, duets, finales, etc. and instead relate the legend in an entire breath . . . [I]n all its external details, it is so unlike anything we now understand by the term "opera."[2]

The central document in Wagner's personal *Holländer* legend is his 1851 *A Communication to my Friends*, written after Wagner's operatic theories had crystallized in *Opera and Drama*. *Der fliegende Holländer* is viewed here as the work which marks Wagner's arrival as a musico-dramatic poet, rather than a mere librettist: the creator of a text already musicalized, that is, bearing within itself the terms of its eventual musical setting.[3] But Wagner goes further than this. In a famous passage, he asserts that the entire work germinated from the "thematic seed" of Senta's Ballad, the first music composed (cf. Chapter 4, above). His attempt to paint the work as a proto-music drama is couched in terms that strongly echo the language of *Opera and Drama* and better suit the music of the *Ring*:

I remember that before I proceeded to write *Der fliegende Holländer* at all, I first sketched Senta's second-act Ballad, composing both the text and the melody; in this piece I unwittingly planted the thematic seed [*thematischen Keim*] of all the music in the opera: it was the poetically condensed image of the whole drama, as it was in my mind's eye; and when I had to find a title for the finished work I was strongly tempted to call it a "dramatic ballad." When I came eventually to the composition, the thematic image [*Bild*] I had already conceived quite involuntarily spread out over the entire drama in a complete, unbroken web [*vollständiges Gewebe*]; all that was left for me to do was to allow the various thematic germs [*Keime*] contained in the Ballad to develop [*entwickeln*] to the full, each in its own direction, and all the principal features of the text were arrayed before me in specific thematic shapes of their own making [*ganz von selbst in bestimmten thematischen Gestaltungen von mir*].[4]

Consideration of the compositional materials for *Der fliegende Holländer* reveals first of all that the preliminary sketch of the Ballad was written *after* a sketch of the theme of the Dutchman's crew and a rudimentary form of the theme for Daland's crew, and secondly that Wagner sketched individual numbers of the opera, and seems not to have done so following their order in the finished work.[5] Nevertheless, in *A Communication to my Friends* Wagner does acknowledge that despite its marked stylistic advance from *Rienzi*, *Der fliegende Holländer* reveals only the "broadest, most vague outlines" of what he was later able to achieve in *Tannhäuser* and *Lohengrin*.[6] He was incapable, however, of seeing the work within the tradition of German Romantic opera that he had inherited from Weber and Marschner.[7] For example, the demonic title figure of *Der fliegende Holländer* is clearly a descendant of Marschner's Vampire and Hans Heiling, and Wagner's representation of the supernatural through diminished triads and tremolo recalls Weber's treatment of it in *Der Freischütz*, to chose just a single influential instance.

Despite Wagner's retrospective reading of *Der fliegende Holländer* as his first music drama, he always retained a certain ambivalence towards the work. He told Liszt in an 1852 letter that "it is only reluctantly that I trouble myself with the *Dutchman*, with *Tannhäuser* and with *Lohengrin* . . . if they had already received their due, the devil himself knows that I should not ask any more about things I've outgrown."[8] That Wagner had really outgrown the first of these is suggested by the fact that it is omitted entirely from his 1865 plan, outlined for King Ludwig, for the rest of his compositional life: while revisions of *Tannhäuser* and *Lohengrin* were planned, the *Holländer* is conspicuous by its absence.[9] Nevertheless, shortly afterwards, Cosima von Bülow wrote to King Ludwig that it was Wagner's "long-held wish" to rework *Der fliegende Holländer* so that it might be a worthy predecessor of *Tannhäuser* and *Lohengrin*.[10] As late as 1880, Wagner spoke to Cosima of his intention to rework the opera and perform it at Bayreuth.[11]

That the Bayreuth Festival was always intended as something more than just a music festival is evident from even a cursory survey of Wagner's views on the subject. At the very least, his establishment of a journal devoted to matters Wagnerian – the *Bayreuther Blätter*, edited for its entire sixty-year history by Hans von Wolzogen – indicates Wagner's broader cultural ambitions. Financial exigencies arising from the 1876 *Ring* prevented a resumption of the Festival until the première of *Parsifal* in 1882, and it is largely to Cosima and her staunch friend and financial advisor Adolf von Groß that we owe the continued nourishment and eventual success of the Bayreuth idea after Wagner's death. For Cosima, however, artistic success was closely bound up with broader aesthetic and cultural matters: the "mission" of Bayreuth, as she saw it, was the promulgation of the Wagnerian gospel throughout the world. To this end, she was aided by the indefatigable Wolzogen, along with Carl Friedrich Glasenapp and others, who, in an outpouring of articles and books, established the "official" view of the composer. Such a view included the smoothing out of awkwardnesses in the composer's biography (achieved through selective presentation of events and outright censorship), a similarly selective emphasis on Wagner's prose writings (especially the late *Regenerationslehre*) and the later music dramas, and a rigidly teleological view of the composer's development, paradoxically yoked with the notion of a unified canon.[12] To be a true Bayreuthian, not simply a Wagnerian, meant adhering to Wagner's views in all matters, ideological as well as musical; Wagner's writings soon ossified into holy writ. Thus Schopenhauer's teachings about art, as mediated by Wagner in *Beethoven* and other writings, became the basis for all interpretation: the notion that music was expression, pure and simple – an external manifestation of an internal emotional state, of the Will itself. Moreover, this Will-music offered a glimpse into the *Ding-an-sich*: philosophical Nirvana.

Following Schopenhauer's valorization of melody as the highest manifestation of the Will, early accounts of Wagner's works placed emphasis almost entirely on their melodic content: the so-called leitmotifs, named and elucidated most notably by Wolzogen in a series of widely copied thematic guides. Wolzogen later widened his focus by situating the leitmotifs within the broader context of the expressive aesthetic position by contrasting them with what he called "parallels": general expressions of the specific emotional content of the leitmotifs.[13] He likens parallels to root words in the language of music, and demonstrates, by example, how the same melodic gestures recur throughout Wagner's works for similar situations. These parallels, arranged according to the rubrics of mood, feeling, situation, action, character, and declamation, are taken from all of Wagner's works (including the three pre-*Holländer* operas), and serve to underline effectively the notion of a unified oeuvre. Curt Mey's contemporaneous *Die Musik als tönende Weltidee* elevates Wolzogen's idea of parallels into universal truth: five metaphysical laws of melody which form the basis of all music. Mey's examples are not just taken from Wagner, but also from (mainly) German music since Bach.[14] In aesthetic terms, then, *Der fliegende Holländer* was treated like all the other works.

On the other hand, *Der fliegende Holländer* occupies a somewhat marginal position in the Bayreuth publicity machine before 1901. During the period between 1878 and 1901, the *Bayreuther Blätter* published only two full-scale articles on the work. The first, from 1882, already betrays a tendency to reinterpret Wagner's early works not only in light of the later ones, but also as part of a unified body of work. Fritz Stade's "psychological study" of Senta's relationships with Erik and the Dutchman – essentially an *explication du texte* – makes a Schopenhauerian distinction between love (*Liebe*), the basis of her bond with Erik, and sympathy (*Mitleid*), the higher feeling that draws her towards the Dutchman; Senta's love for Erik awakens the potential for self-sacrifice, which wells-up unconsciously within her. The first terms of Stade's binaristic oppositions of unconscious/conscious, depth/surface, interior/exterior, feeling/reflection, and, more loosely, culture/civilization are mapped onto Senta, whose naive instincts are everywhere preferred to the considered opinions of others.[15] The second article – a straightforward account of the sources for the legend of the Flying Dutchman – is a *pièce d'occasion*, written for the fiftieth anniversary of the work's première in 1893.[16]

Curiously, Cosima Wagner's 1883 plan for the Festival actually had designated *Der fliegende Holländer* for 1886, before *Meistersinger*, *Tannhäuser*, or *Lohengrin*.[17] Given the controversy surrounding her decision to mount *Tannhäuser* in 1891 – the first of the "Romantic operas" to be given at Bayreuth – it is probably wise that she did not begin with the earlier work, which more closely resembles its German operatic ancestors.[18] The eventual success of the 1891 *Tannhäuser*, followed three years later by *Lohengrin*, paved the way for the *Holländer* in 1901. As she had done with *Tannhäuser*, Cosima chose to perform the revised version of the score: Felix Weingartner's 1896 edition of the opera, which incorporated Wagner's *Tristan*esque retouchings of 1860, was the basic text, but – in keeping with her stated intentions to present Wagner's early works as dramas rather than operas – Cosima and her assistant Julius Kniese revised this score so that it could be performed without a break.

While Wagner originally conceived the work in a single act, by the time he came to write the music he elaborated his scheme into three acts, to be played without a break. Sometime after October 1842, when he retrieved his score from the Berlin Opera, he recast it into three discrete acts, in which form it received its première in 1843 and entered the repertoire.[19] Although in *My Life* Wagner claimed that he chose the single-act form because "the subject itself called for it, for in this way I could render the straightforward dramatic action between the principals without any of the operatic accessories I had come to loath so much" (*ML*, 183), this once again smacks of retrospective myth-making. Siegfried Wagner's later assertion that his father had been forced, against his will, to give the work in separate acts because of the technical limitations of contemporary operatic productions is simply not borne out by the evidence.[20] Wagner never unequivocally stated that the single act was preferable. Nevertheless, to stage the work without interruption, and according to the dictates of Bayreuth style, whereby close attention to declamation was married to a rigidly hieratic style of acting, was to emphasize at once its difference from operatic practice (with its more natural acting style and emphasis on the beauty of the sung line) and its similarity to Wagner's later works (which of course had already been given the Bayreuth treatment).[21]

The production values of the 1901 *Holländer* were reinforced by Wolzogen in the *Bayreuther Blätter*, which published a series of excerpts from Wagner's letters and writings about the work. This collection of Wagnerian scripture was assembled with the explicit intention of preparing visitors for the Festival, that they might approach the work with the correct attitude. Wolzogen's introduction presents *Der fliegende Holländer* as a fully developed music drama, as part of a unified body of works – indeed as the "seed" of the rest. His apologia makes five major points. First, Wolzogen – perhaps remembering the 1891 debates over *Tannhäuser* – asserts unequivocally that the early works belong at Bayreuth because of their close thematic connections with the later works:

This early masterpiece already contains the *seed and basic idea* [*Kern und Grundidee*] of all of his later, great dramatic tapestries [*Weltbilder*], just as in the artist's [own] tragic life: "*the lofty tragedy of Renunciation*" – or, as Wagner added at the time, using Schopenhauer's way of expressing it: "the renunciation of the will, the only means of redemption."[22]

Second, the work is unquestionably worthy of performance there at Bayreuth:

Even the so-called "older works" belong in the *Festspielhaus*, celebrated and created there as new works – dramas – according to their Master's intentions . . . The few "conventional" phrases and cadences in the music of *Der fliegende Holländer* certainly do not render it incapable of sounding across the "mystic abyss" of the *Festspielhaus*, where the deeply characteristic "new sounds" for demonic nature and metaphysical humanity, for storm and sorrow, for longing and redemption (the sounds that since then we have come to know as the Master's language in the perfection of *Tristan*, of the *Ring* and of *Parsifal*) are truly at home, as nowhere else – the only place capable of bringing the musical animation of the drama, not the "opera," of the Flying Dutchman to full expression.[23]

The third point stems from the second: it is only Bayreuth which can "save" *Der fliegende Holländer* from operatic ravishment by performing the work as Wagner intended: by rigidly following Wagner's own directions for staging the work, and thereby forging a unity out of individual details.

It is the Bayreuth Festival, here only, where such wonders take place, in artistic purity – purity above all of intention, of will – as experiences of German spirit and according to the Master's wishes.[24]

It is good that today we have these works – the earliest as well as the last – performed in *Bayreuth*, where the spirit of the performance (in which the work first comes to life as drama) corresponds harmoniously with the spirit of the conception and shaping [of the work], and thereby that is achieved which, in the Master's sense, can be called the *Style* of a work . . . [A]gain and again we hear the Master himself remark that his works appear as "operas" on the operatic stages, and therefore he founded for himself, and for us, his *Bayreuth*.[25]

Above all, you will recognize how Bayreuth understands the style of the works and performs them, and how today, after twenty-five years, the essence and style of its portrayals differ from the independent output of the operatic stage, in that it interprets and resolves the entire stylistic task, as a whole, actually as drama, strictly and fully according to the Master's desire and intent.[26]

Fourth, Bayreuth's performance of *Der fliegende Holländer* is not just important in itself, artistically, but also as the demonstration of an entirely new, yet fully developed, artistic direction on the part of Wagner:

It is in fact the beginning of a new artistic direction, a new artistic creation. Not simply in the sense of the first traces, of a tentative attempt, but both with reference to the basic ideas [*Grundideen*] of all the later works and with regard to their shaping, this work is a primal image [*Urbild*], a seed that contains in itself the essence of all later great and completed blossomings.[27]

Finally, Wolzogen argues (with the composer) that in the *Holländer* Wagner became a true artist and poet for the first time, with his subject matter and musical style firmly rooted in the *Volk*. Senta, the child of the *Volk* and of nature, is identified as a fundamental type found in the rest of Wagner's works in the characters of Elisabeth, Brünnhilde, Isolde, and Eva.

The ideological nature of Wolzogen's piece is highlighted by comparing it with two other Bayreuth guide books for 1901. The first, a *Praktischer Wegweiser für Bayreuther Festspielbesucher*, contains a plot synopsis with only the briefest of allusions to Wagner's own characterization of *Der fliegende Holländer* in *A Communication to my Friends*.[28] The second, in the similarly named *Praktisches Handbuch für Festspielbesucher* is a more lengthy leitmotivic treatment of the work by Max Chop. While Chop's piece relies heavily on Wagner's own *post facto* statements to interpret the opera – arguing that *Der fliegende Holländer* is an *Erlösungswerk* both for Wagner himself and for opera in general (see Chapter 1), for example – he does so in a markedly less aggressive fashion, and is even able to admit to some parts influenced by Meyerbeer or contemporary German operatic taste.[29]

Over the next two years, Bayreuth's ideological line of defense was strengthened by a series of "Nachklänge" published in the *Blätter* that reinforced the main points of Wolzogen's introduction. Several of these evoke strongly the rhetoric of Christian witness, complete with confession and credo. For example, Rudolph Schlößer admits that he attended the 1901 Bayreuth *Holländer* with a certain skepticism, not expecting to find an ideal performance; in previous productions, his strongest impressions had been only of individual details, rather than of a coherent whole. He credits Bayreuth's success to Cosima's decision to produce the work in a single act; the dramatic rhythm of this version is much stronger – the difference between three smaller paintings and a large canvas – and reveals the work to be *echt* Wagner:

What conveyed upon the Bayreuth performance of *Holländer* such a strikingly more powerful emphasis than that of common depictions is first the *uninterrupted* account of the work. Now that one has experienced it, one asks oneself, futilely: how was it possible that no one hit upon a performance like that before Bayreuth? . . . The inexorable progress of the dramatic action in a single movement now strikes the spectator so clearly, that the cleft which separates *Der fliegende Holländer* from Romantic opera widens enormously all of a sudden: in fact, it is now the real Wagner who stands here before us.[30]

This theme is echoed the next year by Reinhold von Lichtenberg, who – along with others – reinforces the notion that a Bayreuth performance is the true première of a work: "here in Bayreuth, each of our Master's works experiences its real birthday for the first time."[31] By following Wagner's intentions explicitly, Lichtenberg avows, the figure of Senta is revealed not as a modern, hysterical being (whose redemptive work happens only as if through a kind of hypnosis) but as a natural, naive girl, free of any trace of "sickly sentimentality." At Bayreuth, one's first impression of Senta is one of the deepest empathy (*tiefen Mitleidens*) with the terrible fate of the Dutchman, and this overarching consciousness of her mission allows one to experience the essential unity of Wagner's works; just as with the earlier premières at Bayreuth, we see how *Der fliegende Holländer* fits into the cycle of works culminating with *Parsifal*.[32] Most of these "echos" of the 1901 première are strikingly silent about the specifics (singers, *Regie*, lighting, and so on) of the production.

For a clear demonstration of the Bayreuth ideology, it is instructive to contrast the above accounts with other contemporary discussions of *Der fliegende Holländer* that do not emanate from the Bayreuth shrine. As odd as it may seem, given his central position in the Bayreuth circle and close personal connections with Cosima (Eva Wagner subsequently became his second wife), Houston Stewart Chamberlain always maintained a touchy critical independence from the Bayreuth party line in his own works (as opposed to those written for Bayreuth publications).[33] His 1896 study of Wagner devotes more space to *Rienzi* than to *Holländer*, and treats Wagner's claims to have suddenly become a Poet in the latter work rather skeptically.[34] In fact, Chamberlain sees *Rienzi* as the decisive work in Wagner's development in the early 1840s, and treats *Holländer* rather cursorily alongside *Tannhäuser* and *Lohengrin*. More interesting, given Bayreuth's reluctance to evaluate the works in a critical manner, is his clear willingness to regard it as a transitional work, on the way to symphonic drama, but not there yet:

Der fliegende Holländer is genuine and deep poetic art; the work is a drama in the most complete sense of the word, and the figure of the "pale sailor" stands so large and plastically concrete before us, just as any one of the Master's later [characters], or any from earlier dramatic art. The whole, however, is yet only a sketch. The significant thing about the new [music] drama is that it can exhaustively depict the processes of the innermost soul, the artistic content of the "thoughts" – and in *Holländer* this does not happen. The inner man, and with him the music, comes off quite badly here:

the poet sketches figures entirely from his heart, but then does not carry out their further elaboration. This poet had only just half emerged from the swaddling clothes of opera, and did not yet dare to venture fully into his own domain.[35]

The introduction to Guido Adler's 1904 publication of his lectures on Wagner, written for the Vienna University, promises a highly contexualized, historical view of the composer and his works.[36] While Adler includes all of the material now irrevocably attached to evaluations of the work – discussion of the sources and Wagner's own commentaries, for example – he does so in an extremely balanced, unpolemical fashion, critical in the best sense, in that he is willing to weigh the work for both success and failure. Adler treats Wagner's own writings seriously, but not scripturally; for him, they are merely one way of approaching a work, but not the only one. This noticeable difference in tone from Wolzogen and other Bayreuthians extends to an ability to allow that Wagner was not perfect: "if such a strong light casts great shadows, that is in the nature of things."[37] Adler makes a real effort to place Wagner's works within operatic tradition by tracing particular musical and textual influences, such as those of Marschner and Weber in *Holländer*, even if this means belying some of Wagner's own claims. For example, the "characteristic web of principal themes" seen by Wagner in *Holländer* is regarded by Adler as simply another example of opera's long-standing use of recurring themes to help unify a work; he asserts that Wagner used this technique in *Der fliegende Holländer* without theoretical reflection or justification, added only later. Likewise he refutes Wagner's claim to have excluded all traditional operatic forms by comparing the admittedly free form of the numbers in the *Holländer* with those in works by Marschner and Weber. He does allow that passages like Erik's Dream in *Holländer*, Tannhäuser's Rome Narration, and Lohengrin's story of the Grail are anticipatory of Wagner's later style, but even then notes that such a through-composed recitative-like style has its predecessor in Gluck, and even Mozart (the Speaker in *Die Zauberflöte*). Adler's scrupulous objectivity extends even to the cultural relativism which formulates his comparison of Verdi and Wagner.[38]

Two final examples of independent viewpoints may be passed over rather more quickly, although each fascinating in its own right. The first is by Alfred Heuß, a critical probing of the relationship of music and stage action in Wagner. Heuß argues against the view, expressed by Wagner in his "Remarks on the Performance of the Opera *Der fliegende Holländer*," that each musical gesture encodes a specific physical response.[39] This he terms "Wagner's error," and illustrates by showing that Wagner himself moved away from such an approach in his staging of the *Ring* in 1876. While Heuß's main point – that Wagner's music does not simply illustrate the action, but rather conveys its essence – would be welcome in Wahnfried, his methodology would be highly suspect, particularly since he does not show the obligatory reverence towards the composer: "The motto of modern Wagner research must now and then be: *for the work of art, against the Master!*"[40] The second example is Max Graf's psychobiographical treatment of Wagner and *Der fliegende Holländer*, first given as a lecture to Sigmund Freud's *Mittwochsgesellschaft*, a group under the auspices of Freud himself, and devoted to expanding his ideas to other fields.[41] That such a modern approach was anathema to the conservative Bayreuth circle needs hardly be said.

The 1901 Bayreuth production was repeated the following summer, after which *Der fliegende Holländer* seems to drop out of consideration again. When Siegfried Wagner revived the work during the ill-fated 1914 season, Wolzogen's *Holländer* breviary was published in book form by Breitkopf und Härtel, but no mention of the work is found in the *Bayreuther Blätter*.[42] A single article furthering the Schopenhauerian interpretation appeared in 1926, although *Der fliegende Holländer* was not produced again at Bayreuth until 1939.[43] By this date much had changed, not only in Bayreuth, with the deaths of Cosima and Siegfried in 1930, but within German society as a whole, of course. As is well known, Hitler's personal ties with the Wagner family stretch back to the immediate post-war years, and with the reopening of the Festival in 1924, Bayreuth became something of a magnet for those disaffected with the Weimar republic. Even before the National Socialists came to power in 1933, the principal Bayreuth publicity organs, such as the *Bayreuther Blätter* and the *Bayreuther Festspielführer*, were firmly in their camp. Yet the publicity surrounding the 1939 Bayreuth *Holländer* for the most part does not partake of Nazi rhetoric, nor is it as aggressively partisan as had been the case in 1901.[44] *Der fliegende Holländer* was now firmly established in the Bayreuth canon. Its treatment in the *Festspielführer* of that year reveals a different sort of canonization: one extending to music-analytical issues.

Throughout the 1920s and 1930s, Wagnerian scholarship was characterized by a new rigorousness: an attempt to answer Wagner's critics in their own terms – that is, analytically and philologically – yet without renouncing Wagnerian principles. Upon examination, this Hegelian confrontation of Wagnerian-Schopenhauerian aesthetics and scholarly objectivity proves to be no less ideological in intent than the more overtly partisan publications of 1901. For example, while Otto Strobel's work with primary sources laid the foundation for the invaluable *Wagner Werk-Verzeichnis*, his Bayreuthian prejudices lead him to claim that the individual sketches for *Der fliegende Holländer* could be seen as a continuous draft, albeit with gaps, in the manner of the later works, when in fact Wagner sketched only individual numbers of the opera out of order.[45] Similar prejudices are to be found in analytical works by Walter Engelsmann and Alfred Lorenz.

Engelsmann's main thesis, expressed across a number of publications appearing during the 1930s, is that the essential principle of Wagnerian music drama is that of thematic evolution: the organic growth of Wagner's works from a single melodic seed, in the manner of a Beethoven symphony; Engelsmann speaks of the "Beethoven-Wagnerschen Evolutionskunst."[46] His approach is a logical extension of the melodic emphasis of the *Leitfaden* literature. Engelsmann argues that Wagner's strong opposition of "opera" (traditionally, a successive, pot-pourri-like form) and "drama" (organically unified music drama) was nothing less than a paradigm shift (*Kulturwende*) between two fundamentally different world views. The discussion of this opposition universalizes the issues, and makes it clear that more is at stake than just theatrical practice. In pot-pourri opera, with its absolute melody and stereotyped melodic and cadential patterns, Engelsmann sees reflected a mechanistic, constructed world, one of passivity, dogma, and arbitrariness. This is the world of the theatre, of diva worship and idolatry wherein everything is derived and varied from old-testament-like *Ur*-dogma. To this is opposed Wagnerian music drama, characterized by organic unity, unending melody, and thematic evolution. It reflects an organic, evolved world, one of activity and controlled, shaped will – the world of essence, of consecration-play (*Weihespiel*) and holy revelation, wherein everything develops by continuous evolution from a single creative source (*Schöpfungs-Urgrund*) and is shaped

in the spirit of the Aryan-German perception of the World-Becoming of the World-Essence in the form of the Created-unity of the primally evolved

World-Tree, represented by Goethe's view of unity, Beethoven's unified works, through the scientific idea of unity, and through Wagner's formal unity.[47]

According to Engelsmann, Wagner made a distinction between "works," which were made or shaped, and "creations," which were grown or evolved: *Rienzi* was shaped, as opera, from tradition; *Holländer* was created, as drama, out of his own experience of the bitterest need of the soul and the evolutionary drive of his innermost powers.[48] Wagnerian melody comes from inspiration; it is a gift from heaven:

> The more now that it is demanded that the creation of entire dramas, like entire symphonies [be created] "from a single point," the developmental possibilities of the thematic seed [*Werkthema*] become more and more significant, likewise the potency of the "inspiration."[49]

Engelmann's assertions, from an article on *Der fliegende Holländer* in the 1939 *Festspielführer*, are accompanied by an analytical demonstration of their validity. He proceeds to demonstrate how the themes in the work evolve from the "inspiration" of Senta's Ballad, just as Wagner had argued in *A Communication to my Friends*; the themes of the Ballad are the *Ur-motive* of the work. In *Der fliegende Holländer*, Wagner reached his compositional maturity ("the *musician* fulfilled in fact that which the *poet* demanded from him"); not, however, by manipulating or varying pre-existing melodies, but through the real reshaping of musical events out of a melodic seed.[50] All the themes in the work are organic:

> Each consists of a third, an octave leap, and an ascending and descending second. Each in a different, poetically determined order and interpenetration of the motives. Each an "inspiration." Nevertheless, none "new." Rather, each referring to the motivic polarity of the primal inspiration. Each develops from the same central point as the others, "spun out," "found," and characterized. Nevertheless, all [are] genetically the same, rooted and "cognate."[51]

Wagnerian music drama, beginning with *Holländer*, marks the evolution from the "unyielding variation technique" (*starren Variationstechnik*) to the "living, evolutionary art of Beethovenian *Werkthematik*":

> Thereby is melody for the first time freed from the bonds of operatic self-sufficiency and brought in service to the idea of the drama (not only instinctively, but also, in fact, musically and motivically).[52]

Engelsmann's main points about *Der fliegende Holländer* – that it is Wagner's first music drama, that it bears within it the seed of all the later works, and that Wagner spoke truly when he described it in his prose writings – are precisely those made by Wolzogen in 1901, but his way of expressing them betrays a new, apparently scientific, and objective orientation.[53]

A similar juxtaposition is found in the work of Alfred Lorenz, arguably the most famous Wagnerian scholar of the interwar years. His four-volume study of the "secret of form" in Wagner's works was an exhaustive attempt to disprove the traditional claim that Wagner's music was formless.[54] Firmly anchored in the Schopenhauerian-Wagner expressive aesthetic position, Lorenz argued that Wagner's music was constructed of a series of instinctively perceived, *Gestalt*-like periods, each of which was shaped according to one of four recurring formal types which generally cohere at a higher level.[55] By 1939, when Lorenz turned his attention to *Holländer* for the *Festspielführer*, his analytical methodology was widely accepted and veritably unassailable (for both aesthetic and political reasons), and his suggestion that the work could be seen as a complex *Bogen* form was sufficient to attach the cachet of his method to the work.[56] Simply by writing about *Der fliegende Holländer*, Lorenz made a gesture towards the analytical canonization of the work – while he admits that it is only partly symphonic, and even has some "operatic" sections.

For the Bayreuth première of *Der fliegende Holländer* in 1901, Cosima and her circle fought tirelessly to present the work as the first music drama, progenitor of an impressive, yet unified heritage. This campaign was waged by performance on the stage of the *Festspielhaus* and by propaganda in the pages of the *Bayreuther Blätter*. For the 1939 revival, little had changed, really, apart from the method of argument. Whereas in earlier years commentators had been content to accept Wagner's own terms for examining the work (a tendency seen most clearly in Wolzogen's 1901 anthology in which his own authorial presence is almost completely effaced), the critical climate of the 1920s and 1930s made it essential to abandon more subjective approaches (no more mystical "echos") in favor of apparently objective analytical ones. Yet the underlying aims of both Engelsmann and Lorenz were not much different from Cosima's in 1901: a need to affirm the *Holländer*'s place in the canon of Wagner's works. Only the means had changed: now thematic and formal unity was asserted in order to validate the work as "symphonic," just as Wagner had claimed. As is typical of pre-war Wagnerism, in all these approaches, ideological considerations take precedence over critical objectivity, and substance is subordinated to image.

Appendices:
Documentary sources relating to the genesis, early performance, and reception of Der fliegende Holländer

A.   Source texts (libretto)

1. Heinrich Heine, "The fable of the Flying Dutchman," *Aus den Memoiren des Herren von Schnabelewopski*, chapter 7. Originally published in *Der Salon I* (Hamburg: Hoffmann & Campe, 1834); translation by Stewart Spencer, from Heinrich Heine, *Sämtliche Werke: historisch-kritische Gesamtausgabe*, ed. Manfred Windfuhr *et al.* (Berlin: Hoffmann & Campe, 1973–), vol. 5, 171–74.

> The significance of Heine's "fable" for Wagner's *Fliegender Holländer* is discussed elsewhere in this volume (see Chapters 1 and 2), and Wagner himself mentions it in several autobiographical accounts of the work.

The tale of the Flying Dutchman is no doubt familiar to you. It is the story of that doom-laden ship which can never gain the shelter of a port and which has roamed the seas since time immemorial. Whenever it encounters another vessel, some of the members of its unearthly crew row over and ask if the others would kindly deliver a bundle of letters for them. These letters have to be nailed to the mast or else ill-fortune overtakes the ship, especially if there is no Bible on board or no horseshoe affixed to the foremast. The letters are always addressed to people who are completely unknown or who died long ago, and it sometimes happens that a great-grandson receives a love-letter addressed to his great-grandmother, who has been buried these last hundred years. A timbered specter, that dreadful ship bears the name of its captain,[1] a Dutchman who once swore by all the devils in hell that he would round some cape or other (the name of which escapes me) in spite of the most violent storm that was then raging, even if he had to keep on tacking until the Day of Judgment. The devil took him at his word, and he is forced to roam the seas until the

Day of Judgment, unless he can be saved by a woman's fidelity. Fool that he is, the devil does not believe in women's fidelity, and so he allowed the doomed captain to go ashore once every seven years to marry and in that way seek his salvation. Poor Dutchman! He is often only too glad to be saved from marriage, to be rid of his redemptress and to return on board ship.

Upon this legend was based the play that I saw at a theatre in Amsterdam. Another seven years have elapsed, and the poor Dutchman, more weary than ever of his endless wanderings, goes ashore and makes friends with a Scottish merchant whom he encounters and to whom he sells diamonds at an absurdly low price; and, hearing that his client has a fair daughter, he requests her as his wife. This bargain, too, is concluded. We now see the Scotsman's house, where the girl awaits her intended husband in a state of some trepidation. She glances frequently and wistfully at a large weathered portrait hanging in the parlor and depicting a handsome man dressed in the style of the Spanish Netherlands; it is an ancient heirloom and, according to her grandmother, a striking likeness[2] of the Flying Dutchman as he appeared in Scotland a hundred years previously, during the reign of William of Orange. And a traditional warning attaches to this painting, to the effect that the women of the family should be wary of the original. That is why the features of this dangerous man have impressed themselves upon the girl's heart since childhood. When the real Flying Dutchman now comes in as plain as life, the girl starts back – but not in fear. He, too, is startled by the sight of the portrait. But when he is told whom it depicts, he succeeds in averting the others' suspicions, laughing at their credulity and even managing a joke at the expense of the Flying Dutchman, that Wandering Jew of the ocean; but his voice involuntarily assumes a note of sadness when he describes how Mynheer is compelled to suffer the most unspeakable torments on this vast, watery waste; how his body is nothing but a tomb of flesh wherein his soul grows weary; how life repulses him and even death rejects him – like an empty barrel that the mocking waves toss back and forth, the poor Dutchman is cast to and fro between life and death, neither of them wanting to take him. His suffering is as deep as the sea on which he sails, his ship has no anchor and his heart no hope.

I think that these were more or less the words with which the bridegroom concluded. The bride looks at him gravely, casting sideways glances at his portrait. It seems as though she has guessed his secret, for when he asks, "Will you be faithful to me, Catharina?," she resolutely replies, "Faithful unto death."

At this point, I remember, I heard laughter, and this laughter came not from below, from Hell, but from above, from Paradise. On glancing up I caught sight of an exquisitely beautiful Eve looking down at me seductively with her big blue eyes. Her arm was dangling over the gallery and in her arm she was holding an apple, or, rather, an orange [*einen Apfel, oder vielmehr eine Apfelsine*]. But instead of symbolically offering me half of it, she merely dropped the peel metaphorically on my head. Was it intentional, or merely chance? I wanted to find out. But in ascending to Paradise to pursue this relationship, I was not a little perturbed to find a pale and gentle young girl, a thoroughly feminine figure, not languid, but as fragile as crystal, a very picture of domestic good breeding and ravishing loveliness. But around the left side of her upper lip there curled a thing like the tiny tail of a lizard as it slips away. It was an enigmatic feature, not the sort of thing you would expect to find on an innocent angel, but no more so on a hideous devil. It was a feature that spoke neither of good nor evil, but simply of pernicious knowledge; it was a smile poisoned by the apple of knowledge which those lips had tasted. Whenever I see such a feature upon the tender, ruby lips of a young girl, I feel in my own lips a trembling and convulsive desire to kiss them; it is an elective affinity.

And so I whispered into the ear of this beautiful girl: "*Juffrow*! I want to kiss your mouth."

"By God, Mynheer, what a splendid idea," was the answer that sprang from her heart, like music to my ears.

But no – I now intend to suppress the whole story that I was planning to tell here and for which the Flying Dutchman was to serve only as the frame. In this way I shall be revenged on all those prudes who delight in devouring such stories and who are ravished right down to the navel, and beyond, but who then revile the narrator, turning up their noses at him in society and decrying him as immoral. It is a fine story, as delicious as candied pineapple or fresh caviar or truffles in Burgundy, and it would make pleasant reading after prayers; but now I will suppress it out of rancor and a desire to settle old scores. Instead I shall place a long dash here ——

This dash indicates a black sofa, and it was there that the story I am not going to tell you took place. The innocent must suffer with the guilty, and there is many a good soul now casting entreating glances in my direction. Very well then, I can confide in the latter that I have never been kissed so passionately as by that blonde Dutch girl, and that she triumphantly overcame the prejudice that I had previously harbored against fair hair and blue eyes. Only now did I understand why an English poet compared such women to iced champagne. The most fiery essence smolders within this mantle of ice. There is no more piquant contrast than that between such external coldness and the inner fire that flares up in bacchanalian frenzy and irresistibly intoxicates the happy reveler. Yes, far more than in most brunettes this torch of sensuality burns in such apparently placid, saintly effigies with their haloes of flaxen hair, their sky-blue eyes and their pious lily-white hands. I know a blonde girl from one of the best Dutch families who, every once in a while, would leave her beautiful castle on the Zuider Zee and travel incognito to the theatre in Amsterdam, where she tossed orange peel on the head of any man who caught her fancy and even spent the occasional dissolute night in sailors' hostels, a regular Dutch Messalina.[3]

I returned to the theatre in time for the last scene of the play, at the point where the wife of the Flying Dutchman, Mrs. Flying Dutchman, is wringing her hands in despair, while out at sea her unhappy husband can be seen on the deck of the uncanny ship. He loves her and is leaving her so as not to be the cause of her undoing; he confesses to her his terrible fate and the fearful curse that weighs upon him. But she cries out in a loud voice: "I was faithful to you until this moment, I know a sure means of remaining faithful unto death!"

With these words the faithful woman hurls herself into the sea and the curse on the Flying Dutchman is lifted, he is redeemed, and we see the ghostly ship sinking to the bottom of the sea. The moral of this piece, for women, is that they should beware of marrying a Flying Dutchman; and we men should draw from it the lesson that women, at best, will be our undoing.

2. R. Wagner, original French prose draft (1840) for a one-act opera on the subject of the Flying Dutchman, "Le Hollandais volant – (nom d'un fantôme de mer)," translated by Peter Bloom.[4]

> Wagner first drafted a prose scenario in French, while he was still pinning his hopes on a Parisian production. The fair copy of the text appears to be Wagner's own French (though Bloom suggests it might have benefited from some outside assistance, perhaps even

by Heine). Wagner's provisional title is not the *Vaisseau fantôme* (phantom ship) – the title used by P. L. Dietsch and subsequently the traditional French title for Wagner's opera – but already the "Flying Dutchman." In this draft the setting of the opera is Scotland, as it would remain until shortly before the Dresden première. At this point no proper names are given. There is still a trace of Heine's sardonic stance to be found at the end of the first paragraph (explaining how Satan capitalizes on the inherent fickleness of women); but even this is muted in a way that suggests Wagner's ultimately serious, non-ironic treatment of the material.

The Flying Dutchman (name of a phantom of the sea)

Once again seven years have gone by, during which the Dutchman – or, according to sailors' tradition, the "Flying Dutchman" – has been wandering upon the high seas, unable to attain either repose or death. Today, from his darkened vessel, whose blood-red sails and ghostly crew are feared by all sailors in foreign waters, he comes ashore on one of the coasts of Scotland. In days gone by, several centuries earlier, the dare-devil swore that he could round any and all possible capes, in spite of strong headwinds and even if it took him an eternity. Satan took him at his word and condemned him to eternal wandering upon the seas, but unable to die – which fate he now longed for passionately. There was only a single condition whose fulfillment would enable the condemned man to achieve redemption: he would have to be "delivered" by a woman who would remain faithful to him unto death. This condition, however, simply provided a means for Satan to collect new victims, because – since women who did not remain faithful unto death were to become the property of the devil – he could not help but acquire them through the vain efforts of the Dutchman to redeem himself in this way.

To this end, the Dutchman was allowed to go ashore every seven years. How many times had he tried by this means to find redemption! And how many times had he been cast back upon the waters due to woman's infidelity! Today he is more weary of his punishment than ever before. If only he could put an end to his existence, even at the price of being reduced to nothingness.

On the coast he meets a very wealthy Scottish merchant who has likewise just landed. He sells the merchant some diamonds and precious jewels, and the Scotsman finds his purchase very profitable. Asked if he has a daughter, he replies positively, and soon comes to terms with the Dutchman on a marriage contract with his daughter, in this way confirming their commercial relations.

His daughter has been raised since infancy together with a young man, good-hearted but poor, who loves her passionately. But the young man fears that he will never obtain the permission to marry his beloved from her rich father. Furthermore, he has often been troubled and angered by the strange and dreamlike inclinations of his beloved; he has never really known with certainty whether his love was in fact returned. The young girl would often sit for hours before a strange portrait in the drawing room, which she would stare at with deep enchantment. This portrait showed a pale and handsome man dressed in black Spanish-style attire. His features, which expressed a profound and ceaseless suffering, touched her to the bottom of her heart. She was especially moved on hearing an ancient ballad, which she had often heard sung by her maid, and which she herself repeated every day. This ballad told of the terrible fate suffered by the pale and handsome man in the portrait. But nothing touched her more vehemently than the end of the ballad, which explained the condition for the salvation of the Dutchman, and which indicated simultaneously that until now he had not as yet found a woman faithful to him unto death. At that moment she would become highly elated and would cry out: "I, yes I, I could deliver this wretched condemned man from his fate!" Such exclamations were heard by everyone with great sorrow; but no one was more afflicted than the poor young man who loved her so much, and who would rush off headlong into the nearby woods and mountains, there to calm his fears and doubts.

It was after one such episode that the father arrived accompanied by the Dutchman. He immediately tells his daughter that she is to marry the stranger: he was enormously wealthy and, furthermore, his apparent sincerity and his ancient lineage would surely convince her not to reject such a marriage. [*The fragmentary German prose draft picks up at about this point*; cf. item 3, below.] But the girl hears none of these praises: the sight of the stranger transfixes her as if by a spell; – she cannot turn her eyes away from his gaze. The two are left alone.

The stranger, profoundly moved by the girl's countenance, hopes to awaken her love. Her appearance reminds him of times long past. Yes, he too has experienced passionate love, but, alas, the devil's cruel mockery would always leave him frustrated in order to make him feel acutely the endless suffering to which he has been condemned. Might she be the one who could remain faithful to him unto death? She declares that she knows but one kind of fidelity, namely that unto death. He attempts to test her by giving her a glimpse from afar of his terrible fate – which captivates her all the more. Swept up by a vague emotion difficult to explain even to herself, she resolves to fulfill the promise made by her father to the stranger.

Night has begun to fall. The father has arranged a celebration. His house is located on the seacoast. The Scotsman's ship and that of the Dutchman are next to each other in port. Happiness reigns throughout the Scottish vessel; everybody sings and drinks to the health of the betrothed couple. But the behavior of the Dutch vessel's crew offers a bizarre contrast, for a deadly silence reigns among them. The lively Scotsmen scoff at the others, and ask if they don't know how to celebrate like real sailors, if they haven't learned to sing and drink, if they don't perhaps belong to the "Flying Dutchman," as the appearance of their ship suggests, and if they don't perhaps have some letters to send to their ancestors, etc. Such taunting angers the Dutchman's sailors, and they reply that they wish indeed to sing a song such as one learns after roaming the seas for centuries on end. They sing a song that is strange, frightful, and terrifying. The Scottish sailors are frightened, and after trying in vain to smother the Dutchmen's horrifying song with their own lively tune, they fall silent and leave the deck, making the sign of the cross – which only provokes the derisive and diabolical laughter of the Dutchmen.

The young girl comes out of the house; her young lover follows her. He is simply desperate: "What have I heard? What have I seen? Is this my reward for so much faithful and long-proved love? Is it really true that you are giving your hand to this stranger who has barely crossed the threshold?" The young girl struggles with her emotions; her friend's protestations fill her with sadness and compassion; but she maintains that it would be impossible for her to belong to him, that this is the will of her father. The young man wishes to hear no more; he reminds her of their childhood and the happy times they spent together, which proved to him that she loved him. This entire conversation is overheard by the Dutchman. When he learns that his fiancée is already bound by the obligations of another love, he rushes to her, and with extreme emotion he cries: "Ah, you cannot be true to me! But it is not yet too late. I love you too much to carry you off to your destruction. Adieu!" The young girl tries to restrain and reassure him, saying that he must not doubt her fidelity, that she belongs only to him. The stranger wishes to hear no more. He orders the crew of his ship to weigh anchor and set sail, for they now have to go out to sea for all time. "Yes," he says, "your kind appearance fills my heart with so much compassion that I absolutely must spare you a terrible fate. You love another, and you will not be able to remain faithful to me. Be happy. I do not want to ruin you. For you should know that the woman who is not faithful to me unto death risks eternal damnation. The number of women I have condemned to this terrible fate is already sufficiently great. But you will be saved! Adieu!" He tries to flee, but she restrains him, begging on her knees: "I am fully aware of your fate, but I am the one who shall deliver you from it!" He wrenches free from her hands: "No, you don't know me!" He points to his ship, whose red sails have been hoisted and whose crew is furiously preparing to cast off. "Behold," he cries, "this ship, with its blood-red sails, strikes terror into the hearts of all sailors. And it is I whom they call the 'Flying Dutchman'!" With these words he leaps aboard his ship as it casts off the shore. Having wrenched herself free from those who are trying to hold her back, the young girl rushes out to a rocky promontory and at the top of her lungs cries out to the departing Dutchman: "I know full well that you can only be saved by a woman faithful to you unto death! Look, then: I love you, and I am faithful to you unto my death!" And as she pronounces the last word she leaps from the cliff into the sea. At the same instant the Dutchman's vessel sinks beneath the waves and disappears.

3. Wagner, fragmentary German prose sketch (from the end of Act II to end); translated by Stewart Spencer in *Wagner* 2 (1981), 26–29.

> In addition to the original French prose scenario, translated above, Wagner wrote a longer, more detailed prose draft in German, of which only a fragment survives. Otto Strobel, who first published the fragment (in the *Bayreuther Blätter* in 1933), identified the fragment as dating from spring 1840, while the editors of the *Wagner Werk-Verzeichnis* suggest that it did not originate until about a year later. The latter claim seems plausible, given the very close resemblance between much of the dialogue sketched here and that of the completed libretto, written down between 18 and 28 May 1841. Wagner's prose drafts often anticipated precise details of the final libretto, which in other cases was often executed directly on the heels of the draft.
>
> The surviving fragment offers proof that Wagner did start out with the notion of casting the work as a single act in three scenes (the beginning of what became Act III in the standard performing

version is here explicitly headed "scene 3"). The final musical-dramatic complex that closes the opera – eventually designated as "Duet, Cavatina, and Finale," is already specified (as "Duet, Trio, and Finale"). The "Trio" indicated here must surely correspond to the Dutchman–Erik–Senta ensemble that follows Erik's Cavatina in the final score ("Fort auf das Meer/Was hör' ich, Gott?/Ha, zweifelst du"), suggesting that Wagner may have imagined the preceding *scena* and Cavatina as a formal duet. It would be interesting to know what other musical numbers or scene complexes might have been identified in the prose draft. One might have expected to find an indication of the big duet at the end of Act II, beginning at the moment Daland leaves the scene and the Dutchman, after a long silence, addresses "Anna" (i.e., Senta). However, it may be that Wagner already conceived of everything after the Dutchman's appearance (following the Senta–Erik duet) as a single scene-complex, as he in fact indicated in the completed score.

As in the French prose draft, the setting is Scotland. Now at least two of the characters have names: Anna (later Senta) and Georg (later Erik). The claim put forth by Julius Kapp (*Richard Wagner und die Frauen*, 1929) that the Senta character was originally named "Minna" (after Wagner's wife) is thus contradicted by the evidence of this draft.

. . . his daughter's jewels: this is the least precious of all the treasures which the *str.*[anger] possesses. Has she no desire to share such wealth? – He [the father] thinks it better to leave the two of them alone together, – he prefers it if the stranger himself talks the girl around. – He thinks it better to leave the two of them alone together, – he prefers it if the stranger himself talks the girl round. He commends her to him as a good, *faithful* child, and to *her* he praises him as a man of generous and noble temperament. – He leaves. It is the *Dut.*[chman] who first breaks the silence. He feels moved to the very depths of his being. This girl's charming appearance speaks to him as though of distant times long past. He, too, has loved, & still feels that, if the devil's cruel mockery has left a beating heart within his breast, it is (alas!) only so that endless suffering might torment him the more acutely. He now feels himself moved by a wonderful, ineffable feeling: would that he might call it love! But no! Rather it is a yearning for the salvation which such an angel might offer him! – *Anna*, too, gives voice to the strange state of mind in which she finds herself; is it a dream, or is she awake? Who is this stranger, with his marvelous features distorted by pain? Does she not feel to have known him for years? How powerfully and unspeakably the sight of him moves her? – He approaches her: "Might you be the angel whose faithful hand will guide me to my salvation? How might it be possible for you to devote yourself to a poor outcast, to a man tossed restlessly about, who now approaches you in the hope of finding in your undying love the peace you have [recte: he has?] always longed for?" – *Anna:* "Whoever you may be, whatever anguish you may have known, whatever the fate which may be in store for me: – I shall always obey my father!" – *Dut:* "So you could give yourself unquestioningly to me, then? What have I done to have deserved this from you? Could it be that my suffering alone is sufficient appeal?" *Anna:* "Oh, what suffering! If only I might console you!" – *Dut:* "You are an angel, & an angel's love is boundless; she is even able to console the profligate! If only you suspected what my fate is." – *Anna:* "Your fate?" *Dut:* "Then you would understand the sacrifice involved in swearing to be faithful to a wretch like me: you would shudder at the lot which you draw on yourself, were you not possessed of woman's finest virtue, were you not possessed of true loyalty!" – *Anna:* "Be comforted, unhappy, wretched man! There is no cruel destiny, no terrible fate which I need fear once I have sworn to be true; the man who receives my love receives my *only* love – steadfast unto death!" – The *Dut.* Feels strangely elated: "Is it then to be she who saves me? Am I then to have found the woman who will help me find salvation? Almighty God, which hast abandoned me – strengthen this angel's heart!" – *Anna:* "Entranced by this unconscious spell, I no longer know whether I am dreaming or awake! Can I grasp and comprehend the powerful feeling which causes my bosom to swell so strangely! Almighty God, let it be love!" – Her *father* enters: "What do you think, my lord? Shall I make preparations for the wedding? My people are celebrating outside: they want to enjoy themselves! They are speaking of bride and groom! Come along, follow me! With your permission, I'll present you to them!" Exit with Anna and Dut.

Scene 3

– The bay; to one side the Scotsman's house. The background occupied by two ships. Merriment and celebrations on the Scottish vessel, – deathly silence and darkness on the Dutchman's. The Scottish steersman and sailors are drinking and singing. Cheerful talk and proposing of toasts. The attitude of the Dutch vessel surprises them. – Are they not celebrating as well? "What sort of fellows are they who do not sing and drink with us?" No answer. – They make fun of the

Dutchman's crew and amuse themselves at their expense. The steersman asks: do you think they belong to the Flying Dutchman? Their ship looks just as if it does; no less than the crew themselves!" The sailors continue joking: "How many centuries long have they all been on board? Do they have any letters or parcels to send? They'd see if they could deliver them to their great-grandfathers and mothers" etc. Things begin to stir on board the Dutchman. The sea grows rough, but only in the immediate vicinity of the ship. A storm blows up in its masts. Its ghost-crew calls to the Scottish sailors, – "Since you asked for it, you shall hear a song such as those which men learn who have roamed the seas for centuries." They sing. Their vessel is tossed up and down on the waves as though it were dancing. A terrible gale howls and whistles through the open rigging, while the rest of the scene, like the sea, remains as calm as ever before. The Scottish crew are dismayed, & believe the ship to be haunted. They try to shout down the strange song and repeat their own lively tune at the tops of their voices. The apparition thunders more dreadfully than ever; – the Scottish sailors finally fall silent and leave the deck, making the sign of the cross, at the sight of which the Dut. crew breaks out in hideous laughter; for a moment all is silent: the sea and the air are everywhere as calm as they were before, & the same deathly silence reigns on the Dut. vessel. –

Duet. Trio and Finale

– *Anna* enters at an agitated pace, followed by *Georg* who raves like a madman. "What did I hear? What did I see? Is it possible? – Tell me, am I dreaming?" – *Anna* turns aside: "Leave me, Georg! Do not ask! I may not answer you!" *Georg:* Merciful God, it is true! No doubt about it! – What baleful power has you in its grasp that you should so lightly deal this mortal blow? – Your father . . . oh, I can guess, – he brought your bridegroom home with him! – But you? – Scarcely had I left you than you gave your hand to a stranger – a stranger who had barely crossed the threshold?" – *Anna:* Stop! No more! I have no choice! No choice!" – *Georg:* "Oh, such blind obedience! No! It's not possible! How could the truest of hearts so swiftly be sacrificed? No doubt to save yourself the trouble of killing me slowly. My heart has been crushed by a single blow." *Anna,* in the most painful dilemma: "My father insists: I have to obey him! I'm not to see you again and not to think of you either, – duty on high demands it of me!" – *Georg:*

"Your duty? Your father? – What words are these?! Do you not recall the times so newly past when, half children still, we swore eternal love?" *Anna* vehemently: "I? *Eternal love?*" – *Georg:* – What? Do you not recall that day when you called me down from the rocky scar into the green valley below, where at your feet I lay the highland flower? Do you recall how we lost our way in the forest? Do you remember how, from high on the cliff, we often gazed out to sea for a sight of your father's ship whenever he went away and entrusted you to my care? What was the name with which you greeted me all that time and with which you flattered my love? You called me your friend, your only friend, and wound your arms round my neck! – Tell me, was it not love you felt when caressing my cheek? Was it not the solemn promise of your undying love which gave strength to your hand's gentle pressure? – The *stranger* has overheard this whole scene: – he now steps forward in a state of terrible agitation: "I'm lost! Alas! I'm done for! Damned for all eternity! Farewell, Anna! – *Anna:* "Wait, unhappy man!" – *Georg:* "What do I see?" – The *Dut:* Leave me! Let me return to sea! To sea for all eternity! – Anna, you cannot be true to me, since your love belongs to another! I have no wish to destroy you, – you are not yet lost!" Turning to the crew of his ship, he gives a piercing signal on his whistle: "Hoist the sails! Weigh anchor! Bid farewell to dry land for all time!" – *Anna:* tries to detain him – Wretched man, do you doubt my undying love?" The *Dut:* – "Your undying love! My salvation! Unhappy girl, learn of the fate from which I have saved you! I am condemned to suffer the most hideous of fates and would more keenly desire a tenfold death. A woman alone can release me from the curse if she keeps faith with me unto death! You have not yet sworn before God, – and so I can still save you; for mark me well: the fate which would befall you, were you not to remain true unto death, is eternal damnation! Countless are the victims already condemned by me to that sentence; but you will be saved! Farewell!" *Anna* in a state of extreme agitation: "Your fate is well known to me: I knew it as soon as I saw you: but the end of your torment is at hand: I am she whose undying love shall release you!" – "You do not know me, – you cannot suspect who I am!" (pointing to his ship, whose blood-red sails have been hoisted and whose crew is engaged in hideous activity, preparing to cast off, weigh anchor, etc.!) "Ask the seas of the world, they'll recognize this ship! With its blood-red sails, it is the terror of all God-fearing sailors, – & it is I, I – whom men call the *Flying Dutchman*!" With the speed of lightning he is on board his ship, which in the very same moment casts off. *Anna's* father and nurse and the chorus, who have hurried up in answer to Georg's cries for help, attempt in vain to hold her back; with the strength of one possessed she tears herself free and reaches a rocky promontory: at the top of her voice she calls after the disappearing *Dut:* "I know full well that you can only be saved by a woman who is faithful to you unto death! Look at me; I have been faithful to you until now, faithful unto death!" She leaps into the sea; and even as she does so the Dutchman's ship sinks without a trace beneath the waves.

B.   Autobiographical texts and correspondence

1. From R. Wagner, "Autobiographical Sketch" ("Autobiographische Skizze"), originally published in *Zeitung für die elegante Welt* (1 and 8 February 1843) (*GS*, vol. 1, 13–14, 16–19).[1]

> In the wake of his great public success with *Rienzi*, Wagner was asked by his friend Heinrich Laube to supply a short autobiographical sketch for the literary-cultural periodical he was editing at this time ("Newspaper for the Elegant World"). The account of the conception and composition of *Der fliegende Holländer* here is of interest since it is nearly contemporaneous with the work itself.

[**Spring 1839**] Around this time my contract with the director of the [Riga] theatre came to an end, and particular circumstances made it inconvenient for me to remain any longer in Riga. For two years already I had been nurturing the plan of going to Paris; to this end I had sent, from Königsberg, the draft of an operatic subject to Scribe with the suggestion that, if the idea pleased him, he should accept it free of charge and work it up into a libretto, if he would then arrange a commission for me to compose it for the Paris Opéra.[2] Of course, Scribe paid no attention to this idea whatsoever. Nonetheless, I did not give up on my plans, but on the contrary, continued to pursue them with determination in the summer of 1839, convincing my wife to join me aboard a sailing-vessel that was to transport us to London. This sea-voyage I shall never forget; it lasted for three-and-a-half weeks and was fraught with mishaps. On three different occasions we suffered terrible storms, and on one of them the captain was forced to seek shelter in a harbor on the Norwegian coast. The passage through the rocky Norwegian skerries made a tremendous impression on my imagination; the legend of the Flying Dutchman, which I heard repeated by the sailors, acquired for me a distinctive coloring such as only the experience of such an adventure at sea could provide. [. . .]

[**Mid-summer 1840**] Suddenly Meyerbeer showed up in Paris again for a short time. He inquired with the most genial concern after the state of my affairs and declared himself ready to assist me. He then put me in contact with the director of the Opéra, Léon Pillet: it was decided that I should supply the theatre with an opera in two or three acts.[3] I had already provided myself with the draft of a subject for just such an opportunity as this. The "Flying Dutchman," whose intimate acquaintance I had made during my sea-voyage, had continued to preoccupy my imagination; in addition, I had become acquainted with H. Heine's treatment of the subject, in his characteristic fashion, in a part of his *Salon* [*see Appendix A, no. 1, pp. 166–69*]. In particular it was the conception of how this Ahasuerus of the ocean might be redeemed, which Heine had taken from a Dutch play on the same theme, that gave me just what I needed to adapt the material as an operatic subject. I came to an understanding here with Heine himself, drafted a sketch of the subject, and gave this to M. Léon Pillet with the suggestion that he have a French libretto fashioned from it for me to set.

Things had proceeded thus far when Meyerbeer departed from Paris again, leaving the fulfillment of my hopes and plans to fate. Soon I learned from Pillet, to my surprise, that he was so pleased with the sketch I had submitted to him that he wished I would immediately cede to him my own claim to it. According to a previous agreement he was obligated to provide another composer with a libretto as soon as possible. My sketch seemed to him perfectly suited to this purpose, and no doubt any objections on my side to parting with the subject would be quelled by the knowledge that I could not possibly hope to receive any commission for an opera of my own for at least four years due to other outstanding commitments to several protégés [*Kandidaten*] of the Opéra administration; surely I would not want to carry this subject around with me for such a long time; surely some other idea would occur to me in the meantime and help console me for the sacrifice of this one. I stubbornly resisted this presumption, but achieved nothing more than a temporary deferral of the matter. Setting my hopes on the hasty return of Meyerbeer, I remained silent.

In the interim I was asked by Schlesinger to write for his *Gazette musicale*.[4] I provided him with various substantial essays – "On German Music," and others. Especially well received was a short story entitled "A Pilgrimage to Beethoven." These writings contributed not a little to making my name known in Paris. In November of this year [1840] I completed the full score of my *Rienzi* and sent it immediately off to Dresden. This period saw the culmination of my exceptionally unfortunate circumstances. For the *Gazette musicale* I wrote another short story, "The End of a German Musician in Paris" ("Das Ende eines deutschen Musikers in Paris"), whose hapless protagonist dies uttering this credo: "I believe in God, Mozart, and Beethoven." It was a good thing that my opera was completed, for now I found myself obliged to forgo all creative artistic activity for an extended time; instead I was reduced to undertaking for Schlesinger arrangements for all sorts of instruments, even the *cornet à pistons*. These activities secured for me some slight improvement in my situation. Thus winter of 1841 I passed in the most ignoble of circumstances.

In the spring I moved out to the country, to Meudon. With the warm approach of summer I yearned once again for creative work – and the occasion to realize this wish came sooner than expected. I learned that my sketch for a libretto on the "Flying Dutchman" had already been given over to a poet, Paul Fouché [Foucher], and it became evident that if I were not willing to abdicate my rights to the material I would simply be cheated of it under some pretext or other. So I at last agreed to surrender the rights to my draft for a certain sum of money. I quickly turned around and executed my own libretto in German. In order to compose the libretto I needed a piano, since after a compositional hiatus of three-quarters of a year I needed to re-immerse myself in the proper creative frame of mind. And so I rented a small piano. Once it had arrived I rushed about in a state of the greatest anxiety – I dreaded to discover that I had perhaps ceased to be a musician at all. I started out with the Sailors' Chorus [Act III] and the spinning-song [Act II]; after that, everything flowed along quite smoothly, and I shouted for joy upon gaining the inner conviction that I was indeed still a musician after all. Within seven weeks I had composed the entire opera.

At the end of this time, however, I was once again inundated with the most petty cares; it was another two months before I could manage to compose the overture to the completed opera, even though I was carrying it around all but finished in my head. Naturally I had no greater desire than to see the opera produced as quickly as possible in Germany. From Munich and from Leipzig I received negative responses – the opera was not suited to Germany, I was told. Poor fool that I was, I had thought that the opera was suited *only* for Germany, as it struck a chord that can only resonate among Germans.

Finally I sent my newest work to Meyerbeer in Berlin with the request that he arrange for its acceptance by the court theatre there. And before long this was accomplished. As my *Rienzi* had just been accepted by the Dresden court theatre I was now able to anticipate productions of two of my works by the leading German stages, and I was overcome by the realization that – strangely enough – Paris had turned out to be of great assistance for my career in Germany. In Paris itself, however, I had no prospects for several years at least; so I left the city in the spring of 1842. For the first time I set eyes on the Rhine – and with warm tears in my eyes I, poor artist, swore eternal allegiance to my German fatherland.

2. From *A Communication to my Friends* (*Eine Mittheilung an meine Freunde*, 1851, published 1852: *GS*, vol. 4, 265–68).

> The "Communication," written soon after *Opera and Drama* and Wagner's other theoretical tracts on the "art-work of the future," is a stylized artistic and intellectual autobiography, less concerned with facts and dates. In this way it complements the more down-to-earth factual narrative of the 1843 "sketch."

I have already indicated in general terms the mood in which I conceived the "Flying Dutchman." The conception was quite as old as the mood as such, which I had been cultivating for some time, and which, stimulated by certain captivating impressions, was finally ripe for communication in appropriate artistic form.

– The figure of the "Flying Dutchman" is a mythic-poetic creation of the folk: a primeval trait of human nature finds the most gripping and powerful expression in this figure. In its most general significance this trait can be identified as the longing for peace in the wake of life's storms. We encounter the figure in the bright, cheerful Hellenic world in the guise of Odysseus and his wanderings, and his longing for homeland, house, hearth, and wife – for all that this civic-minded son of ancient Greece could truly hope for, and that which he did finally achieve. Christianity, lacking a strong feeling for an earthly homeland, re-created this figure in the guise of the "Wandering Jew" [*des "ewigen Juden"*]. For that wanderer, condemned to an endlessly joyless and pointless, long-since outlived existence, there bloomed no hope of redemption on earth; his only remaining desire was a longing for death, his only hope the prospect of ceasing to exist. Then toward the end of the Middle Ages a new, active feeling directed the attention of various nations towards *life*: the successful, world-historical consequence of this new orientation was a drive toward discovery. The sea became the arena of life; this, however, no longer meant just the confined Mediterranean horizons of the Hellenic world, but the vast oceans that girdle the entire globe. This marked a break with the old world; the longing of Odysseus to return to homeland, hearth and conjugal mate had been transformed, after the sorrows of the "Wandering Jew" and his longing for death, into a longing for something new and unknown, something never before experienced and yet heralded by a sense of anticipation. We meet this extraordinary, broad new psychological trait in the myth of the Flying Dutchman, this poem of sea-faring people from the world-historical epoch of the voyages of discovery. What we have here is a remarkable hybrid, cultivated by the spirit of the folk, of the character of the Wandering Jew with that of Odysseus. For his temerity this Dutch seaman is condemned by the devil (by which we are to understand here the element of tides and storms) to navigate the seas aimlessly throughout all eternity. Just as Ahasuerus, he yearns for an end of his sorrows through death. But this redemption, withheld from the Wandering Jew, is put within reach of the Dutchman in the form of – a woman who will sacrifice herself for love. The longing for death drives him to seek out such a woman. But that woman is no longer the domestic paragon, Penelope, as courted in ancient times by Odysseus; it is now the epitome of woman [*das Weib überhaupt*], woman as yet unmanifest, only longed-for, dimly intuited, an infinitely feminine being – let me just say it outright: the *woman of the future*.

This, then, was the "Flying Dutchman" who continued to rise from the waves and other wetlands of my life so regularly and with such irresistible attraction. It was the first *popular myth* [*Volksgedicht*] to penetrate my heart and compel me, as a creative artist, to reshape it and interpret it in artistic form.

From this point my career as a *poet* begins, while that as a mere manufacturer of opera libretti ceases. And yet it was no radical leap that I was making. At no point did I operate on the basis of conscious reflection. Such a reflective move could only be effected on the basis of some combination of exemplary phenomena lying ready at hand. Yet the phenomena that might have served as examples for my new creative path [*auf meiner neuen Bahn*] were nowhere to be found. My procedure was new; it was indicated to me by my own innermost state of mind [*Stimmung*], impressed upon me by the need to communicate this state of mind. In order to liberate myself from within (that is, to communicate with like-minded people out of a need for understanding) I had to set out in a new direction as an artist, one not suggested by my prior experience. What drives one to do this is a sense of necessity – a deeply felt, compelling necessity, though not fully understood in terms of practical reason.

If I mean to present myself to my friends here as a poet, I should perhaps feel some compunction about doing so on the basis of a poem such as my *Flying Dutchman*. So much here remains unformed, the structuring of the situations so loose and amorphous, the poetic verse and diction so lacking in individuality that any of our modern-day playwrights – who structure everything according to a predetermined plan, seeking out whatever material their lightly acquired professional skill judges as promising – might well see fit to upbraid me harshly for my presumption in dignifying my work with the designation of "poem." I should much sooner be checked by my own misgivings about the form of this poem than by any fear of such critical censure, were it at all my intention to present it as a finished product. On the contrary, however, I am perfectly pleased to exhibit to my friends the course of my artistic development [*mich in meinem Werden vorzuführen*]. Yet the form of the "Flying Dutchman" poem was, like that of all my subsequent works, conditioned in every particular, down to the last detail of its musical execution, by the material itself, as this had become part of a distinctive personal frame of mind [*Lebensstimmung*], and as I continued to acquire a capacity for artistic formation along the lines of my newly chosen path, through practice and experience.

I will return to the characteristic features of this artistic formation, as I have already promised. But for the moment let me continue to follow up the genesis of my dramatic poems, having now indicated the crucial turning point of my artistic evolution with respect to formal considerations. –

I next proceeded to execute both the poetry and music of my *Flying Dutchman* with the utmost rapidity under external circumstances that I have already described for my friends in another context.[5] I had

moved out of Paris into the country, and from here I began to establish my first new contacts with my German homeland. My *Rienzi* had
been accepted for performance in Dresden. This acceptance struck
me as a quite unexpected and heartening sign of love and friendship
from Germany, warming my heart all the more towards my homeland
as the cosmopolitan winds of Paris were blowing with an ever more
icy chill. Already I felt myself back in Germany in all my thoughts
and my work [*Tichten und Trachten*]. I was overcome with an emotional, longing sense of patriotism such as I had never entertained
before. This patriotism was devoid of any political coloring; for even
by that time I was sufficiently enlightened that the current state of
political Germany possessed not the slightest attraction for me, as
compared, say, to that of political France. It was rather the feeling of
homelessness in Paris that aroused in me a longing for the German
homeland. Yet this longing was not aimed at some long familiar thing
that was to be regained – rather at something new, as yet unknown,
which I intuitively longed for, but of which I only knew one thing for
sure: that I would certainly never find it here in Paris. It was the
longing of my Flying Dutchman for a woman – not, as I have suggested, for the wife of Odysseus, but for the redeeming woman whose
features I beheld as yet only indistinctly, and which hovered before me
only as the feminine element in general. And now this element
expressed itself to me in terms of the *homeland* [*Heimat*], that is to say,
the sensation of being embraced by some intimately familiar community, although a community I did not truly know, but only longed for
as the realization of the concept of "homeland." Previously it had
been the notion of something thoroughly foreign that, in the
confining circumstances of my earlier existence [i.e., in Magdeburg
and Riga] had beckoned to me with the promise of salvation, and
which had driven me towards Paris in order to find it. Yet just as I had
met with disappointment in Paris, so I was to again in Germany. My
Flying Dutchman had not by any means yet discovered the *new*
world: *his* woman could only redeem him by bringing about his end,
and her own. – But, let us proceed!

After the completion of my *Flying Dutchman*, preoccupied only
with the thought of returning to Germany and of acquiring the necessary means to accomplish this, I found myself obliged once again
to turn to musical hack-work. I prepared piano scores of Halévy
operas. Yet a new-won sense of pride preserved me now from the

bitterness with which these demeaning tasks had previously filled me. I maintained my good humor and kept up a correspondence with my homeland regarding the upcoming preparations for the production of my *Rienzi*. And from Berlin I received a confirmation of the acceptance of my *Flying Dutchman* for performance there. [In my imagination] I lived now entirely in the longed-for, native sphere which I was about to re-enter [in reality].

From Wagner's correspondence (1841–44)

Translations by the editor (except where noted), from R. Wagner, *Sämtliche Briefe* (*SB*), vols. 1 and 2 ed. Gertrud Strobel and Werner Wolf (Leipzig: VEB Deutscher Verlag für Musik, 1967, 1970).

To Cäcilie Avenarius

Dresden, 5 January 1843

My dearest Cäcilie,
[. . .] During that time [while *Rienzi* had been taken off the boards to afford the singers a rest] my *Flying Dutchman* was put into rehearsal. [Schröder-] Devrient took on the role of Senta. After the brilliant, splendid, intoxicating operatic experience of *Rienzi* none of us held out great hopes for the effect of the *Dutchman*; I confess that I myself approached the matter with much trepidation, since it requires a good deal of imagination [*Fantasie*] to appreciate this opera, which offers little in the way of brilliant effects. It is something altogether different, a whole new genre (as many are saying), which will likely be slow to make headway: you all have been of different opinions on the issue. The première took place on 2 January, and I confess that I take much greater pride in the success with which this opera met than in the case of *Rienzi*, where I had so much at my disposal. We gave the opera in three acts so that it filled an entire evening.[6] After the second and third acts I was greeted with stormy applause, as were the singers. The second performance took place just yesterday, and I experienced the triumph of an even greater public response. As before I was called out twice with the singers; I let the singers take a bow on their own, but the public would not be satisfied until I made a solo appearance. And so with this opera, too – which came into the world practically before your very eyes – I have managed to score a success; indeed, I

may perhaps claim to have founded a new genre. Its success really means a lot, given the kind of expectations that had been aroused by *Rienzi*. The plan is now for the *Dutchman* to be put on in Berlin at the beginning of March.[7] [. . .]

Your brother,
Richard W.

(*SB*, vol. 2, 203–04)

To Robert Schumann

Most valued friend,

Since I know you take a kindly interest in me, it is with a joyous heart I can inform you that yesterday my new opera, *The Flying Dutchman*, scored a success that fills me with greater pride than the success of *Rienzi*, precisely because I have sharply departed in this newest opera from everything that the public is accustomed to seeing and hearing. I, along with my friends, had only hoped that public approbation might follow upon closer acquaintance with the opera; the fact that the very first performance has met with such significant approval surpasses all our expectations – after the second and third acts I was called out, together with the singers, to stormy applause. [Schröder-]Devrient achieved with her role perhaps the most original creation of her whole career [*vielleicht das Originellste, was sie je produciert*]. Her success was enthusiastically registered: shivering with both excitement and warm sympathy. the audience found themselves running hot and cold. [. . .]

Yours most truly,
Richard Wagner

Dresden, 3 January 1843
(*SB*, vol. 2, 197)

Most esteemed friend,

I am thinking of imposing a piece of work on you – I see no other way for it, but to turn to you. Here I sit in Dresden, produce my operas, have success, become Kapellmeister[8] – and yet remain God-forsaken, for all that. They write about me in all the papers, but what do they write? The usual figures or speech, turns of phrase, mainly good and perhaps even too well meant, sometimes not well meant. All this, it is true, affords me some recognition. But most of those who speak about me understand nothing of what really matters in the case of composer, and thus it pains me to see nothing but empty phrase-making reaching the public. I need a real musician. I know of none in Dresden, but I do in Leipzig. I know you do what you can for me[9] – I appreciate that, but I like to think that you *might* do more, i.e. that you get to *know* my works. [. . .] I am about to send the score of my *Flying Dutchman* back to Berlin, where the work is to be produced in March. But I cannot resist the temptation to hold on to the score for a few more days in order to send it first to you. Perhaps it will interest you, and dispose you to carrying out my request, if I were to leave the score with you for three days so that you might look through it. Just so that you could become acquainted with my [new] direction – that's the main thing for me. If you were moved to write something more or less substantial about my music – I leave that up to you. [. . .]

Yours,
Richard Wagner
Marienstrasse no. 9

Dresden, 27 January 1843
(*SB*, vol. 2, 215–18)

My most worthy friend,
[. . .] Permit me to mention at this juncture that it says much for the seriousness of our local audiences that a composition such as my *Flying Dutchman* was given such a warm reception here. Your remarks on the piece, after you had perused the score, confirm this observation of mine, and to judge by the reservations you expressed concerning its excessively somber coloring – reservations which I admit to be well-founded – one might have expected that such a work would have had no great appeal here. But since audiences have grown increasingly accustomed to the work the more often they have heard it, I believe it not inappropriate to mention this fact in order to encourage you to think more highly of the seriousness of taste which is increasingly gaining ground here. – I may add that I agree with everything which – in light of your present knowledge of the work – you have found to say on the subject; there is only one point which alarmed me, and which – I must confess, because of the issues it raises – embittered me: that you can tell me quite calmly that there is a good deal in the work that smacks of – Meyerbeer. In the first place I do not know what in the whole world is meant by the word "Meyerbeerian,"

except perhaps a sophisticated striving after superficial popularity; but no existing work can be "Meyerbeerian" since . . . not even Meyerbeer himself is "Meyerbeerian," but Rossinian, Bellinian, Auberian, Spontinian etc. etc. But if there really were some solid reality that could be called "Meyerbeerian" just as we describe something as Beethovenian, or, for all I care, as Rossinian, I confess that it would have required a wonderful freak of nature for me to have drawn my inspiration from *that* particular source, the merest smell of which, after wafting in from afar, is sufficient to turn my stomach. This would be the death-knell of my creative powers, and the fact that you have condemned me demonstrates clearly that your view of me is far from impartial, a fact which is perhaps attributable to your knowledge of the *external* circumstances of my life, since these, I admit, brought me into contact with Meyerbeer the *man*, to the extent that I now find myself in his debt. [. . .][10]

> Your most obedient servant
> *Richard Wagner*

Dresden, 25 February 1843
(Translation from Spencer and Millington, *Selected Letters*, 105)

To Johann Philipp Samuel Schmidt (Berlin)

Most honored sir,
[. . .] Since you wish it, . . . I hasten to submit a brief and factual report on the success of my *Flying Dutchman*, which has just received its third performance. I am enclosing a copy of the libretto, from which you will see how completely this opera differs in style from that of *Rienzi*, indeed, how far it diverges in many essential points from all that our audiences have come exclusively to regard as the leading operatic genre. You will find that I have allowed a simple tale to unfold of its own accord, without endowing it with this or that operatic ingredient such as is generally considered necessary nowadays. The French versifier who adapted my sketch[11] (the authorship of which is common knowledge) has completely destroyed the marvelous aura of the tale by weaving into it episodes such as are to be found in every contemporary French opera. Although I felt I had solved the problem by simplifying the plot as far as possible, I could not conceal from myself the fact that I was risking a great deal more by appearing before the general public in what is at present so alien a guise . . . In

this opera I have included no pageantry, nor any thunderous finales straining for theatrical effect, etc . . . I was all the more surprised to meet with the most brilliant success at the very first performance, and to be assured that I had succeeded in winning over the audience right from the outset. The first act, as you will see from the libretto, is really only an introduction, but once it had put the audience in the right mood of suspense they were swept along irresistibly by the work, not least because of the highly original and affecting acting of Schröder-Devrient. I and the singers were called on stage and greeted with tumultuous applause, which was repeated at the end of the third act, which, moreover, contains the scene with the ghost ship and a rapid unfolding of the dramatic catastrophe. [. . .]

Your most humble servant
Richard Wagner

Dresden, 9 January 1843
(Translation from Spencer and Millington, *Selected Letters*, 103)

To Minna Wagner (from Berlin)[12]

[. . .] It was after midnight when I finally got to bed last night, and at five in the morning I sent for a light and had the fire lit since it was pointless remaining in bed any longer, unable to sleep. You know, if you had been there, we could have chattered all night together, – but I was on my own! [. . .] It was one of the most decisive evenings of my entire life. – Imagine, I was appearing before a *completely unknown* audience with this fantastical opera of mine, a work totally remote from anything they had previously heard or grown to enjoy and offering, on the face of it, so little that is appealing or rewarding! I felt their hostility quite keenly: there was not a single person in the audience I knew personally, none of them was predisposed in my favor; – they all sat there feeling their customary cold curiosity and thinking: well, what sort of affair is this *Flying Dutchman* going to be? – No one lifted a finger at the end of the overture, – they listened to the melancholy first act in a mood of expectant curiosity and amazement, without knowing what decision to reach: – now and again one of the singers was greeted with effortful applause; – in a word, I realized the position I was in, – but I did not despair, since I could see that the performance was going extraordinarily well. The second act began, and it gradually dawned on me that I had achieved my aim: I had woven a spell around my audience such that the first act had transported them into that strange mood which forced them to follow me wherever I chose to take them. Their interest grew, tension turned into excitement, heightened involvement – finally to enthusiasm, and even before the curtain had fallen on the second act I was celebrating a triumph such as few, I am sure, have ever been granted. Never before – not even with *Rienzi* in Dresden – have I seen and heard such a prolonged outburst of enthusiasm as manifested itself here once the final curtain had fallen: – of all the assembled company, there was not a single one of them, be he high or low, prince or pauper, who could not be seen and heard shouting and roaring with the rest of them. [. . .]

The last act was child's play: the scenery worked a treat and made a splendid impression; the whole thing was played at great speed, and the ending – which was very well staged – came with surprising rapidity. [. . .] In short, my dear wife, I have won a remarkable victory: the extraordinary and almost unprecedented nature of it can be appreciated only by those who are in a position to assess all the circumstances involved, and the present state of our operas, as well as to understand how totally different and unfamiliar is the direction I have embarked upon with my *Dutchman*! [. . .]

Today I am dining with *Meyerbeer*, tomorrow with Küstner. [. . .] Mendelssohn, with whom I also dined on one occasion, favored me be coming on stage after the performance, embracing me, and congratulating me most warmly. – [. . .]

your Richard

Berlin, 8 January [1844], 7:00 in the morning
(Translation from Spencer and Millington, *Selected Letters*, 116–17)

C.   Interpretation

Wagner to Ferdinand Heine (early August? 1843), trans. from Spencer and Millington, *Selected Letters of Richard Wagner*, 114–15.

> This letter was apparently provided to Ferdinand Heine as the basis for a "publicity piece" describing the opera that was later published in the Leipzig *Illustrirte Zeitung* (7 October 1843) in anticipation of the upcoming Berlin production (January–February 1844). (See Chapters 1 and 4.)

Dear Heine,

When I wrote my *Flying Dutchman* I was of the conviction that I could not write it any other way. It was in the course of my famous sea-voyage and among the Norwegian cliffs that the subject-matter – long familiar to me from the writings of your namesake[1] – took on a quite special color and character – somber, admittedly, but copied from that same nature of which we are all a part, and not the speculative vision of some gloom-infected dreamer. But the wide wild ocean with its far-flung legends is an element which cannot be reduced compliantly and willingly to a modern opera; and although the legend of the Flying Dutchman, filled as it is with the pounding of the sea, now took hold of me in such a way as to demand an artistic reworking, it seemed to me that the legend would have to be dreadfully mutilated and hacked to pieces if it was to be turned into a libretto meeting the modern requirements for piquant situations and unexpected surprises etc. And so I preferred not to alter the subject-matter as it already existed, except insofar as the development of a dramatic plot required it; instead I allowed the whole aura of the legend to spread unchecked over the entire piece, since only in that way did I believe I could hold the listener's attention, inducing in him that strange frame of mind which alone would persuade even the least poetical listener to conceive a sympathy – nay, even a real fondness – for this most somber of legends. And I ensured that my music was endowed with a similar character: in order to achieve this aim I refused to look to the right or to the left of me, or to make the least concession to modern taste since I knew that to have done otherwise would be not only inartistic but unwise. From the outset I had to abandon the modern arrangement of dividing the work into arias, duets, finales, etc., and instead relate the legend in a single breath, just as a good poem should be. In this way I produced an opera whose popularity – now that it has been performed – I find impossible to explain since, in all its external details, it is so unlike anything we now understand by the term opera; indeed, only now do I realize what demands I have been placing on audiences, asking them suddenly to forget all that they had previously found entertaining and attractive in the theatre. But the fact that this opera has won so many friends for itself not only in Dresden but, especially, in Kassel and Riga, and that even the wider public has taken the work to heart seems to me to be a very important pointer for us, suggesting that we should henceforth write only what we Germans are inspired to write by our innate sense of poetry, and that we should never again make concessions to any foreign fashions but simply choose and treat those subjects that appeal to us; in that way we shall be quite certain of satisfying our fellow countrymen, too. If we proceed in this way we may yet regain an original German opera, and all who lose heart and who turn in their despair to foreign models may learn from my Dutchman's example – since it is without doubt conceived in a way that no Frenchman or Italian would ever have conceived it. –

A straightforward account of the action of the opera is sufficient to etc. etc.

Yours,
Richard Wagner

Overture to *Der fliegende Holländer* ("programmatic commentary" by R. Wagner, 1852), *GS*, vol. 5, 176–7, translation by Thomas Grey.

> During his early years in exile in Zurich Wagner was persuaded to collaborate with local musicians in a number of concerts featuring vocal and orchestral excerpts from his operas. To assist a better appreciation of the various orchestral overtures and preludes to his Dresden operas Wagner devised brief "programmatic commentaries" on them. The following descriptive-interpretive gloss on the *Holländer* overture was written in conjunction with performances of the work on 18, 20, and 22 May 1853.

The terrible ship of the "Flying Dutchman" is tossed about by storms; it approaches the coast where it lands, and where its captain has been promised he might one day find happiness and salvation; we perceive the sympathetic strains of this promise of redemption, which suggest the feelings of prayer and lament at once: the accursed one listens, somber and despondent; tired and longing only for death he steps ashore, while his crew silently battens down the ship, likewise exhausted and weary of living.

– How many times has not the unfortunate one gone through with this routine! How many times has he steered his ship from the ocean's waves to the peopled shores, where once each seven years he is allowed to land; how many times has he imagined that his sufferings were at an end, and yet! – how many times, bitterly disappointed, has he not had to set sail once again on his endless, senseless sea-voyage! Hoping to bring about his own end, he steers madly toward the tempestuous swells: he plunges his ship into the ocean's gaping maw, – and yet this maw will not swallow it; now he steers for the breakers crashing upon the rocks, – and yet the rocks will not splinter it. All the terrifying dangers of the sea, at which he once laughed in the abandon of heroic hubris [*wilder Männertatengier*], now mock him in turn – they refuse to harm him: for now he is immune to such dangers, cursed to chase forever across the vasty deep in search of treasures that he can never enjoy, but never to find that one thing that could save him!

– A spry and hearty ship sails by; the Dutchman harks to the merry, carefree singing of its crew, who are on their return voyage and elated by the thought of their imminent arrival in their homeland. Such jollity inspires him with rage; he causes his ship to storm furiously past theirs, terrifying and intimidating that happy crew into silence and flight. In his distress the Dutchman utters a dreadful cry for salvation: he is surrounded only by men and by the empty seas – but it is only a woman who can achieve his redemption. Where is this savior, in what land does she reside? Where does a feeling heart beat in sympathy with his woes? Where is she who will not flee from him in horror, like these cowardly men who cross themselves in fright at the sight of him?

– Then a light breaks through the night: like a lightning-bolt it strikes his tortured soul. For a moment it is extinguished, then flares up again; the seafarer fastens his gaze on this beacon and steers for it with vigorous determination through wave and current. What draws him on so powerfully is the glance of a woman, radiating a sublime pity and divine sympathy. A heart has fathomed the infinite depths of sorrow experienced by this accursed being, and that heart is breaking with sympathy, it is impelled to offer itself in sacrifice, to annihilate itself and his suffering in one. The wretched man collapses before this divine apparition, just as his ship shatters into pieces; the ocean swallows up the wreck – but the Dutchman rises from the waves, safe and sound, the victorious redemptrix leading him by the hand toward the rosy dawn of sublime love.

Richard Wagner, "Remarks on the Performance of the Opera *Der fliegende Holländer*" (1852), *GS*, vol. 5, 160–68, translation by Thomas Grey.

> Wagner's remarks on the staging of his opera were written on 22 December 1852 for the benefit of his new-found friend and advocate, Franz Liszt, who was overseeing a production of *Der fliegende Holländer* in Weimar (premièred 16 February 1853). As with his similar production notes for *Tannhäuser* (August 1852),

the exiled composer hoped in this way to exert some control over the stagings of his works that were now beginning to take place in a number of German theatres. According to his later testimony, though, these brochures were little regarded at the time. In the meantime they have come to provide a valuable, and relatively rare, glimpse into the composer's notions about the co-ordination of stage action and music (even for the *Ring* and *Parsifal* we don't have authoritative records of this kind). Although by the later twentieth century few directors cared to be bound by what most considered an outmoded, melodramatic stage aesthetic, the composer's remarks retain a significant historical and critical interest.

Above all I have to recall for conductors and stage directors that to which I have already admonished them in my production notes on *Tannhäuser* with regard to the precise co-ordination of stage events and the orchestra.[2] In particular the ship and the ocean must be given scrupulous attention by the stage director: he will find all the necessary indications in the corresponding passages of the piano-vocal score or orchestral score. The opening scene of the opera should evoke the proper mood in which the audience will be able to appreciate the marvelous apparition of the "Flying Dutchman" himself, and for this reason the scene needs to be treated with great care. The sea, in between the rocky promontories, must be shown in as wild a state as possible; the handling of the ship cannot be too realistic, and such details as the shaking of the vessel when struck by a violent wave (between the two verses of the Steersman's song) should be realized in a very drastic manner. Particular attention must also be paid to the lighting and its varied nuances: in order to make effective the meteorological shifts across the first act the skillful implementation of painted scrims [*Schleierprospekten*] is imperative, reaching as far as the middle of the stage. But as my remarks here are not primarily intended to address the purely decorative aspects of production (on which matter I refer the reader to the staging of this opera at the Berlin Schauspielhaus), I will content myself here with re-iterating my opening plea that the stage directions given in the printed score be observed closely, while I leave the specific execution of these directions up to the imaginative discretion of stage designers and machinists.

Instead, I address myself here simply to the singers, and above all to the interpreter of the difficult leading male role, that of the Dutchman. The success of the opera really depends on the satisfactory realization of this leading role: the interpreter must succeed in arousing and sustaining the deepest sympathy; he will be enabled to do so if he observes punctiliously the character-traits of the role I enumerate below.

The external appearance of this character is already indicated with adequate precision. His first appearance is extraordinarily serious and solemn: his first hesitant steps on *terra firma* can present a characteristic contrast to the uncanny swiftness of the ship as it moves over the waters. During the low trumpet notes (B minor) at the end of the introduction[3] he steps, on a plank set down by the crew, from the deck of the ship onto a rocky outcropping of the shoreline: the first note of the aria's ritornello (the low E♯ in the basses) corresponds to the Dutchman's first step onto land. His slow and deliberate deportment, typical of seafarers when they first set foot ashore after a long voyage, is accompanied by the wave-figure in the cellos and violas. To the first beat of the third measure he takes a second step, still with arms crossed and head bowed; the third and fourth steps correspond to the analogous notes in the eighth and tenth measures. From here on the performer may allow his movements to be guided instinctively by his performance as such, but he should never let himself be tempted into any excessive pacing to and fro; rather, a certain grim external composure, even against the most passionate expression of his inner pain and despair, will be best suited to conveying the characteristic quality of this figure.

The first [vocal] phrases should be sung in an utterly dispassionate manner, as by one utterly fatigued (and almost exactly in tempo, as should be the whole recitative). At the words of bitter anguish, "Ha, stolzer Ozean!" etc., he does not yet break out into a true passion; rather, he should turn his head partially back toward the sea with a gesture of terrible scorn. During the ritornello – following "doch ewig meine Qual" – he lowers his head, sad and tired; he sings the words "euch, des Weltmeers Fluten" etc. staring straight ahead. For the gestural accompaniment of the Allegro ("wie oft in Meeres tiefsten Grund [*recte*: Schlund]") I would not want to restrict too much the singer's motions, though he should still keep in mind my overall injunction to maintain an external tranquillity even while animating his vocal performance with the most gripping passion and sorrowful emotions: a single, not too broad motion of the arm or hand should suffice to accompany the stronger individual accents of the vocal line. Even the words "Niemals der Tod, nirgends ein Grab!," which should certainly be very powerfully accentuated, are still part of an indirect, descriptive account of his sufferings – not yet a direct outpouring of his actual despair as such. He only arrives at the latter in what follows, for which the maximum energy of [visible] action should be held in reserve. By the repetition of the words "Dies der Verdammnis Schreckgebot!" he has lowered somewhat both his head and his whole bearing. He remains in this position for the first four measures of the orchestral postlude [mm. 115–18]; then with the E♭ violin tremolo of the fifth measure [m. 119] he raises his eyes toward the heavens, while the rest of the body remains bent down; with the quiet drum-roll in the ninth measure of the postlude he falls into a shivering tremble, he forms a tight fist with his low-held hands, and his lips quiver as he finally begins the phrase "Dich frage ich" etc. (his fixed gaze still turned toward heaven).

This entire address to the "angel of God" should be executed in the position thus indicated, with a terrifying expression in the voice, but without any perceptible change of stance, except for those individual spots where the performance demands some slight movement. We must see before us a veritable "fallen angel," who, in his tormented condition, vents his fury to the almighty powers above. But at last, with the words "Vergebne Hoffnung" etc., the whole power of his despair is given full expression: he raises himself up in a rage and, with an action of the most energetic sorrow (his gaze still directed heavenwards), he thrusts all such "vain hope" [*vergebne Hoffen*] aside. He cares to hear no more of the promised salvation, and collapses as if completely annihilated (at the entrance of the timpani and basses). At the return of the Allegro-ritornello his features are re-animated, as with a last, desperate hope: the hope for the apocalypse that alone will bring about his own demise.

This Allegro-coda [*Schlußallegro*] requires the most terrifying energy in the vocal production as well as in gestural action – for here it is all a matter of immediate effect. Yet the singer should make it possible to perceive this whole section, however energetic the performance, as a culmination of the energy of the whole [scene], which finds its most shattering climax at the words "Ihr Welten! endet euren Lauf!" etc. Here the sublimity of expression must reach its peak. Following the closing words, "ewige Vernichtung, nimm mich auf!," the performer remains in a fixed, erect position, imposing and statue-like, throughout the *fortissimo* portion of the postlude; only with the onset of the *piano*, and the muffled song from within the ship's cabin, does the rigidity of his stance begin to yield. He begins to lower his arms; with the four measures of *espressivo* in the first violins he lowers his head, exhausted, and during the last eight measures he staggers over to the rocky cliffs on one side; he leans his back against these and remains here for a long time, with his arms crossed over his chest. –

I have discussed this scene at such length in order to demonstrate how I would like to see the Dutchman interpreted, and what importance I attach to the scrupulous co-ordination of action and music. The performer ought to strive to carry out the entire role along similar lines. This aria also happens to be the most difficult part of the entire role since, for one thing, the success of this number will determine whether or not the audience is able to develop a sympathy and understanding for all that follows; if this monologue fully achieves its aim of reaching the audience and attuning it to the proper receptive frequency, then the most important thing has been accomplished in terms of laying a foundation for the rest [. . .]

In the following scene with Daland the Dutchman remains at first in the same position he has assumed at the end of his monologue. When Daland addresses him from shipboard he responds only by raising his head slightly. As Daland then joins him ashore, he steps with dignified calm toward center stage. His whole demeanor exudes a quiet, placid dignity; his expression is neutral – noble, but without any strong accentuation. He is acting here as if by force of habit: he has gone through such transactions so many times before, and even the most seemingly calculated questions and answers he delivers as if by rote [. . .]. Yet equally instinctive is the sudden eruption of his continued longing for salvation; after his earlier terrible outburst of despair his manner has now become milder, more yielding, and he expresses his longing for peace with a moving sadness. He throws out the question, "Hast du eine Tochter?" ['Do you have a daughter?"], still with apparent equanimity. Daland's enthusiastic answer, "fürwahr, ein treues Kind" ['indeed, a loyal child'] throws the Dutchman immediately back into a state of hope (so often proven futile before); he cries out in spasmodic haste: "let her be my wife!" He is seized again by that old longing, and he now delivers with moving expressivity an account of himself (retaining a manner of surface calm) in the cantilena [*Gesang*]: "Ach, ohne Weib, ohne Kind bin ich." The warm description the father provides of his daughter further kindles in the Dutchman this ancient longing for "salvation through a woman's fidelity," increasing in intensity in the Allegro-coda of the duet as an impassioned conflict between hope and despair, in which hope seems almost ready to prevail.

In his first encounter with Senta in the second act the Dutchman appears once again solemn and composed; with conscious exertion he has reined in all his passionate feelings. During the long first fermata [no. 6, Finale, m. 1] he remains motionless upon the threshold. With the timpani solo [mm. 2ff] he strides slowly toward the front of the stage. In the eighth measure of this solo [m. 9] he stops (the two-measure *accelerando* figure in the strings [mm. 10–11] applies to Daland's gestures; he remains at the door, waiting in astonishment for some greeting from Senta, whom he beckons with open arms, and with some impatience). During the next three measures of timpani [mm. 12–14] the Dutchman advances all the way downstage and to one side, where he remains motionless, with his eye trained the whole time on Senta. (The repeated string figure [mm. 14–15] applies to the intensified repetition of Daland's gesture; with the pizzicato note and ensuing fermata [m. 17] he ceases his entreaties and shakes his head in puzzlement; then with the entry of the basses after this fermata he himself approaches Senta.)

The postlude to Daland's aria [no. 6b, mm. 126–54] must be played in its entirety. During the first four measures, *forte*, he turns decisively to leave; but with the fifth and sixth measures he stops and turns around. The following seven measures [132–39] accompany his partly good-humored, partly curious and expectant play of gestures, alternately glancing at Senta and at the Dutchman; during the next two measures, to the [repeated] bass notes [139–40], he proceeds to the door, shaking his head. Then with the renewed entry of the woodwind theme [m. 141] he pokes his head into the room one last time, withdraws it perplexed, and closes the door, so that by the F-sharp chord in the woodwinds [m. 143] he has disappeared from view. The remainder of this postlude is, together with the ritornello of the subsequent duet, accompanied by utter silence and motionlessness on stage: Senta and the Holländer, positioned at opposite sides of the front of the stage, are both utterly transfixed in their mutual gaze. (The performers need not worry that this staging will seem dull; experience has shown that precisely this arrangement is most able to seize the audience's attention and to prepare them for the ensuing scene.)

The Dutchman should maintain a thoroughly placid and stationary posture throughout the following E-major movement [No. 6c,

Duet], even against the most gripping and emotional vocal performance; only the hands and the arms (the latter somewhat spar-
ingly) should be used to support the stronger accents. – Only at the
two-measure timpani solo preceding the E-minor section [mm.
140–41] does the Dutchman finally move, in order to approach Senta:
he takes a few steps toward center stage, with a certain constraint and
doleful formality. (I must inform conductors here that I was mistaken
in giving the tempo marking "un poco *meno* sostenuto" at this point
[m. 142], as experience has taught me; the whole preceding section is
fairly slow – especially the Dutchman's opening solo; but then it
should become gradually, unobtrusively more animated, to the extent
that by the E-minor section [m. 142] the tempo will actually have to be
held back slightly in order to give at least the beginning of this section
the necessary solemn, deliberate expression. The [initial] four-
measure phrase should be played hesitatingly, so that the fourth
measure itself is given a distinct *ritenuto*; the same is then repeated
across the first phrase of the Dutchman's vocal line.) With the
timpani solo in the ninth and tenth measures [150–51] the Dutchman
takes another two steps toward Senta. The tempo may be tightened
somewhat over the eleventh and twelfth measures, such that at the
words "du könntest dich" etc., in A minor, the original (intended)
moderate tempo takes hold, now by comparison slightly less drag-
ging; and this should be maintained for the duration of the section.
With the *più animato*, "so unbedingt, wie?" etc. [mm. 200ff], the
Dutchman betrays the animating effect of Senta's first actual address
to him – this passage should be sung already with great emotion.
Senta's passionate exclamation "O! welche Leiden! Könnt' ich Trost
ihn bringen!" stirs him deeply; he trembles with dumb amazement at
the quiet words, "welch holder Klang im nächtlichen Gewühl?" By
the *molto più animato* [m. 218] he can no longer control himself; he
sings with passionate fire, and at the words "Allewiger, durch diese
sei's!" he sinks to his knees. Then at the B-minor *agitato* [m. 244] he
raises himself up energetically: his love for Senta expresses itself in his
terrible dread at the fate to which she will expose herself by extending
her hand to save him. This comes over him like a terrible reproach,
and in his passionate warning to her of the stipulation that she must
share his fate [should she prove faithless], he becomes truly human,
while up to now he has generally conveyed the eerie impression of a
ghost. Thus the performer should entirely surrender himself at this

point to human passion, and collapse before Senta as if completely annihilated at the words "nennst ew'ge Treue du nicht dein!," so that Senta stands over him like a sublime angel, as she goes on to reassure him what *she* understands by fidelity. – In the ritornello of the subsequent *allegro molto* [mm. 322ff] the Dutchman raises himself up erect in solemn emotion and exaltation: his singing intensifies into a sublime song of victory. There can be no misapprehension as to the rest: in his last appearance in the third act everything is passion, sorrow, and despair. I particularly recommend that recitative phrases not be stretched, but that instead everything be taken in the most animated, forward-driving tempo.

It would be hard not to hit the mark with the role of Senta. I ought to warn of one thing only: don't construe her dreamy character in terms of a modern, sickly sentimentality! On the contrary, Senta is a very solid Nordic girl, and her apparent sentimentality is thoroughly naive. Only on a wholly naive girl, especially when surrounded by all the peculiar splendors of Nordic natural scenery, could the impression of such things as the ballad of the Flying Dutchman or the portrait of this pale seafarer produce such a remarkable effect as her drive to redeem this accursed being. With Senta this drive is expressed in terms of a powerful delusion [*Wahnsinn*], such as is natural only to wholly naive beings. It has been observed how Norwegian girls have on occasion succumbed to feelings of such overwhelming strength that a sudden seizure of the heart causes their death. Something like this is very much the case with the seemingly "sickly" Senta. – Erik, too, must be no sentimental whiner; on the contrary, he is of a stormy temperament, sturdy and somber, like the lonely northern highlands themselves. He who performs the cavatina in the third act in a saccharine manner does me a grave disservice; it should rather breathe sadness and lament. (Anything in this piece that is likely to lead to such false conclusions – such as the falsetto passage or the closing vocal cadenza, I entreat the performer to alter or simply omit.)[4] – I would further entreat the interpreter of Daland not to push this role into the out-and-out comic vein: he is just a rough figure from everyday life, a seafarer who braves storms and other dangers for the sake of profit, and for whom, for example, the sale of his daughter (as it might appear) to a rich man should by no means be thought of as pernicious – he thinks and acts just as hundreds of thousands of others do, without imagining in the least that he does anything wrong.

Notes

1   The return of the prodigal son: Wagner and Der fliegende Holländer

1 Undated letter (early August?, 1843) to Ferdinand Heine, in *Sämtliche Briefe* (*SB*), vol. 2, ed. Gertrud Strobel and Werner Wolf (Leipzig, 1970), 314–15. Wagner's phrase "famous sea-voyage" suggests that the episode, not surprisingly, figured as one of the composer's favorite anecdotes among his early circle of friends in Dresden. This letter was designed to provide the basis for an essay on the opera that was printed (anonymously) in the Leipzig *Illustrirte Zeitung* in October 1843 (see the translation included in Appendix C, pp. 190–92).

2 Wagner, *My Life* (*ML*), trans. Andrew Gray (Cambridge, 1983), 160.

3 *Ibid.*, 162. See also the brief account of the voyage given in the 1843 "Autobiographical Sketch" (included in Appendix B, pp. 178–81). Although Wagner does not mention the rhythm of the sailors' call in the earlier account, he does claim to have heard them recounting the tale of the "Flying Dutchman." It is difficult to assess the veracity of either claim, but of the fierce storms and the emergency landing along the Norwegian coast there is no reason to doubt.

4 It is surprising that Wagner cites the Sailors' Chorus (*Matrosen-Lied*) from Act III in the this context rather than the more "realistic" adaptation of the experience in the introductory scene of Act I. Yet on reflection, is seems that Wagner is being more honest here than he is generally given credit for: it is indeed more plausible that he would first have worked the sailors' cry – in whatever form he actually heard it – into a conventional song like that opening Act III, rather than into the more complicated, artificial (so to speak) context in which it was eventually deployed in the first number of the opera.

5 "On Conducting," trans. Robert L. Jacobs, in *Three Wagner Essays* (London, 1979), 55.

6 *ML*, 190. Heinrich Heine and E. T. A. Hoffmann are frequently identified as models for the short fictional pieces on musical subjects Wagner published the *Revue et gazette musicale*. Heine is the closer model, on the whole, although Wagner leavens the detached, ironic mode of Heine with a dose of conventional Romantic sentiment. The cultural-literary background of Wagner's musical fiction for the *Gazette musicale* is explored by Matthias Broszka in *Die Idee des*

Gesamtkunstwerks in der Musiknovellistik der Julimonarchie (Laaber, 1995).

7 Whether or not Wagner actually heard accounts of the Flying Dutchman legend "confirmed" by the crew of the *Thetis* during the voyage is more questionable (cf. n. 3). The fact that he makes this assertion only in the "Autobiographical Sketch" published in the *Zeitung für die elegante Welt* in early February 1843 (at the time of the *Holländer* première) and not in the more detailed description of the voyage in *My Life* is grounds for suspicion. The decision to change the locale of the opera to conform with the composer's own biography was, as suggested above, quite possibly intended as a validation of his "rights" to the subject, in a sense. The claim to have heard variants of the story itself *in situ* would add another layer of authentication.

8 Reprinted in *SSD*, vol. 12, 46–64.

9 *SL*, 90. The text printed in the *Neue Zeitschrift* is reproduced in Wagner, *SSD*, vol. 16, 58–60.

10 Even in his final years Wagner was still contemplating revisions to the score in order to establish a definitive text. See below ("Conception and composition," pp. 23–4) and Isolde Vetter, "Der 'Ahasverus des Ozeans' – musikalisch unerlöst?" in *Richard Wagner: Der fliegende Holländer*, ed. Attila Csampai and Dietmar Holland (Reinbek bei Hamburg, 1982), 116–29.

11 *PW*, vol. 1, 19 (*GSD*, vol. 1, 19). This same context, however, sounds an opposing theme that will continue to sound through the rest of Wagner's career: the failure of the German people, on the whole, to acknowledge adequately Wagner's contribution to the advancement of a distinctly national culture. Before *Holländer* was finally (and in the event, only provisionally) accepted by the Berlin Opera, Wagner was faced with rejections from Munich and Leipzig, on the grounds that the opera was not "suitable for Germany." "Fool that I was," he sighs, "I had fancied it was fitted for Germany alone, since it struck on chords that can only vibrate in the German breast" (*ibid.*). In *My Life*, Wagner again recalled how Councilor Küstner, Intendant of the Munich theatre, returned the score to the composer, assuring him that "it was not suitable for German stage conditions and did not correspond to the taste of the German public" (*ML*, 214).

12 In the *Communication*, as Dieter Borchmeyer points out, Wagner explicates all three of his mature operas to date (*Der fliegende Holländer*, *Tannhäuser*, and *Lohengrin*) as, among other things, allegories of the isolated condition of the "true" artist and his longing for "redemption" in the form of a genuine, instinctive appreciation of his aims – in short, "love" (*Richard Wagner: Theory and Theatre*, trans. Stewart Spencer [Oxford, 1991], 206). The Dutchman, in particular, serves "as a symbolic projection of his own situation during his years in Paris from 1839 to 1842" (p. 205). On the idea of the Romantic operas as allegories of the artist, see also D. Borchmeyer, "Totenreich und Venusberg – Wagners 'romantische Opern' als Künstlerdramen," in *Das Theater Richard*

Wagners (Stuttgart, 1982), 185–206 (chapter omitted from the English translation).

13 This metaphorical construction is discussed at length in Chapter 3 ("Engendering Music Drama: *Opera and Drama* and its Metaphors") of Thomas Grey, *Wagner's Musical Prose: Texts and Contexts* (Cambridge, 1995), and by Jean-Jacques Nattiez in *Wagner Androgyne*, trans. Stewart Spencer (Princeton, 1992), 37–42, 76–90, 132–39, and 158–62. On the cultural background of this metaphorical practice, see Mark Joel Webber, "The Metaphorization of Woman in Young Germany: The Intersection of Rhetoric and *Naturphilosophie*," in *Geist und Gesellschaft: Zur deutschen Rezeption der französischen Revolution*, ed. Eitel Timm (Munich, 1990), 125–38.

14 The passage reads like a tacit, invidious comparison of himself with Heine, whose "frivolously ironic" adaptation of the Flying Dutchman story he had appropriated but also quite brazenly de-ironized.

15 One might also invoke the representational tradition of angelic androgyny here, or Jean-Jacques Nattiez's contention (in *Wagner Androgyne*) that Wagner's creative thought-process was consistently informed by the motif of androgyny. A nexus of associations might also plausibly be constructed between the German musical tradition (culminating in Beethoven) as Wagner's "redeeming angel," the redemptive mission of Senta in *Holländer*, and the dual-gendered role of Leonore in Beethoven's *Fidelio*, whom Florestan explicitly invokes as the "angel" of his temporal and even spiritual salvation ("Ich seh' wie ein Engel im rosigen Duft . . . ein Engel, Leonoren, der Gattin so gleich, der führt mich zur Freiheit ins himmlische Reich") in his great aria at the opening of Act II.

16 The refrain of the expository *Légende* (a short strophic ballad) in Act I of Halévy's grand opera, *Le juif errant* (1851, libretto by Eugène Scribe and Jules de Saint-Georges) describes the protagonist Ashvérus [*sic*] as being driven away from every potential resting-place by "un ange invisible, l'ange du très-haut," ordering him to take up his endless wanderings once again. The folkloric and literary genealogy of the "Wandering Jew" figure is extensively documented and analyzed by George K. Anderson in *The Legend of the Wandering Jew* (Providence, 1965). A large number of literary treatments of the motif between the time of Goethe and the 1840s are described in Chapters 8 ("Ahasuerus in the Romantic Heyday") and 9 ("Early Variations on Romantic Themes"). The theme of redemption through the love of a faithful woman is foreshadowed in the ambitiously scaled poetic drama of Edgar Quinet, *Ahasvérus* (1833), while the poem "The Undying One" (pub. 1830) by Mrs. Caroline Norton (Lady Stirling-Maxwell) introduces the Bluebeard-like motif of the Wandering Jew's fatal effect on a series of women whom he courts over the ages (203–05, 208–09), anticipating this aspect of Wagner's Dutchman.

17 Guido Adler observed that *Der fliegende Holländer* exhibits a "poetic affinity with Victor Hugo, in both poetic and musical terms" (*Richard Wagner* [Munich, 1923], 63).

18 In a letter to Louis Spohr expressing Wagner's appreciation that the Kassel theater (at Spohr's bidding) had requested permission to stage *Der fliegende Holländer* soon after its première, the composer speaks of himself as a "pupil of the revered Master [Spohr]" and adds: "may my attempts to sacrifice to our beloved German muse at least give you proof of my good intentions" (letter of 22 April 1843, *SB*, vol. 2, 243).

19 See also "Sources and Genesis of the Text" (Chapter 2, below), as well as Eduard Reeser, "Die sagengeschichtlichen und literarischen Grundlagen des *fliegenden Holländers*," in *Richard Wagner: Der fliegende Holländer*, ed. Csampai and Holland, 63–70.

20 See the letters to Meyerbeer of 3 May and 4 June 1840 (*SB*, vol. 1, 386, 394; cf. *SL*, 67). The former is an extraordinary document – in view of Wagner's subsequent attitude toward Meyerbeer – in which he grovels obsequiously before the established and successful composer, offering himself "body and soul" as Meyerbeer's "slave" ("for I confess that I have something of a slave-nature in me" [!]), even signing himself "Your property, Richard Wagner." In addition to petitioning for Meyerbeer's intercession on behalf of his operatic endeavors he requests an outright a loan of 2,500 francs to see him through the next winter. In view of Wagner's construction of the "good angel of German music" that saved him from the commercial-philistine infernal quagmire of Parisian musical culture, there is more than a little irony in the fact that Wagner, in the earlier of these two letters, invokes Meyerbeer as his "guardian Angel" ("daß mir Gott in Ihnen meinen mächtigsten Schutzengel zuge-sandt habe"). In the second letter he apologizes that his natural tendency toward "exaltation" may have led him to transgress the boundaries of propriety in his earlier communication.

21 ". . . so ersuche ich Sie in tiefster Demuth ein gutes Wort für mich und meinen 'geflügelten Holländer' (1 Act) fallen zu lassen, von dem ich einige Nummern zur Audition fertig habe" (*SB*, vol. 1, 401). The "winged Dutchman" appears to be Wagner's German version of his working title ("Le Hollandais volant"), though the work that eventually materialized from these transactions with the Opéra was known as *Le Vaisseau fantôme* ("The phantom ship"), following a number of other pre-existing literary treatments of the story. See Chapter 2, below, and Peter Bloom, "The Fortunes of the Flying Dutchman in France," *Wagner* 8/2 (April 1987), 42–66.

22 *ML*, 201. Deschamps had just recently provided the libretto of Berlioz's "dramatic symphony," *Roméo et Juliette* (1839). In the autobiography Wagner implies that these pieces originated "towards the end of the past winter . . . when I still had hopes of producing this subject for the Paris Opéra," which in context suggests a date of February or March 1841. It is of course possible that he was mis-remembering the chronology or that he meant to say only that they were "already composed" by this time. Cf. *WWV*, 227, and Barry Millington, *The Wagner Compendium* (London, 1992), 278, where a date of between 3 May and 26 July is suggested on the basis of the correspondence.

23 The story of Wagner's negotiations with Pillet over the sketch has been scrutinized at length by Isolde Vetter, Barry Millington, and Peter Bloom, among others. See Chapter 2 below as well as Bloom, "The Fortunes of the Flying Dutchman in France."

24 Issued 15 January 1845; Meser had also produced a piano-vocal score in the fall of 1844. On these and subsequent editions of the score, see *WWV*, 233–36.

25 The principal evidence of these revisions is contained in letters to Theodor Uhlig (24–25 March, 9 April, 6–7 May, and 22 July 1852) and Franz Liszt (8, 9, and 13 January 1853). For further details see Paul S. Machlin, "Wagner, Durand and 'The Flying Dutchman': The 1852 Revisions of the Overture," *Music and Letters* 55 (1974), 410–28; Isolde Vetter, "Der 'Ahasverus des Ozeans' – musikalisch unerlöst?"; and Vetter, "*Der fliegende Holländer* von Richard Wagner. Entstehung, Bearbeitung, Überlieferung," Ph.D. diss. Technische Universität, Berlin, (1982). Machlin implies that the final twenty-two measures of the 1860 revised coda were already present in 1852, although this now appears not to have been the case.

26 These few measures are transcribed in Vetter, "Der 'Ahasverus des Ozeans'," 126, and in Werner Breig, "Das 'verdichtete Bild des ganzen Dramas' – Die Ursprünge von Wagners Holländer-Musik und die Senta Ballade," in *Festschrift Heinz Becker*, ed. J. Schläder and R. Quandt (Laaber, 1982), 174. Vetter registers surprise that Wagner could thus recompose what he had called the "thematic seed of the whole opera," overlooking the probability that the refrain of the Ballad (the only part cited and transformed in other contexts) might have stayed as it was, as would, of course, the introductory "Dutchman" motive.

27 See Vetter, "Der 'Ahasverus des Ozeans'," 124, 127.

2   The sources and genesis of the text

1 Fritz Mende, *Heinrich Heine: Chronik seines Lebens und Werkes*, 2nd ed. (Berlin, 1981), 56.

2 Edward Fitzball, *Thirty-five Years of a Dramatic Author's Life*, vol. 1 (London, 1859), 168.

3 Bernd Laroche, who reproduces Fitzball's play in German translation in his useful but unreliable *Der fliegende Holländer: Wirkung und Wandlung eines Motivs* (Frankfurt am Main, 1993), proposes in different places 1827 (p. 54) and 1828 (p. 203). The British Library catalogue suggests *c.* 1829. The printed volume itself is undated.

4 For a more extended synopsis see Barry Millington, "Did Wagner Really Sell his 'Dutchman' story? A Re-examination of the Paris Transaction," *Wagner* 4 (1983), 114–27.

5 William Ashton Ellis, "From Fitzball to Wagner: A 'Flying Dutchman' Fallacy," *The Meister* 5 (1892), 4–21; citations on pp. 5 and 21.

6 Mende, *Heinrich Heine*, 61.

7 *WWV*, 227. See, however, Paul S. Machlin, "A Sketch for the

Dutchman," *Musical Times* 117 (1976), 727–29, for an alternative thesis as regards the chorus of the Dutch crew.

8 These details are contained in Peter Bloom's fascinating article "The Fortunes of the Flying Dutchman in France," *Wagner* 8/2 (1987), 42–66.

9 See Stewart Spencer, "Wagner Autographs in London," *Wagner* 5/1 (1984), 14–17.

10 *Ibid.*, 15.

11 The mysterious circumstances surrounding this transaction were examined in full by the present author in "Did Wagner Really Sell his 'Dutchman' Story?"

12 See Isolde Vetter, "For the Last Time: Wagner did Sell his 'Dutchman' story," *Wagner* 7 (1986), 16–22.

13 Translated in Otto Strobel, "Wagners Prosaentwurf zum 'Fliegenden Holländer'," *Wagner* 2 (1981), 26–29.

14 Bloom, "The Fortunes of the Flying Dutchman in France," 54–55.

15 *Ibid.*, 58.

16 See, for example, his letters to Karl Theodor von Küstner (17 May 1842; *SB*, vol. 2, 98) and Johann Philipp Samuel Schmidt (9 January 1843; *SB*, vol. 2, 213).

17 See, for example, Julius Kapp, *Richard Wagner und die Frauen* (Berlin, 1929), 305, and Curt von Westernhagen, *Wagner: A Biography*, trans. Mary Whittall (Cambridge, 1978), vol. 1, 65.

18 For a detailed discussion of all these sources and their deployment by Foucher and Révoil, see B. Millington, "Did Wagner Really Sell his 'Dutchman' Story?"

19 The Commission report is quoted in Bloom, "The Fortunes of the Flying Dutchman in France," 59–61.

3 Text, action, and music

1 On this latter point, and on the relation of this overture to earlier models as well as to Wagner's 1841 essay "On the Overture," see Thomas Grey, "Wagner, the Overture, and the Aesthetics of Musical Form," *19th-Century Music* 12/1 (Summer 1988), 3–22.

2 The original version of the overture is given in the G. Schirmer vocal score. Most modern performances and recordings implement the revised 1860 ending of the overture and final scene, as printed (for instance) in the Dover full score, a reprint of the Fürstner 1896/97 score edited by Felix Weingartner. References to the score in this chapter follow the Weingartner edition for the most part, although Isolde Vetter's edition of the 1842 *Urfassung* for the new Wagner *Sämtliche Werke* (B. Schott's Söhne, Mainz) will be cited where appropriate.

3 For details see Paul S. Machlin, "Wagner, Durand and The *Flying Dutchman*: The 1852 Revisions of the Overture," *Music and Letters* 55 (1974), 410–28.

4 The reprise, in the chorus, of various elements from this opening number toward the end of the act suggests that one might loosely interpret the

whole first act as an expansion of the traditional ensemble-introduction. Wagner several times referred to the "introductory" aspect of the first act in his correspondence about the opera, and the author of a critical-explanatory essay in the *Illustrirte Zeitung* (1843) – written with the direct input of the composer (see Appendix C) – makes the same point: "This whole first act is thus only an introduction, and Wagner has posed a difficult task for himself here since everything depends on the interest generated by the character of the Dutchman at his first appearance" (*Illustrirte Zeitung*, Leipzig, 1/15 [7 October 1843], 235).

5 Gudrun Busch notes how the entire opera, from the tempestuous instrumental "sea picture" of the overture to the Dutchman's tragic departure at the end, is framed by the characteristic tone or "topic" of the storm, which maintains a continuous presence either as foreground or background throughout most of the work (Busch, "Die Unwetterszene in der romantischen Oper," in *Die couleur locale in der Oper des 19. Jahrhunderts*, ed. Heinz Becker [Regensburg, 1976], 161–212, esp. 192–96).

6 Isolde Vetter's edition of the 1841 *Urfassung* (*Richard Wagner: Sämtliche Werke*, vol. 4/1) gives this elided reading of Acts I and II (likewise for Acts II and III) as representing the composer's original plan, prior to the Dresden première.

7 The Ballad is given in its original key (A minor) in Vetter's edition of the opera (*Richard Wagner: Sämtliche Werke*, vol. 4/1, 216–40), which also contains the original modulation to B (or V of E minor) immediately preceding the Ballad.

8 After the first of these episodes in G flat Erik reproaches her: "You are evading me? you try to flee?" ("Du weichst mir aus? Du willst mich fliehn?"). As the German verb "ausweichen" (to evade) can also signify a local shift of key, Wagner may have intended a kind of musical pun here.

9 Before Wagner transposed the Ballad down a step, its coda and the parallel passage here were both in the same key (C).

10 See *WWV*, 227–28 and the letter to Giacomo Meyerbeer of 26 July 1840 (*SB*, vol. 1, 401).

11 Cf. *GSD*, vol. 4, 323 (*A Communication to my Friends*) and Chapter 4, below.

12 The letters from the phantom crew addressed to now aged or long-dead relatives is a motive found in a wide variety of earlier versions (see Chapter 2, as well as Heine's "Fable of the Flying Dutchman" in Appendix A).

13 Wagner calls for the Dutch crew to sing through a megaphone-like "speaking tube" (*Sprachrohr*) to create an eerie, hollow sound – the same device he later prescribed for the dragon in *Siegfried*.

14 These last details appear to have been added with the 1852 revisions to the score. Paul Machlin gives four variants of the closing stage directions in an appendix to "Wagner, Durand, and *The Flying Dutchman*," 427–28. In addition to the "transfigured" version of the Senta theme, with harp accompaniment, Wagner's later revision augments the rhythm of the

Dutchman motive in its final iteration, and bolsters its heavenward ascent with swirling string figurations. The original conclusion, as given in the *Sämtliche Werke* edition, sounds disappointingly flat and peremptory in comparison.

4   Romantic opera as "dramatic ballad": Der fliegende Holländer and its generic contexts

1 See especially Carl Dahlhaus, *Richard Wagner's Music Dramas* (1971), trans. Mary Whittall (Cambridge, 1979), 18–19, and "Wagner's *Communication to my Friends*," *The Musical Times* 124 (1983), 89–92. Dahlhaus's skepticism has been frequently echoed in the *Holländer* literature since then.

2 "I have been charged with stepping *backwards* in these works onto the path of 'Romantic opera,'" which, one supposed, had reached its zenith in Meyerbeer's *Robert le diable* and which I myself had left behind with *Rienzi*" (*GSD*, vol. 4, 264–65).

3 A longer excerpt from this letter is given in Appendix B, pp. 185–86.

4 Letter to Minna Wagner of 8 January 1844 (*SL*, 116). A longer excerpt is given in Appendix B, pp. 189–90.

5 "Musikalische Zustände in Riga," *Neue Zeitschrift für Musik* 19/2 (6 July 1843), 8 (cf. Chapter 1 on Wagner's own views to this effect.) The text of this and other early reviews of *Der fliegende Holländer* can be found in Helmut Kirchmeyer, *Situationsgeschichte der Musikkritik und des musikalischen Pressewesens in Deutschland*, part IV, vol. 2: *Das zeitgenössische Wagner-Bild, Dokumente 1842–45* (Regensburg, 1967).

6 E. Hanslick, "*Der fliegende Holländer* von Richard Wagner," review of Vienna performance, 2 November 1860, reprinted in *Richard Wagner: Der fliegende Holländer – Texte, Materialien, Kommentare*, ed. A. Csampai and D. Holland (Reinbek bei Hamburg, 1982), 141.

7 "Operntheater," *Recensionen und Mittheilungen über Theater und Musik* (Vienna), 6 (1860), 704–05.

8 *Zeitung für die elegante Welt* 42/2 (11 January 1843), 47 (original emphasis).

9 *Illustrirte Zeitung*, 7 October 1843, 234 (emphasis added). Partially reprinted in *Richard Wagner: Der fliegende Holländer*, ed. Csampai and Holland, 102–07 (see esp. p. 103). Complete text given in Kirchmeyer, *Musikkritik*, part 4, vol. 2, cols. 240–60.

10 Sieghart Döhring and Sabine Henze-Döhring have also drawn attention to the presence of this phrase in the *Illustrirte Zeitung* piece, and mention the possible model of Heinrich Heine's *William Ratcliff* (which the author called a *dramatisierte Ballade*). They assume that Wagner's later use of the phrase was suggested by the newspaper essay, without considering that he himself may have been responsible for this earlier use of the term. "The term 'dramatic ballad',"" they write, "proves to be an apt designation above all because it is not the interaction of the *dramatis personae*, but rather the Ballad and [Erik's] Dream-Narration that deter-

mine the dramaturgy and musico-poetological substance [*Faktur*] of the work" (*Oper und Musikdrama im 19. Jahrhundert* [Laaber, 1997], 169–70).

11 Eduard Gehe, "Dresdner Theater-Skizzen," literary supplement to *Unser Planet* (January 1843), 9 (emphasis added).

12 "Capellmeister Wahrlieb's Dresdner Opernskizzen: *Die Jüdin* von Halévy; *Der fliegende Holländer* von Richard Wagner," *Allgemeine Theater-Chronik* 20 (February 1843), 86.

13 *Dresdener Abendzeitung* (November 1843), 25.

14 Dieter Borchmeyer also notes the accuracy of Wagner's claim as regards "the work's poetical design" (*Richard Wagner: Theory and Theatre*, trans. Stewart Spencer [Oxford, 1991], 191).

15 See for example Werner Breig, "Das 'verdichtete Bild des ganzen Dramas' – Die Ursprünge von Wagners 'Holländer'-Musik und die Senta Ballade," in *Festschrift Heinz Becker*, ed. J. Schläder and R. Quandt (Laaber, 1982), 162–78, esp. 163–65; Carolyn Abbate, "Erik's Dream and Tannhäuser's Journey," in *Reading Opera*, ed. A. Groos and R. Parker (Princeton, 1988), 129–67, esp. 134–35; Abbate, *Unsung Voices: Opera and Musical Narrative in the Nineteenth Century* (Princeton, 1991), 69–87; as well as Thomas Grey, "Musical Background and Influence," in *The Wagner Compendium*, ed. Barry Millington (London and New York, 1992), 75–76. On the genres of *Romanze* and ballad in German Romantic opera generally, see Siegfried Goslich, *Die deutsche romantische Oper* (Tutzing, 1975), 249–66, and Döhring, *Oper und Musikdrama*, 146–47.

16 This shift of generic-stylistic idiom in the coda from pseudo-traditional ballad to the heroic manner of the "rescue" aria (à la Leonore) is noted by Arthur Groos, see "Back to the Future: Hermeneutic Fantasies in *Der fliegende Holländer*," *19th-Century Music* 19/2 (Fall 1995), 191–211.

17 Act II of Edward Fitzball's semi-farcical melodrama *The Flying Dutchman; or the Phantom Ship* (1827), for instance, includes stage business involving not only a portrait of the Dutchman (Vanderdecken), but also the picture of a "shepherdess" resembling the heroine, Lestelle. The Dutchman's portrait mysteriously changes aspect in order to further a burlesque mistaken identity sub-plot.

18 See for example Borchmeyer, *Richard Wagner: Theory and Theatre*, 206–10, also Chapter 1, n. 12 above.

19 This point is developed by Berthold Hoeckner in "Elsa's Scream, or the Birth of Music Drama," *Cambridge Opera Journal* 9 (1997), 97–132.

20 There is a discrepancy on this point in the text that Wagner was unable or unwilling to resolve. When Senta sings the Ballad in Act II we are meant to perceive this as a spontaneous, unprecedented act. Having heard it "so often" from Mary, she suddenly discovers that she knows it by heart. Erik, on the other hand (in the lines cited above), chides Senta for singing the old Ballad "yet again," just now. Wagner evidently wanted it both ways: the moment of decisive, spontaneous inspiration ("Ich sing' sie selbst!"), and history of obsessive preoccupation ("heut' noch sangst du sie!"). In

the early French prose draft Wagner spoke of "an ancient ballad which [Senta] had often heard sung by her maid, and which she herself repeated every day" (see Appendix A, p. 171).

21 Senta's transgression from reality into the domain of myth (or from ballad into drama) at this moment is a point of discussion for several recent writers (Abbate and Groos, for example cf. notes 15 and 16 above). It was already registered by Liszt in his 1854 brochure on the work, where he connects it to Senta's demonstration of seemingly psychic, clairvoyant powers. Of her outburst at the end of the Ballad he writes: "Die Fiction wird fast zur Wirklichkeit" (Franz Liszt, *Sämtliche Schriften*, ed. Dorothea Redepenning and Britta Schilling (Wiesbaden, 1989), vol. 5, 93). Describing her response to Erik's *Traum-Erzählung* (as he identifies it), Liszt writes: "Her gestures accompany the narration while she appears immersed in a clairvoyant sleep, and soon she even anticipates Erik's own words. His vision is present to her. This Norwegian maiden becomes subject to magnetic powers, a sibylline vision, [a kind of] Swedenborgian spiritualism. The longed-for ship and its captain are no longer merely fictional entities for her" (*ibid.*, 95).

22 A parallel conjunction of "ballad" and ominous "picture" occurs in Meyerbeer's *Robert le diable*, incidentally. When the heroine Alice first sets eyes on Robert's Mephistophelian sidekick, Bertram, prior to the Act I finale, she asks in startled tones who this *sombre personage* might be. To fragmentary reminiscences of the ballad theme in E minor, G, and A minor below a hushed tremolo, Alice remarks on an uncanny resemblance: she has seen this same face before in a painting adorning her village church back home, portraying the Archangel Michael in battle with Satan. "He resembles the Archangel?" Robert inquires, disingenuously. "No indeed," responds Alice, with a shudder; " . . . the other!"

23 Groos notes the even larger pattern of interrupted song that extends to the first and third acts, and its function of conjoining separate musical numbers along the lines of contemporary grand opera ("Back to the Future," 194). Such interruption of "natural song" in opera draws attention to the artifice of its setting (as song within opera), while at the same time lending a naturalistic touch: in real life, songs may be interrupted by other events, they may be re-begun, or they may be left unfinished.

24 Groos also registers the generic transformation of ballad into opera in pointing out how Senta turns "the ballad's measured refrain into the triumphant stretta of a rescue opera" ("Back to the Future," 201).

25 In German Romantic opera as a whole, according to Siegfried Goslich, this expository function is most commonly found in numbers identified as romances (*Romanze*) rather than as ballads (*Der Vampyr* would be a case in point), though the generic distinction between them is not strongly marked (Goslich, "Romanze und Ballade," in *Die deutsche romantische Oper* [Tutzing, 1975], 249–68).

26 James Parakilas, *Ballads Without Words: Chopin and the Tradition of the Instrumental Ballad* (Portland OR, 1992), 35.

27 Abbate, *Unsung Voices*, 73.

28 On Senta's hallucinatory or somnambulistic participation in Erik's dream-narration (also its background in notions of "animal magnetism" in contemporary psycho-physiological science, and as a Romantic literary theme), see Reinhold Brinkmann, "*Sentas* Traumerzählung," in *Bayreuther Festspiele 1984, Programmheft I*, 1–17.

29 On Fitzball and his *Flying Dutchman* see also Bernd Laroche, *Der fliegende Holländer: Wirkung und Wandlung eines Motivs* (Frankfurt, 1993), 54–61. The text of Fitzball's play is given by Laroche, in German translation (pp. 85–160). One might speculate as to whether the eloquent muteness of the Dutchman upon first seeing Senta exhibits some trace – direct or indirect – of the muteness feigned by Fitzball's Vanderdecken throughout the play, including his first encounter with the heroine, Lestelle Vanhelm. (This motif of muteness was a remnant of the earliest French boulevard melodrama.) It is interesting, in this regard, that a review of the early Kassel production of the opera speaks of "the melodramatic scene between the Holländer and Senta" (*Casseler Depeschen* Aug. 1843; see Kirchmeyer, *Musikkritik*, vol. 4/2, col. 204).

30. This early treatment of the Flying Dutchman legend, first published in *Blackwood's Edinburgh Magazine* in 1821, is reprinted in *Wagner* 5:4 (1984), 121–26.

31 Dahlhaus, *Richard Wagner's Music Dramas*, 9.

32 Anon. review in the *Haude und Spenersche Zeitung* (9 January 1844). The paper's editor points to a still earlier treatment of it in Washington Irving's *Bracebridge Hall*.

33 "Der fliegende Holländer. Kritische Skizze von Braun von Braunthal," *Der Komet* 14/10 (12 January 1843), 37.

34 *Allgemeine Preußische Zeitung* (10 January 1844), 64 (cited from Kirchmeyer, *Musikkritik*, vol. 4/2, col. 321).

35 Hanslick, "Der fliegende Holländer von Richard Wagner" (*Die Presse* [6 November 1860]), cited from *Richard Wagner: Der fliegende Holländer*, ed. Csampai and Holland, 140.

36 "Ich fand alles in der Oper gespenstisch bleich" (cited from Martin Gregor-Dellin, *Richard Wagner: Sein Leben, Sein Werk, Sein Jahrhundert* [Munich, 1983], 185).

37 "Der fliegende Holländer. Romantische Oper in drei Aufzügen von Richard Wagner," *Illustrirte Zeitung* (7 October 1843), 235. On the relation of this "red thread" image to the evolving critical discourse of the Wagnerian leitmotif see Thomas Grey, ". . . *wie ein rother Faden*: On the Origins of 'Leitmotif' as Critical Construct and Musical Practice," in *Music Theory in the 19th Century*, ed. Ian Bent (Cambridge, 1996), 187–210.

5   Landfall on the stage: a brief production history

1 This was the same Lachner to whom the rehearsals of the 1864 royal-command Munich production had been first entrusted, and who famously complained about "the incessant wind that blew out at you

wherever you happened to open the score" (Ernest Newman, *The Life of Richard Wagner*, vol. 3 [New York, 1941], 312).

2 Letter of 5 January 1843. See the translation in Appendix B, 185–86.

3 Marie Schmole was writing in 1895. She says she was ten in summer 1842 and so would not have been more than eleven at the time of the *Holländer* première. Her reminiscences are in *Letters of Richard Wagner: The Burrell Collection*, ed. John N. Burk (London, 1951), 118–35. (Translations are my own where not otherwise indicated. Warm thanks to Stewart Spencer for his scrutiny of the translations and to him and Mike Ashman for their valuable comments on the chapter as a whole.)

4 *Illustrirte Zeitung* (Leipzig) (7 October 1843). The costumes are reproduced in *Richard Wagner: Der fliegende Holländer, Texte, Materialien, Kommentare*, ed. Attila Csampai and Dietmar Holland (Reinbek bei Hamburg, 1982), 104–06, and the closing scene in Detta and Michael Petzet, *Die Richard Wagner-Bühne König Ludwigs II.* (Munich, 1970), 22. The latter gives an excellent account, verbal and visual, of the early productions up to 1901 (pp. 20–32 and pls. 4–31).

5 *ML*, 242–43.

6 *The Memoirs of Hector Berlioz*, ed. and trans. David Cairns (London, 1969/1977), 303–04.

7 *Allgemeine Zeitung* (Kassel) (12 June 1843).

8 Oswald Georg Bauer, *Richard Wagner: Die Bühnenwerke von der Uraufführung bis Heute* (Frankfurt, 1982), 48. Gerst's sketches and notes are dated 24 September 1842 and transcribed and illustrated in Petzet, *Wagner-Bühne*, 23–24 and ill. 5.

9 26 April 1852, quoted in Petzet, *Wagner-Bühne*, 24.

10 The sets were probably based not on the Berlin 1844 production, as Wagner had advised, but on Caessmann's 1852 designs for Zurich (Petzet, *Wagner-Bühne*, 26).

11 His handwritten annotations in a vocal score used for the production are reproduced in the C. F. Peters edition of the vocal score, ed. Gustav Brecher (Frankfurt, 1914).

12 It was Hans Richter's memory of Wagner's obsession with the lighting that prompted him to consult Bram Stoker, author of *Dracula* (1897) and who ran London's Lyceum Theatre with Henry Irving from 1878, about the lighting for a revival of this same 1864 production which he conducted in London in the 1890s.

13 *Münchener Neueste Nachrichten* (8 December 1864); *Bayerische Zeitung* (8 December 1864) (quoted in Petzet, *Wagner-Bühne*, 28, 31). It remains unclear whether this staging was or was not influential on others in the later part of the nineteenth century. Petzet (*Wagner-Bühne*, 32) believes that its influence was minimal, while Bauer (*Bühnenwerke*, 50) says it was much imitated elsewhere.

14 Alfred Loewenberg, *Annals of Opera: 1597–1940* (London, 1978), cols. 825–27.

15 For an account by the singer who took the title role in 1870 see Sir Charles Santley, *Reminiscences of my Life* (London, 1909).

16 *The World* (4 November 1891), quoted in *Shaw's Music*, ed. Dan H. Laurence, vol. 2 (London, 1989), 444–46.

17 Bauer, *Bühnenwerke*, 50. The title of this standard French translation is the same as that of the opera inspired by (though scarcely based on) Wagner's original French scenario, set by Pierre-Louis Dietsch and produced in Paris in 1842. See Chapter 2 above, and Peter Bloom, "The Fortunes of the Flying Dutchman in France," *Wagner* 8 (1987), 42–65.

18 The effigies can be seen in the museum at Haus Wahnfried.

19 Dietrich Mack, *Der Bayreuther Inszenierungsstil 1876–1976* (Munich, 1976), 38–39, pls 164–75. For the development at Bayreuth of the cyclorama and its lighting possibilities, see Carl-Friedrich Baumann, *Bühnentechnik in Festspielhaus Bayreuth* (Munich, 1980), 165–70. The most radical scenic conception for the opera around this time was that of the Russian constructivist, Vladimir Tatlin. Himself a naval man, Tatlin's designs (1915–18, unfulfilled) included masts and rigging which he expected the singers to climb. See Rosamund Bartlett, *Wagner and Russia* (Cambridge, 1995), 221–23.

20 Bauer, *Bühnenwerke*, 52.

21 Hans Curjel, *Experiment Krolloper 1927–1931* (Munich, 1975), 58.

22 "Rettung Wagners durch surrealistische Kolportage," in Ernst Bloch, *Zur Philosophie der Musik* (Frankfurt, 1974), 176–84.

23 Quoted in Curjel, *Experiment*, 52.

24 Peter Heyworth, *Conversations with Klemperer* (London, 1973), 65.

25 A color illustration of Act II is included in Charles Osborne, *The World Theatre of Wagner* (London, 1982), 31.

26 25 July 1955, quoted in Mack *Der Bayreuther Inszenierungsstil*, 40.

27 Wieland reinvented the production for theatres abroad, notably in Stuttgart and Copenhagen (1961) and in Hamburg (1966), whence it traveled to the Edinburgh Festival in 1968. It is still in the Copenhagen repertoire as of 1999. Wieland's ideas about the opera (from an essay in the program book for Copenhagen, 1961) are quoted in Geoffrey Skelton, *Wieland Wagner: The Positive Sceptic* (London, 1971), 145–46.

28 Walter Panofsky, *Wieland Wagner* (Bremen, 1964), 83.

29 *Ibid.*, 83.

30 *Ibid.*, 84.

31 Wagner, "Remarks" (see Appendix C, p. 199).

32 Walter Erich Schäfer, *Wieland Wagner* (Tübingen, 1970), 82–83.

33 Joachim Herz says that the principles of music theatre "can be reduced to one basic law: that of the truthfulness of the action." See *The Music Theatre of Walter Felsenstein*, ed. and trans. Peter Paul Fuchs (London, 1991), 150.

34 See Patrick Carnegy, "Stage History," in *Richard Wagner: Die Meistersinger von Nürnberg*, ed. John Warrack (Cambridge, 1994), 135–52.

35 Joachim Herz, "Zur filmischen Gestaltung von Richard Wagners Oper *Der fliegende Höllander:* Gespräch mit Horst Seeger," in *Theater – Kunst des erfüllten Augenblicks* (Berlin, 1989), 104.

36 Personal communication, 5 February 1998. I am grateful to Professor Herz for helping me see a copy of his film and for answering my questions about it and his stage productions.

37 Following the "thaw" at the end of the repressive Zhdanov years, *Der fliegende Holländer* had been the first Wagner opera to be chosen for production in the Soviet Union since World War II – a 1957 production at the Maly Theatre in Leningrad conducted by Kurt Sanderling (Bartlett, *Wagner and Russia*, 290).

38 "From her dreams Senta finds at last the strength to leave the world of money-grubbing and strict convention, and to start a new life. In this way the folk-legend becomes also an expression of hope for a better future" (promotional brochure for film of *Der fliegende Höllander*; Joachim Herz's personal archive).

39 Herz, "Zur filmischen Gestaltung," 107.

40 Joachim Herz, "Der fliegende Höllander," in *DDR-Revue* (Berlin) 4/65, 43.

41 Bauer, *Bühnenwerke*, 56–57.

42 Michael Lewin, *Harry Kupfer* (Vienna, 1988), 138.

43 *Ibid.*, 145.

44 147 substantive reviews are listed in Lewin, *Harry Kupfer*, 442–45.

45 Lewin, *Harry Kupfer*, 135.

46 Personal communication, 14 March 1999.

47 The lighthouse is now an exhibit in the park of the theatre museum in Vienna.

6   Der fliegende Holländer in performance

1 David Cairns, trans. and ed., *The Memoirs of Hector Berlioz*, corrected ed. (New York, 1975), 303.

2 In *Mein Leben* (*ML*, 242), Wagner is particularly annoyed by the physical unsuitability of Michael Wächter, the singer of the Dutchman, but in a letter to Wilhelm Fischer (*SB*, vol. 4, 9 May 1852), he recalls Wächter's performance as "brilliant and energetic," and Berlioz, without being distressed by Wächter's appearance, offered high praise for his voice and singing; see *Memoirs*, 303–04.

3 Rosa Sucher, *Aus meinem Leben* (Leipzig, 1914), 31.

4 Clara Louise Kellogg, *Memoirs of an American Prima Donna* (New York, 1913), 263–65.

5 Eugen Segnitz, review of Bayreuth performance of 22 July 1901, *Musikalisches Wochenblatt* 32 (1 August 1901), 417.

6 *Cosima Wagner: Das zweite Leben. Briefe und Aufzeichnungen, 1883–1930*, ed. Dietrich Mack (Munich, 1980), 35.

7 See *Ibid.*, 491.

8 *Ibid.*, 538–39.

9 Einhard Luther, *So singe, Held! Biographie eines Stimmfaches (Teil 1): Wagnertenöre der Wagnerzeit (1842–1883)* (Trossingen and Berlin, 1998), 35. See also David Breckbill, "The Bayreuth Singing Style

Around 1900" Ph.D. Dissertation, University of California, Berkeley (1991), 475.

10 Richard Graf Du Moulin Eckart, *Cosima Wagner: Ein Lebens- und Charakterbild. Band II: Die Herrin von Bayreuth, 1883–1930* (Munich, 1931), 638.

11 The only recording of "Willst jenes Tag's" by any of Cosima's Eriks (the Edison cylinder by Alois Burgstaller purporting to preserve this excerpt in fact contains the Act II solo "Mein Herz voll Treue" instead) is from Emil Borgmann, who sang several performances (including the first) in 1902, but his piano-accompanied Beka recording, taken briskly, includes full cadenza, the higher alternatives Wagner suggests, and is sung in the original key. Paul Knüpfer, who alternated as Daland in 1902, twice recorded "Mögst du, mein Kind"; his more common 1915 version, although abbreviated, includes a full rendering of the cadenza.

12 Susanna Großmann-Vendrey, *Bayreuth in der deutschen Presse*, vol. 3, part 1: *Von Wagners Tod bis zum Ende der Ära Cosima Wagner (1883–1906)* (Regensburg, 1983), 171.

13 Breckbill, "The Bayreuth Singing Style," 431.

14 *Cosima Wagner: Das zweite Leben*, 845.

15 Quoted in Harold Rosenthal, *Two Centuries of Opera at Covent Garden* (London, 1958), 376.

16 Breckbill, "The Bayreuth Singing Style," 486–87.

17 Frederic Spotts, *Bayreuth: A History of the Wagner Festival* (New Haven, 1994), 129.

18 Once available on LP: EJS 489. The later performance from this production mentioned earlier, dating from 18 July 1942, is available complete on Preiser 90232 (CD). It is a scrappy performance under the baton of Richard Kraus and lacks many of the qualities that make the Elmendorff excerpt so satisfying, and some of the singers' voices seem quite worn on this occasion. A further oddity is the fact that there is a break between Acts I and II. Presumably this intermission added for the convenience of the "friends of the Führer" (soldiers in the German army) who made up much of the audience.

19 Peter Heyworth, *Otto Klemperer: His Life and Times* (Cambridge, 1983), vol. 1, 278. There is a discrepancy in Heyworth's account: if Klemperer used the 1844 score and the "original orchestral material was borrowed from Zurich" (which incorporates the 1852 revisions in scoring), the score and parts would have been poorly coordinated at several points, and it is unclear which version was given primacy in such cases.

20 Joachim Herz, "Wagner and Theatrical Realism, 1960–1976," *Wagner* 19/1 (January 1998), 29.

21 Heyworth, *Otto Klemperer*, 279.

22 This extra exclamation comes a measure before the standard entrance, so that what is a shocked outburst in the later version is simply a more emphatic reiteration in the early version. In hindsight, the later version, first introduced in the Meser vocal score, is preferable.
    The first Italian (1869) and French (1897) editions of the *Holländer*

contain the extra "Senta!" Wagner is known to have been annoyed at
features of the former (see *CWD*, 22 January 1869); that unhappiness
might well stem from its reliance on certain readings, like this one, from
the early Meser scores (particularly the full score) that Wagner had subsequently revised. (Later Bayreuth productions, incidentally, have been
inconsistent in which reading of Erik's entrance to use.)

23 Barry Millington, "*Der fliegende Holländer,*" *The Metropolitan Opera
Guide to Recorded Opera*, ed. Paul Gruber (New York, 1993), 675–76.

24 Isolde Vetter, "'Der fliegende Holländer' von Richard Wagner:
Entstehung, Bearbeitung, Überlieferung," dissertation, Technical
University Berlin (1982) contains a large inventory of these variants.

25 George Bernard Shaw (review of 25 April 1894), in Dan H. Laurence,
Shaw's Music: The Complete Music Criticism (London, 1981), vol. 3, 188.

26 Olin Downes, *New York Times* (10 November 1950); quoted in William
H. Seltsam, comp., *Metropolitan Opera Annals, First Supplement:
1947–1957* (New York, 1957), 39.

27 David Hamilton, "Enter the Dutchman," *Opera News* (7 April 1979),
25–28.

7 Canonizing the Dutchman: Bayreuth, Wagnerism, and Der fliegende Holländer

1 The genesis of the *Holländer* is discussed above in Chapter 1.

2 *SL*, 114–15 (see also Appendix C, pp. 190–92). A similar view suggesting
instantaneous creation is found in Wagner's famous letter to Karl
Gaillard of 30 January 1844: "[B]efore I set about writing a single line of
the text or drafting a scene, I am already thoroughly immersed in the
musical aura of my new creation, [and] I have the whole sound & all the
characteristic motives in my head so that when the poem is finished & the
scenes arranged in their proper order the actual opera is already completed" (*SL*, 117–18). This correspondence began as a consequence of
the Berlin production of the *Holländer* on 7 January 1844.

3 *GSD*, vol. 4, 266–67; *PW*, vol. 1, 308–09.

4 *GSD*, vol. 4, 323; trans. cited from Carl Dahlhaus, *Richard Wagner's
Music Dramas*, trans. Mary Whittall (Cambridge, 1979), 18.

5 *WWV*, 237.

6 *GSD*, vol. 4, 319. Wagner makes a similar point in the "Introduction" to
GSD, vol. 1, 3.

7 Unlike, for example, Hanslick's review of the 1860 Vienna première (cf.
Chapter 4).

8 *SL*, 269.

9 Letter to Ludwig II, 6 January 1865. *SL*, 632–33.

10 Richard Graf du Moulin Eckhart, *Cosima Wagner: ein Lebens- und
Charakterbild*, vol. 1 (Munich, 1929), 320.

11 *CWD*, vol. 2, 464. Entry of 9 April 1880.

12 An early example of such an interpretation may be found in Franz Liszt's
essay "Wagner's Fliegender Holländer," in Franz Liszt, *Sämtliche*

Schriften, Bd. 5: *Dramaturgische Blätter*, ed. Dorothea Redepenning & Britta Schilling (Wiesbaden, 1989), 68–114.

13 Hans von Wolzogen, *Musikalisch-dramatische Parallelen: Beiträge zur Erkenntnis von der Musik als Ausdruck* (Leipzig, 1906).

14 Curt Mey, *Die Musik als tönende Weltidee: Versuch einer Metaphysik der Musik. Erster Teil: Die metaphysischen Urgesetze der Melodik* (Leipzig, 1901).

15 Fritz Stade, "Senta in ihrem Verhältniß zu Erik und zum Holländer: eine psychologische Studie," *Bayreuther Blätter* 5 (1882), 305–10, 353–60.

16 Wolfgang Golther, "Die Sage vom 'Fliegenden Holländer'," *Bayreuther Blätter* 16 (1893), 307–19.

17 Cosima Wagner, *Das zweite Leben: Briefe und Aufzeichnungen 1883–1930*, ed. Dietrich Mack (Munich, 1980), 35.

18 For an account of this production and the politics around Cosima's campaign to perform the works as drama rather than as opera, see Friedrich Spotts, *Bayreuth: A History of the Wagner Festival* (New Haven, 1994), 107–10.

19 These events are discussed in Chapter 1.

20 Siegfried Wagner, *Erinnerungen* (Stuttgart, 1923), 142.

21 See Spotts, *Bayreuth*, 97–100.

22 Hans von Wolzogen, introduction to Richard Wagner, "Über den 'Fliegenden Holländer'," *Bayreuther Blätter* 24 (1901), 189 (original emphasis).

23 *Ibid.*, 187, 190.

24 *Ibid.*, 191.

25 *Ibid.*, 191–92.

26 *Ibid.*, 193.

27 *Ibid.*, 189–90.

28 Heinrich Schmidt, "Kurze Einführung in Rich. Wagners Musikdramen: I. Der fliegende Holländer," in *Praktischer Wegweiser für Bayreuther Festspielbesucher* (Bayreuth, 1901), 53–61.

29 Of course, Chop's basic format – that of a thematic guide – is pure "party line." Max Chop, "Richard Wagners 'Fliegender Holländer' geschichtlich und musikalisch analysiert," in *Praktisches Handbuch für Festspielbesucher*, ed. Friedrich Wild (Leipzig, 1901), 1–44.

30 Rudolph Schlößer, "Holländer-Nachklänge," *Bayreuther Blätter* 24 (1901), 304–05 (original emphasis).

31 Reinhold Freiherr von Lichtenberg, "Holländer-Nachklänge," *Bayreuther Blätter* 25 (1902), 338–39. See also José Vianna da Motta, "Holländer-Nachklänge," *Bayreuther Blätter* 25 (1902), 232–34.

32 Lichtenberg, "Holländer-Nachklänge," 340.

33 On this, see Geoffrey G. Field, *Evangelist of Race: The Germanic Vision of Houston Stewart Chamberlain* (New York, 1981), 123–68.

34 Houston Stewart Chamberlain, *Richard Wagner* (Munich, 1896), 231. "The series of events [between *Rienzi* and *Holländer*] is therefore not to be taken as if Wagner had been suddenly transformed from a 'musician' to a 'poet' by some magic spell, but above all and foremost [as] the

expressive *intensification of the musician* [das *Erstarken des Musikers zum Ausdruck*]."

35 *Ibid.*, 241. As a whole, Chamberlain's book reveals a similar balance between critical objectivity and partisan subjectivity (as when he speaks flatteringly of those then active at the Festival and includes a chapter on the "Bayreuther Gedanke"). Paul Stübe ("Der Spinnerinnen-Chor im 'Fliegenden Holländer'," *Bayreuther Blätter* 24 [1901], 247–48), disagrees with Chamberlain's characterization of the chorus as "operatic" and "unmotivated."

36 Guido Adler, *Richard Wagner: Vorlesungen gehalten an der Universität zu Wien* (Leipzig, 1904). Bayreuth's response to Adler's book may be measured by Curt Mey's scathing review of it in the *Bayreuther Blätter* 28 (1905), 259–62.

37 Adler, *Richard Wagner*, 350.

38 *Ibid.*, 71.

39 Alfred Heuß, "Zum Thema, Musik und Szene bei Wagner: im Anschluss an Wagners Aufsatz, Bemerkungen zur Aufführung der Oper 'Der Fliegende Holländer'," *Die Musik* 10 (1910–11), 3–14, 81–95. Wagner's "Remarks" are given in Appendix C, pp. 193–200.

40 Heuß, "Zum Thema," 95.

41 Max Graf, *Richard Wagner im "Fliegenden Holländer": ein Beitrag zur Psychologie des künstlerischen Schaffens*, Bd. 9: *Schriften zur angewandten Seelenkunde*, ed. Sigmund Freud (Leipzig and Vienna, 1911). This work is discussed by Isolde Vetter in "Wagner in the History of Psychology," in *The Wagner Handbook*, ed. Ulrich Müller and Peter Wapnewski, trans. and ed. John Deathridge (Cambridge, MA, 1992), 132–33.

42 *Richard Wagner über den "Fliegenden Holländer": die Entstehung, Gestaltung und Darstellung des Werkes aus den Schriften und Briefen des Meisters zusammengestellt* (Leipzig, 1914).

43 Robert Saitschick, "Der fliegende Holländer – ein Symbol unseres Zeitalters," *Bayreuther Blätter* 49 (1926), 169–75. To Saitschick, the Dutchman symbolizes the restless striving forward into the unknown; he is the embodiment of true masculinity, just as Senta is that of the *Ewig-Weibliche*.

44 Although, to be sure, production of Wagner was resolutely politicized during the 1920s and 1930s. (On the 1929 Krolloper production of the *Holländer*, directed by Jürgen Fehling, see Chapter 5.)

45 In Strobel's typewritten internal catalogue of primary sources (undated, but likely made during the 1930s and 1940s); see *WWV*, 238.

46 Walter Engelsmann, "Schaffenswende," *Bayreuther Festspielführer* (1939), 110. Engelsmann's other works include: *Goethe und Beethoven* (Augsburg, 1931); *Wagners Klingendes Universum: Der Ring aus Gott – Welt – Macht – Besitz – Liebe – Weib – Mutter und Mensch* (Potsdam, 1933); and "Kunstwerk und Führertum," *Die Musik* 26 (October 1933), 18–22.

47 Engelsmann, "Schaffenswende," 111.

48 *Ibid.*, 114.

49 *Ibid.*, 112–13.
50 *Ibid.*, 120.
51 *Ibid.*, 119.
52 *Ibid.*, 120.
53 Engelsmann's method, although rooted in the same aesthetic and philosophical tradition, moves away from the vagueness characteristic of Wolzogen's *Musikalisch-dramatische Parallelen* and Curt Mey's *Die Musik als tönende Weltidee*. It most strongly anticipates *Substanzgemeinschaft* analysis, such as that of Rudolph Réti, *The Thematic Process in Music* (New York, 1951).
54 Alfred Lorenz, *Das Geheimnis der Form bei Richard Wagner* (Berlin, 1924–33; repr. Tutzing, 1966).
55 For a discussion of Lorenz's aesthetic and philosophical background and principles, see Stephen McClatchie, *Analyzing Wagner's Operas: Alfred Lorenz and German Nationalist Ideology* (Rochester, 1998), chapters 2 and 3.
56 Alfred Lorenz, "'Der fliegende Holländer' – Oper oder Worttondrama?" *Bayreuther Festspielführer* (1939), 102–08. Lorenz's methodology received no substantive criticism until after the Second World War, possibly on account of Lorenz's personal and professional ties with National Socialism; see McClatchie, *Analyzing Wagner's Operas*, chapters 1 and 6.

A Source texts (libretto)

1 Heine seems to allude to the tradition (as represented, for example, by the 1821 story "Vanderdecken's Message Home") of identifying the name of the ship itself as the "Flying Dutchman."
2 *Konterfei* – the same term Mary applies to the portrait in Act II of Wagner's opera; the detail of seventeenth-century Spanish dress is also maintained, and is mentioned in the original prose draft (see below). William of Orange (1650–1702) reigned as King of England (William III) from 1689 jointly with his wife, Queen Mary.
3 Messalina, the third wife of the Roman emperor Claudius, was renowned for her profligacy, scheming ambition, and sensual indulgences.
4 Wagner's original French text (Bibliothèque nationale, Paris, Département des manuscrits, Nouvelles acquisitions françaises 22552) is given in Peter Bloom, "The Fortunes of the Flying Dutchman in France: Wagner's *Hollandais volant* and Dietsch's *Vaisseau fantôme*," *Wagner* 8/2 (April 1987), 63–66, as well as in Bernd Laroche, *Der fliegende Holländer. Wirkung und Wandlung eines Motivs* (Frankfurt and Berlin 1993), 71–74.

B Autobiographical texts and correspondence

1 Passages from Wagner's prose writings here (as in the main body of the text) are identified according to location in the *Gesammelte Schriften* (Leipzig, 1887–1911), vols. 1–10 (*GS*), *Sämtliche Schriften und*

Dichtungen (Leipzig and Berlin, 1911–16), vols. 1–16 (*SSD*), or *Richard Wagner's Prose Works*, trans. William Ashton Ellis (London, 1895–99), vols. 1–8 (*PW*). Translations in the appendix are by the editor, unless otherwise indicated.

2 In the latter part of 1836 Wagner had sketched a plan for a four-act grand opera on the subject of Heinrich König's novel, *Die hohe Braut*, which he sent (in French translation) to the celebrated playwright and librettist, Eugène Scribe, in the naive hope of thus paving the way for a brilliant Parisian career (à la Meyerbeer.)

3 Léon Pillet had worked in the administration of the Paris Opéra (Academie royale de musique) since 1838, although he was not appointed full director of the institution until 1 August 1841. Wagner was certainly never commissioned to provide "an opera in two or three acts," as he implies here, but he was given to understand that he would have a better chance of having a relatively short work accepted by the Opéra (in one or two acts, rather than the five-act "grand opera" format of *Rienzi*) that could serve as a curtain-raiser to a ballet performance. The *Vaisseau fantôme* of Dietsch, Foucher and Révoil that eventually resulted, somewhat indirectly, from Wagner's proposal of the "Flying Dutchman" subject to Pillet was in two acts and was performed eleven times on a double-bill with various ballets (including Hérold's *La fille mal gardée* and Adam's *Giselle*) in the winter of 1842–43 (see Peter Bloom, "The Fortunes of the Flying Dutchman in France," *Wagner* 8/2 [April 1987], 61, and cf. Millington, "Sources and Genesis of the Text" above, pp. 33–35).

4 Maurice [Moritz] Schlesinger (1798–1871), son of the Berlin publisher Adolf Schlesinger, carried on his father's business in Paris. He served as editor and publisher of the *Gazette musicale de Paris* from 1834 onwards (later *Revue et gazette musicale*, to 1880*)*. Wagner's contributions to the *Gazette musicale* are collected in vol. 1 of the *Gesammelte Schriften*, vol. 7 of *Richard Wagner's Prose Works*, and in *Wagner Writes from Paris . . . (Stories, Essays and Articles by the Young Composer*), trans. and ed. Robert Jacobs and Geoffrey Skelton (London: Allen & Unwin, 1973).

5 In the *Gesammelte Schriften* Wagner references at this point his account of *Der fliegende Holländer* in the 1842/3 "Autobiographical Sketch" (see above, pp. 178–81).

6 Wagner alludes to the fact that even after completing the opera he had kept in mind the possibility of a continuous, one-act performance in three consecutive "scenes."

7 In the event, the first Berlin performance did not take place until almost exactly two years later, 7 January 1844.

8 Wagner was appointed director of the Dresden court opera following the death of Joseph Rastrelli in November 1842, though his responsibilities were shared with the composer and conductor Carl Gottlieb Reissiger.

9 Notices on Wagner and his *Rienzi* had appeared in issues 36 and 41 (21 October, 18 November) of the *Neue Zeitschrift für Musik* in 1842.

10 The end of the letter also contains a paranoid dig at Mendelssohn,

whom Wagner holds somehow responsible for the lack of attention paid to the Dresden premières of *Rienzi* and *Der fliegende Holländer* in the *Allgemeine musikalische Zeitung*. Thus this one letter documents the first stages of Wagner's antipathy toward the two leading "Jewish musicians" of the day, such as he would go on to vent at length in *Judaism in Music* (1850) and parts of *Opera and Drama* (1850–51).

11 Paul Foucher, together with Benédict-Henri Révoil. See Chapter 2, "Sources and genesis of the text," as well as Wagner's original prose draft given in Appendix A, above. (Foucher and Révoil can hardly be said to have "adapted" Wagner's prose sketch at all, in fact; their libretto is independent of Wagner's draft in almost all particulars.)

12 As Spencer and Millington note, Wagner's account of the public enthusiasm for his new opera is not reflected in the critical reviews of the Berlin première, and the work was not performed again in Berlin between the following February and 1868.

C Interpretation

1 I.e. Heinrich Heine's satirical vignette published in *Aus den Memoiren des Herrn von Schnabelewopski* (1834); see the translation in Appendix A above (pp. 166–69).

2 "On the Performance of *Tannhäuser*: A Communication to Conductors and Interpreters of This Opera, *GS*, vol. 5, 122–59 (*PW*, vol. 3, 167–205). Written in August 1852, this is a longer analogue to the present notes on the production of *Der fliegende Holländer*.

3 *Ed.* – That is, to the iterations of the "Dutchman" motive in trumpet and French horn across the closing nine measures of the Introduction, no. 1.

4 *Ed.* – The "falsetto passage" (*Falsettstelle*) presumably refers to the high B-flat at "mir Liebe nicht auf's neu"; the "cadenza" is the decorated descending scale of the penultimate measure, "die Versich'rung deiner Treu'?"

Select bibliography

Abbreviations:

CWD   Cosima Wagner, *Diaries* (2 vols.), ed. M. Gregor-Dellin and D. Mack, trans. Geoffrey Skelton (New York and London, 1978, 1980)

GSD   Richard Wagner, *Gesammelte Schriften und Dichtungen*, 10 vols. (Leipzig, 1887ff)

ML   Richard Wagner, *Mein Leben*, ed. Martin Gregor-Dellin (Munich, 1976); *My Life*, trans. Andrew Gray (Cambridge, 1983)

PW   *Richard Wagner's Prose Works*, trans. William Ashton Ellis, 8 vols. (London, 1892–99)

SB   Richard Wagner, *Sämtliche Briefe*, vols. 1–5, ed. G. Strobel and W. Wolf (Leipzig, 1967–93)

SL   *Selected Letters of Richard Wagner*, trans. and ed. Stewart Spencer and Barry Millington (New York, 1988)

SSD   *Sämtliche Schriften und Dichtungen*, 16 vols. (Leipzig, 1911–16)

WWV   J. Deathridge, D. Mack, and E. Voss, eds., *Wagner Werk-Verzeichnis* (Mainz, 1986)

Abbate, Carolyn. "Erik's Dream and Tannhäuser's Journey," in *Reading Opera*, ed. C. Abbate and R . Parker (Berkeley and Los Angeles, 1988), 129–67

    Unsung Voices (Princeton, 1991)

Abraham, Gerald. "The Flying Dutchman: Original Version," *Music and Letters* 20 (1939), 412–19

Anderson, George K. *The Legend of the Wandering Jew* (Providence, 1965)

L'Avant-scène Opéra no. 30 (1980), *Richard Wagner: "Le Vaisseau fantôme'*

Bloom, Peter. "The Fortunes of the Flying Dutchman in France: Wagner's *Hollandais volant* and Dietsch's *Vaisseau fantôme*," *Wagner* 8 (1987), 42–66

Borchmeyer, Dieter. "The Transformations of Ahasuerus: *Der fliegende Holländer* and his Metamorphoses," in *Richard Wagner: Theory and Theatre,* trans. S. Spencer (Oxford, 1991) 190–215

Breig, Werner. "Das 'verdichtete Bild des ganzen Dramas': Die Ursprünge von Wagners 'Holländer'-Musik und die Senta-Ballade," in *Festschrift Heinz Becker*, ed. J. Schläder and R. Quandt (Laaber, 1982), 162–78

222

Brinkmann, Reinhold. "*Sentas* Traumerzählung," *Bayreuther Festspiele: Programmheft I: "Der fliegende Holländer"* (1984), 1–17

Busch, Gudrun. "Die Unwetterszene in der romantischen Oper," in *Die "Couleur locale" in der Oper des 19. Jahrhunderts*, ed. Heinz Becker (Regensburg, 1976), 161–212

Cheesman, Tom. *The Shocking Ballad Picture Show: German Popular Literature and Cultural History* (Oxford and Providence, 1994)

Csampai, Attila, and Dietmar Holland. *Richard Wagner: Der fliegende Holländer* (Reinbek bei Hamburg, 1982)

Dahlhaus, Carl. "The Flying Dutchman," in *Richard Wagner's Music Dramas*, trans. Mary Whittall (Cambridge, 1979), 7–20

"Wagner's 'A Communication to my Friends': Reminiscence and Adaptation" (trans. Mary Whittall), *The Musical Times* 124 (1983), 89–92

Deathridge, John. "An Introduction to *The Flying Dutchman*," in *Der fliegende Holländer/The Flying Dutchman* (ENO Opera Guide), ed. Nicholas John (London and New York, 1982), 13–26

Döhring, Sieghart, and Sabine Henze-Döhring. *Oper und Musikdrama im 19. Jahrhundert* (Laaber, 1997)

Ellis, William Ashton. "From Fitzball to Wagner: A 'Flying Dutchman' Fallacy," *The Meister* 5 (1892), 4–21

Fitzball, Edward. *The Flying Dutchman, or The Phantom Ship: A Nautical Drama in Three Acts* (London, 1827)

Glümer, Claire von. *Erinnerungen an Wilhelmine Schröder-Devrient* (Leipzig, 1862)

Golther, Wolfgang. "Die Sage vom 'Fliegenden Holländer'," *Bayreuther Blätter* 16 (1893), 307–19

Goslich, Siegfried. *Die deutsche romantische Oper* (Tutzing, 1975)

Graf. Max. "Richard Wagner im 'Fliegenden Holländer': ein Beitrag zur Psychologie des künstlerischen Schaffens," in *Schriften zur angewandten Seelenkunde*, vol. 9, ed. Sigmund Freud (Leipzig and Vienna, 1911)

Grey, Thomas. "Wagner, the Overture, and the Aesthetics of Musical Form," *19th-Century Music* 12/1 (Summer 1988), 3–22

Groos, Arthur. "Back to the Future: Hermeneutic Fantasies in *Der fliegende Holländer*," *19th-Century Music* 19/2 (1995), 191–211

Heine, Heinrich. *Aus den Memoiren des Herren von Schnabelewopski*, in *Sämtliche Werke: historisch-kritische Gesamtausgabe*, ed. Manfred Windfuhr *et al.* (Berlin, 1973–), vol. 5, 171–74

Herz, Joachim. "Zur filmischen Gestaltung von Richard Wagners Oper *Der fliegende Holländer*: Gespräch mit Horst Seeger," in Joachim Herz, *Theater: Kunst des erfüllten Augenblicks* (Berlin, 1989)

Heuß, Alfred. "Zum Thema, Musik und Szene bei Wagner: im Anschluß an Wagners Aufsatz, 'Bemerkungen zur Aufführung der Oper *Der fliegende Holländer*'," *Die Musik* 10 (1910–11), 3–14, 81–95

Howison, John [?]. "Vanderdecken's Message Home; Or, the Tenacity of Natural Affection," Blackwood's *Edinburgh Magazine* (May 1821), 127–31

Kirchmeyer, Helmut. *Situationsgeschichte der Musikkritik und des musikalischen Pressewesens in Deutschland*, pt. 4: *Das zeitgenössische Wagner-Bild* (Regensburg, 1967–85)

Laroche, Bernd. *Der fliegende Holländer: Wirkung und Wandlung eines Motivs. Heinrich Heine–Richard Wagner–Edward Fitzball–Paul Foucher & Henri Revoil/Pierre-Louis Dietsch* (Frankfurt, 1993)

Leprence, Gustave. "The Flying Dutchman in the Setting by Pierre-Louis Dietsch," *The Musical Quarterly* 50 (1964), 307–20

Lorenz, Alfred. "*Der fliegende Holländer*: Oper oder Worttondrama?" *Bayreuther Festspielführer* (1939), 102–08

Machlin, Paul. "'The Flying Dutchman': Sketches, Revisions and Analysis." Ph.D. diss. UC Berkeley (1976)

"Wagner, Durand and 'The Flying Dutchman': The 1852 Revisions of the Overture," *Music and Letters* 55 (1974), 410–28

"A Sketch for the Dutchman," *The Musical Times* 117 (1976), 727–29

Millington, Barry. "Did Wagner Really Sell his 'Dutchman' Story?" *Wagner* 4/4 (October 1983), 114–27

"*The Flying Dutchman, Le Vaisseau fantôme*, and Other Nautical Yarns," *The Musical Times* 127 (1986), 131–35

Newman, Ernest. "The Flying Dutchman," in *The Wagner Operas* (New York, 1949), 3–49

Petzet, M. and D. "Die Richard-Wagner-Bühne König Ludwigs II.," *Studien zur Kunst des 19. Jahrhunderts* 8 (1970)

Saitschick, Robert. "Der fliegende Holländer: ein Symbol unseres Zeitalters," *Bayreuther Blätter* 49 (1926), 169–75

Spencer, Stewart. "Some Notes on "Der fliegende Holländer," *Wagner* 3 (1982), 78–86

Stade, Fritz. "Senta in ihrem Verhältniß zu Erik und zum Holländer: eine psychologische Studie," *Bayreuther Blätter* 5 (1882), 305–10, 353–60

Stübe, Paul. "Der Spinnerinnen-Chor im 'Fliegenden Holländer'," *Bayreuther Blätter* 24 (1901), 247–48

Thorslev, Peter L. Jr. *The Byronic Hero: Types and Prototypes* (Minneapolis, 1962)

Vetter, Isolde. "Der fliegende Holländer von Richard Wagner: Entstehung, Bearbeitung, Überlieferung." Ph.D. diss. Technische Universität, Berlin (1982)

"Senta und der Holländer – eine narzißitische Kollusion mit tödlichem Ausgang" and "Die Entstehungsgeschichte der Oper 'Der fliegende Holländer'," in *Richard Wagner: Der fliegende Holländer* (Texte – Materialien – Kommentare), ed. A. Csampai and D. Holland (Reinbek bei Hamburg, 1982)

"For the Last Time: Wagner *Did* Sell his 'Dutchman' Story," *Wagner* 7/1 (January 1986), 15–22

Warrack, John. "Behind *The Flying Dutchman*," in *Der fliegende Holländer/The Flying Dutchman* (ENO Opera Guide), ed. Nicholas John (London and New York, 1982), 7–12

Winkler, Gerhard. "Wagners 'Erlösungsmotiv': Versuch über eine musikalische Schlußformel – Eine Stilübung," *Musiktheorie* 5 (1990), 2–35

Wolzogen, Alfred von. *Wilhelmine Schröder-Devrient: Ein Beitrag zur Geschichte des musikalischen Dramas* (Leipzig, 1863)

Wolzogen, Hans von. "Richard Wagner über den 'Fliegenden Holländer'," *Bayreuther Blätter* 24 (1901); rpt. Leipzig, 1914 (*Richard Wagner über den "Fliegenden Holländer": die Entstehung, Gestaltung und Darstellung des Werkes aus den Schriften und Briefen des Meisters zusammengestellt*).

Index